D1606424

The Reconstruction of Economic Theory

Recent Economic Thought Series

Warren J. Samuels, Editor
Michigan State University
East Lansing, Michigan, U.S.A.

This series is devoted to works that present divergent views on the development, prospects, and tensions within some important research areas of international economic thought. Among the fields covered are macromonetary policy, public finance, labor and political economy. The emphasis of the series is on providing a critical, constructive view of each of these fields, as well as a forum through which leading scholars of international reputation may voice their perspectives on important related issues. Each volume in the series will be self-contained; together these volumes will provide dramatic evidence of the variety of economic thought within the scholarly community.

THE RECONSTRUCTION OF ECONOMIC THEORY

edited by

Philip Mirowski
Tufts University

Kluwer-Nijhoff Publishing
a member of the Kluwer Academic Publishers Group
Boston/Dordrecht/Lancaster

Distributors

for the United States and Canada: Kluwer Academic Publishers,
101 Philip Drive, Assinippi Park, Norwell, MA 02061

for the UK and Ireland: Kluwer Academic Publishers, MTP Press Limited,
Falcon House, Queen Square, Lancaster LA1 1RN, UK

for all other countries: Kluwer Academic Publishers Group, Distribution
Centre, P.O. Box 322, 3300 AH Dordrecht, The Netherlands

Library of Congress Cataloging-in-Publication Data
Main entry under title:

The Reconstruction of economic theory.

  (Recent economic thought)
  Bibliography: p.
  Includes index.
  1. Economics—Addresses, essays, lectures.
I. Mirowski, Philip, 1951– . II. Series.
HB171.R38 1986   330.1   85-30032
ISBN 0-89838-211-4

PRINTED IN THE UNITED STATES.

Contents

Contributing Authors

Randall Bausor, Dept. of Economics, University of Massachusetts—Amherst, Amherst, MA 01003

David Ellerman, Industrial Cooperative Association, Somerville, MA 02144

Donald Katzner, Dept. of Economics, University of Massachusetts—Amherst, Amherst, MA 01003

David Levine, Dept. of Economics, University of Denver, Denver, CO 80208

Philip Mirowski, Dept. of Economics, Tufts University, Medford, MA 02155

The Reconstruction of Economic Theory

1 INTRODUCTION: PARADIGMS, HARD CORES, AND FUGLEMEN IN MODERN ECONOMIC THEORY

Philip Mirowski

Every age has scoffed at its predecessor, accusing it of having generalized too boldly and too naively. Descartes used to commiserate the Ionians. Descartes in his turn makes us smile, and no doubt some day our children will laugh at us. Is there no way of getting at once to the gist of the matter, and thereby escaping the raillery which we foresee? No, that is impossible; that would be a complete misunderstanding of the true character of science.

—*Henri Poincaré*, Science and Hypothesis

Apologia

Books with titles such as that sported by the volume you hold in your hands are, let us admit, frequently disappointments. Not only in the discipline of economics, but in the wider academic world as well, there is a persistent jostle and clamor to proclaim the "revolutionary" this or the "pathbreaking" that. The exigencies of self-promotion have escalated beyond all bounds of circumspection and propriety; it seems no one is content to admit to continuity with tradition. The last three decades have even witnessed the spectacle of the natural scientists chiming in, with all the fashionable talk of "scientific revolutions", "paradigms", "degenerating research programs",

1

"incommensurability", and so forth. The widespread academic disdain for any semblance of mere yeoman service in the cause of furthering knowledge is exemplified by Thomas Kuhn's description of "normal science" as "puzzle-solving": a mundane activity, similar to the solution of a crossword puzzle, or the successful negotiation of a maze by a rat. After all, who wants to grow up to be a normal scientist?

The reality, of course, falls far short of this mark. Once past the title page of *The Reconstruction of "X"*, usually the boredom sets in. The disillusionment comes in one of two brands. In the first, the alleged novelty of the analysis is wildly exaggerated, with the results varying only insignificantly from the reigning orthodoxy. In the second, the conventional wisdom is flayed and pilloried without mercy, while the work stops well short of any operational suggestion as to how one might avoid the errors of those subjected to scorn. In either case, the reader has been duped, and is sure to think twice about picking up another book with a similar title. A few more such incidents, and another cynic is born.

So why pick such a rash title? The mandate given to the editor of the present volume was succinct and to the point: gather together some of the most recent attempts to remake economic theory at its most fundamental levels, and avoid the two debased brands of academic revolutions. Now, anyone would have realized that this would be a devilishly difficult task, more likely than not to backfire; but, in retrospect, the editor still marvels at the complacency with which he embarked on the enterprise. It was quite easy to identify the critics of conventional economics who had little more than criticism to offer; it was much more difficult to feel certain that he had actually stumbled upon a substantive divergence from the orthodoxy that appeared to promise further fruitful developments. Thus the purpose of this introduction is to provide justification for the title, which the editor has come to believe is appropriate. The modus appologia will be to present the reader with an outline of the principles of selection the editor finally settled upon, along with some indication as to how the present essays fulfill those criteria. Forewarned and forearmed, the prospective reader should then be equipped to judge for him- or herself whether truth in advertising has been further abused, or if something a little more interesting and entertaining is afoot.

What Is the Orthodoxy in Economics?

Any assertion of novelty of analysis must presume an orthodoxy as a benchmark. However prosaic this may seem, it is by no means a simple matter, because orthodoxies have a habit of not standing still. Kuhn captured our problem in a phrase: "... to answer the question 'normal or revolutionary?' one must first ask 'for whom?'" (in Lakatos and Musgrave, 1970, p. 252). Certainly there is a surfeit of economists who harbor the conviction that their ideas are original and profound, just as there is surely a second surfeit of economists poised to challenge that conviction. However many economists we might canvass, there is no guarantee that we would eventually converge upon a solid orthodox credo. This problem is compounded by some blind spots in most economists' field of vision when it comes to the history of modern economic thought, an issue we shall shortly have occasion to discuss.

To circumvent the problem, we shall provisionally define the orthodoxy in economic theory (to which the essays in this volume claim to provide an alternative) as the composite of standard curriculum prevalent in American or American-influenced graduate programs. This choice severely restricts the field of possibilities, because after World War II the American graduate economics curriculum has become much more homogeneous than was the case previously. With only minor risk of exaggeration, in that curriculum there are now only two schools of thought to choose from: the predominant neoclassical economic theory, and a European variant of an attenuated form of Marxian economic theory. Although other schools of thought have flourished in the past and still claim adherents, in a surprisingly short interval German historicism, American Institutionalism, Austrian subjectivism, and yes, even Keynesian macroeconomics have been displaced and superseded as active research programs in the schools that train the majority of the next generation of economists. Hence, irrespective of the fact that the ranks of economists have swelled at an exponential rate in the postwar period, the dispersion of the types of credentials of the Western economist has narrowed to a bipolar distribution. However one might evaluate the desirability of such a trend, it is the critical backdrop against which the essays in this volume should be understood.

To merely attach names to these two schools of thought is nowise sufficient to characterize them; nor does it illustrate the thesis that economics has grown more homogeneous. In order to do so, we must have some idea of the features that comprise their identity, as well as the features that are adventitious or expendable. Lakatos (Lakatos and Musgrave, 1970, p. 133) has coined a marvelously ironic term for the concept we seek: the "hard core" of a research program. Lakatos believed that research programs are usually accompanied by a package of prescriptions as to which inquiries to avoid, and which research paths to pursue. The "hard core" of a program is that collection of concepts, theories, and practices that are ruled off limits to empirical falsification or conceptual refutation. The problems or anomalies linked to this assemblage which happen to arise in the course of inquiry are deflected onto a second set of concepts, theories, and practices which Lakatos calls the "protective belt": these can be radically altered, or, if need be, dropped. The philosophical assertion of a certain inviolate set of concepts and practices in science was not original with Lakatos; much of the basic idea could be found in the discussions of the Duhem-Quine thesis which, briefly summarized, states that any single hypothesis is immune to falsification, because of the plethora of auxiliary hypotheses attached to any scientific theory (see Harding, 1976). We do not need to subscribe to Lakatos' methodological strictures in detail to see that this concept of the "hard core" could be very useful in an attempt to identify the orthodoxy in an intellectual discipline. If there exists some constellation of concepts and practices that are treated as privileged and, as such, embody the unity and coherence of an inquiry, then that hard core will serve adequately as a shorthand referent for the entire research project.

Is there a hard core characteristic of neoclassical economics or Marxian economics as they are manifested in the conventional economics graduate program? The quest for either of these hard cores is a notoriously tricky business. Many historians of economic thought and some methodologists have tried it, especially for neoclassical economics, with none too impressive results. The candidates for neoclassicism have ranged from Robbins' "scarce means for given ends" to Benthamite methodological individualism to Hollis' and Nell's empiricism. It is the contention of this editor (Mirowski, 1984 and forthcoming) that none of these characterizations of the hard core of neoclassicism really fill the bill, in that they neglect the actual historical practices of those whom no one would dispute were progenitors of neoclassicism. (Parenthetically, this was the same criticism Kuhn, Lakatos, Laudan, and others made of the Popperian and logical positivist philosophers of science.) While disputes over the history of doctrine are not a major concern in this volume, they do occupy one very central role in it: they will serve to identify the orthodox concepts and practices that undergo reconstruction in this volume. In this instance the editor has drawn upon a thesis he has elaborated at length elsewhere (Mirowski, forthcoming), as well as summarized in his essay on mathematical formalism in this book, for the purpose of providing the demarcation criteria for the hard cores of neoclassical and Marxian economic theory.

This thesis, baldly stated, is that both of these research programs grew out of attempts to approriate and apply the metaphors, practices, and methods of the physics of two different historical periods, and to bend them to the discussion of economic phenomena. Thus the hard cores of the respective research programs in economics are the metaphors and methods of the natural science of the respective historical periods. Even more bluntly, Marxian economic theory is a bowdlerized version of Cartesian substance theories of motion; whereas neoclassical economic theory is a bowdlerized version of nineteenth-century energy physics.

Clearly some brief elaboration is in order, although for details the reader is urged to consult the cited texts. First, the Marxian theory. Descartes, as is well known, wanted to portray the world as ultimately reducible to manifestations of matter and its extension. Although the Cartesian research program was superseded in many respects by the Newtonian paradigm, the "rational mechanics" of the eighteenth and early nineteenth centuries did preserve and elaborate upon the process of physical explanation as reduction of phenomena to an undifferentiated material substance in motion. The classical economists, anxious as they were to build their explanations upon solid "natural" foundations, adopted the substance metaphor as the basis for their theories of value. One need only recall the Physiocratic *Tableau Oéconomique*, with its generic substance "blé" wending its way among the three classes of society, to conjure an explicit example of Cartesian explanation (Foley, 1976). Marx, both through intensive study of the classical economists and through his Hegelian influences (especially *The Phenomenology of Spirit*), imbibed the metaphor of value as substance in motion, and took as his task the rendering of its economic implications internally consistent. His version of the labor theory of value was the pinnacle of Cartesian substance theories in economics, and it is this that remains the hard core of the Marxian economic tradition. This is even true of its modern Cambridge or Sraffian variant (Steedman, 1977), which claims to jettison the labor theory of value, only to fall back upon the natural substance of the "standard commodity."

Next, the neoclassical theory. After physical theory was consolidated in the mid-nineteenth century around the mathematical formalisms of energy and the field concept, the revised picture of the physical world was rapidly incorporated into a new economic theory much more mathematical and formal in character than classical economics. In this theory, energy became transmuted into "utility". This utility was suffused throughout an abstract commodity space, and was the primary motive force behind economic activity: that is, it constituted a field. Theoretical analysis assumed the format of variational or extremal principles, such as Lagrange's technique of locating extrema under constraints, employing the principle of undetermined multipliers. Constrained optimization became the hallmark of neoclassical theory, its hard core being the postulation of a psychological field which behaved, for all intents and purposes, just like potential energy.

These two characterizations of the hard cores of the predominant research programs in economics have many intriguing implications for the history of economics, its epistemology, its sociological structure, as well as its persistent imperialistic relationship to the remainder of social theory, but these are not our present concern. In the development of criteria for the inclusion of contributions to this volume, the editor employed these theses in order to decide what was and what was not just another version of orthodox theory. The criteria were deployed to identify divergence from the respective hard cores, as well as to estimate the prospect of the contribution being "absorbed" back into the orthodox research tradition. The editor hoped that the result of this process would be the identification of a reasonably coherent third stream or alternative economic theory. The criteria derived from this understanding of the respective hard cores were:

1. The presence of an alternative to the physical reductionism inherent in the scientific metaphors that comprise the hard cores of neoclassicism and Marxism. In the contributors' essays, this often appears as a reluctance to remain satisfied with exogenous natural determinants of economic phenomena.
2. The development of a mathematical formalism not simply appropriated from a physical model without comment.
3. The reevaluation and reconceptualization of an economic phenomenon whose format had previously been dictated by some idiosyncracy of the parent physical model: for instance, the presumed temporal reversibility of trade, the notion of statics adopted from mechanics, or the construct of growth as the spatial accumulation of identical units.
4. A consideration of the philosophical problems specific to social research, which are often discussed in the context of the controversy over which principles, if any, distinguish social inquiry from the natural sciences.
5. Finally, a confident and sure grasp of the structure of neoclassical and Marxian economic theory, as an antidote to the temptation to reinvent the wheel.

Is There a "Third Stream"?

So much for the wish list. Suppose for the sake of argument that the above characterizations of the hard cores are correct, and that the five criteria above are sufficient to identify a third stream of economic theory, neither Marxian nor neoclassical. Wishful thinking aside, does such a creature really exist?

The editor was extremely gratified to discover that some very substantial components of such a theory do exist, but that they were scattered haphazardly throughout the insurmountable heap of economics literature published since the 1960s. Hence the rationale for yet another book tossed upon the heap: the existence of a viable alternative to the bigemony of neoclassicism and Marxism is in danger of getting lost in the sheer volume. In many cases, partisans of one or the other of the orthodox positions have been incapable of recognizing the significance of a suggested alternative, and therefore our contributors have not until now had their ideas appear in the same venue. Searchers for a third stream have in the past had to be omnivorous readers of many far-flung (and sometimes inaccessible) journals such as *Australian Economic Papers*, the *Journal of Post Keynesian Economics*, *Journal of Economic Issues*, *Cambridge Journal of Economics*, *Economic Development and Cultural Change*, *Social Concept*, and in one case, even *Mathematics Magazine*.

That is not to say, however, that all of the present essayists agree on all, or even most, points of economic theory. As an example, the relative aversion to the neoclassical (or Marxian) research program varies drastically among the contributors, as will become apparent from perusal of their papers. If the editor were forced to rank the present company as to the degree of equanimity with which they regard the last forty years' evolution of neoclassical theory, he would list himself as the most implacably opposed to its theoretical imperatives, followed in rapidly increasing order of sympathy by Levine, Bausor, Ellerman, and Katzner. More than once the editor found himself playing the Montagnard to their Girondists, prodding them in directions about which they had strong reservations. It is a tribute to each of their commitments to scholarship that they suffered this importunity with patience, grace, and cheerful good humor. In this and other respects, perhaps all the talk of revolutions and the shattering of paradigms is wrong; rather than a band of guerrillas, the present company is better understood as an array of fuglemen: exemplars, reconnoiterers into unknown territory, pursuing the thankless and unrewarded task of the innovation of an economics that deserves the name of social theory.

Somewhere between the particularity of individual vision and the generality of a unified, disciplined intellectual school lies the actuality of third stream economic theory. At the risk of conjuring a system where none really exists, the editor is convinced that there are common themes emerging from the various manifestations of third stream theory. While they may not be the central themes, which would command allegiance from all those who might identify with third stream theory, the editor has found them to be sufficiently widespread as to constitute a point of departure and a basis for commu-

nication. We offer a brief précis of each here, for the benefit of those unacquainted with the third stream literature.

A.   Third stream economic theory does not appear to be synthetic, in
that it evinces a distinct lack of interest in encompassing the neoclassical and
Marxian models as special cases of a more general or covering law model.
The portrait of science as necessarily cumulative has provoked increasing
skepticism in recent history and philosophy of science (Laudan, 1984). Problems of incommensurability and meaning-invariance arise even in the natural sciences when one research tradition claims to fully subsume another. In
economics, there is the further problem that the neoclassical and Marxian
schools have patterned themselves on particular conceptions of natural science methods and concepts, which the third stream eschews. Hence, for the
most part, contributors to this volume generally avoid fostering the appearance of unbroken tradition of economic analysis.

B.   Third stream economics generally does not accept "price" as a coherent phenomenological entity to be elevated to the position of the central
object of explanation by economists. This volume provides instances of a
movement to categorize price into its various functions, and then to break it
down into its more fundamental constituent phenomena. Levine, for one,
in his essay herein as well as in (Levine, 1980), presents a trenchant critique of equilibrium price as an a priori reconciliation of the forces buried
within the natural givens of the analysis, as if equilibrium were merely
something hidden from our superficial perception, an entelechy in the
already-written book of our days. Levine's suggested alternative is to reconceptualize price as one of many instruments available to the firm to achieve
some of its many objectives: firm growth, market expansion, market stability, financial manipulations, restructing of its market environment, or
even the transmutation of its clientele. As he forcibly argues, there is no
comprehensive way to reduce all of these diverse objectives to a single ranking or objective function, just as there is no sensible algorithm that reduces all of the firm's instruments to a single prototypical control variable,
such as, say, a "shadow price". From this perspective, the very idea that a
firm would either treat prices as parametric or simply acquiesce to some
"market clearing price" seems outlandish.

In two other examples from this collection, Bausor and Mirowski dissect
the conventional notion of price, and in particular the "law of one price", in
order to display its subliminal content. Bausor skeptically evaluates the
commonplace that price can act either as a seaworthy vessel of information
or as a dependable mechanism of coordination. His insight is that one must
start with a model of individual psychology which freely allows the existence
of differences of opinion, expectations, and interpretative capacities, before

one can reasonably pose the question of coordination success or failure. Only if the people in economic models are not zombies would the problem of economic coordination even arise. The conventional construction of a market clearing price rapidly breaks down in such an environment. Bausor concludes by outlining an equilibrium model in historical time, revealing the circumscribed role of price in such a framework. Mirowski, on the other hand, questions the near-universal conviction that price is merely the simple ratio of physical quantities of goods. In asking the question why are prices expressed as numbers, he raises the possibility that the seemingly "natural" ratios mask a whole complement of institutional prerequisites which belie any simple barter economy. A detour through abstract algebra is used as an occasion to suggest that numerical prices embody a working distinction between legitimate and illegitimate trade, which in turn is a prerequisite for the reification of growth and profit.

C. The third stream of economic theory has many diverse sources of inspiration—within this volume alone one can easily discern classical, Marxian, and neoclassical themes—but there does seem to be a common denominator of discourse, which might be dubbed *neoinstitutionalism*. Each contributor has independently adopted the goal of constructing models that do not portray the market as a self-sufficient isolated entity, but rather an institution predicated upon the operation of other social institutions, the components operating in a sometimes symbiotic, sometimes contradictory relationship. Pride of place in this respect goes to Ellerman, who has developed a theory of property rights and appropriation which is analytically prior to the theory of the market, and indeed, value theory itself. Appropriation has always been a wretched skeleton in the neoclassical closet, ever since Walras tried to avoid it with the lame excuse that "nature makes things appropriable' (Walras, 1969, p. 76). The conundrum for Walras was to explain why his prices were "natural" even though "the appropriation of scarce things ... is a phenomenon of human contrivance." Although there have been attempts in the interim to solve this problem, neoclassicals are not much further along than they were in Walras' day. Ellerman clarifies the flaw inherent in these attempts, as well as in any analysis that depends upon the distributive-shares metaphor. In its place, Ellerman proposes a labor theory of property, distinctly different in form and content from the Marxian labor theory of value. Although he does not cite them, his work has some resemblance to that of Thorstein Veblen and John R. Commons in their quest for an institutional legitimization of economic distribution.

Other contributors also address themes reminiscent of institutionalist concerns. Levine's stress on the firm as an institution capable of semi-autonomy from the market recalls the pioneering work of Berle and Means of a half-century ago. Katzner's model of the firm, which he uses mainly as a vehicle to discuss problems in the application of formalism to economic analysis, innovates a technique for the discussion of the roles of rules and social hierarchy in production, a concern of the institutionalist branch of labor economics. Mirowski confronts the institutional underpinnings of economic analysis in two essays: one explores the socially contingent character of economic quantification; the second, compares the treatment of institutions in game theory and in the writings of Veblen, Commons, and Mitchell.

   D.   Third stream economic theory diverges from the pattern of previous challengers to the bigemony of neoclassicism and Marxism in that it explicitly evaluates the impact of the escalating standards of mathematical sophistication upon the content of economic theory. The essays in this volume are particularly noteworthy because they meet a high standard of fluency in mathematical expression, while avoiding the arrogance of the axioms/proof/ illustration format without corresponding discussion of the theoretical significance of the economics. Most representative of this trend, the contribution by Katzner echoes the thesis (Katzner, 1983) that mathematical formalization and quantification are two separate theoretical issues in economics. The present paper furthers that thesis by explicitly focusing attention on the influence of formalization upon the concepts found in conventional neoclassical models; his work lends coherence to the frequently fuzzy discussion of the interaction and interpenetration of mathematics and economics. In particular, his trenchant observations on the great divide between dialectical and arithmomorphic concepts carry on the tradition of that unsung classic by Nicholas Georgescu-Roegen, *The Entropy Law and the Economic Process* (Georgescu-Roegen, 1971).

   Other contributions to this volume also more or less explicitly comment on the economic content of mathematical models. The essay by Mirowski considers at length the conventional defenses of the use and abuse of mathematics in neoclassical economic theory, and finds them wanting. It is contended in that essay that such harmless choices as the unit of measurement, or the appropriation of a particular subset of mathematical technique, are freighted with profound theoretical content. The paper by Ellerman entertains the notion that accounting, the shunned relative of economics, embodies the fundamentals of a group algebra which can serve to formalize trading relationships. Bausor's essay explores the implications of probabalistic arguments for the problem of coordination in historical time. Any one of these could alone falsify the common impression that there exists no alternative to mainstream mathematical economics.

   Ultimately, no amount of systematization after the fact by the editor will conjure a third stream of economic theory; that is for the reader to decide for him- or herself. Nevertheless, the editor retains the conviction that there are more novel *ideas* contained herein per page than in most of the journal literature in economics, and it is on this basis that he recommends this book to you, the reader.

References

Foley, Vernard. 1976. *The Social Physics of Adam Smith*. West Lafayette, Ind.: Purdue University Press.

Georgescu-Roegen, Nicholas. 1971. *The Entropy Law and the Economic Process*. Cambridge, MA: Harvard University Press.

Harding, Sandra, ed. 1976. *Can Theories Be Refuted?* Boston: Reidel.

Katzner, Donald. 1983. *Analysis Without Measurement*. New York: Cambridge University Press.

Lakatos, Imre, and Musgrave, Alan, eds. 1970. *Criticism and the Growth of Knowledge*. Cambridge: Cambridge University Press.

Laudan, Larry. 1984. *Science and Values*. Berkeley: University of California Press.

Levine, David. 1980. "Aspects of the Classical Theory of Markets," *Australian Economic Papers*, (19):1–15.

Mirowski, Philip. 1984. "Physics and the Marginalist Revolution." *Cambridge Journal of Economics*, Dec. (8):361–379.

Mirowski, Philip. Forthcoming. *More Heat Than Light*.

Poincaré, Henri. 1952. *Science and Hypothesis*. New York: Dover.

Steedman, Ian. 1977. *Marx After Sraffa*. London: New Left Books.

Walras, Leon. 1969. *Elements of Pure Economics*. Trans. W. Jaffée. Clifton, NJ: Kelley (reprint).

2 RECONCEPTUALIZING CLASSICAL ECONOMICS

David P. Levine

From the point of view of method and analytical structure, classical political economy provides the most clear-cut alternative to neoclassical economics. The central distinction between classical and neoclassical theory has to do with the way in which the former attempts to account for the reproduction of the economy through time. By including the notion of reproduction, the classical theory attempts to conceive of the economy as a determinate and enduring system, two qualities missing from the neoclassical conception. While the classical theory falls short in its effort to provide an account for the reproduction of a market economy, that effort can help guide us to a reconstruction of economic analysis with implications significantly different from those of the neoclassical theory. In the following, we present the barest outline of a reconceptualization of classical economics.[1]

Natural Price and Market Price

Recent efforts to revive the method of classical political economy focus on the way in which technical/material relations enter into the determination of prices and commodity exchange.[2] By so doing, these efforts attempt to

13

provide an objective framework within which economic relations can be determined and thus avoid the contingency of the neoclassical theory with its emphasis on purely subjective conditions.

By focusing on this technical or material aspect of the classical theory its modern practitioners emphasize only one side of classical analysis and exclude another which more directly incorporates the idea of property ownership. In a recent paper (Levine, 1980) I have attempted to investigate these two sides of the classical theory and to show how they stand opposed one to the other. Briefly, we can summarize the two aspects of the classical theory as follows:

1. The classical theory conceives of the economy as a system of relations between independent property owners pursuing their private interests. This is the conception of civil or civilized society and it emphasizes property ownership and self-seeking. Its focus is therefore on the market and what it terms market price rather than on the process of production and reproduction of those things that exchange in the market.
2. Simultaneously, the classical theory conceives of the economy as a system of the reproduction and expanded reproduction of a set of material relations having to do with the subsistence of persons. Here, it focuses on production price, the subsistence wage, and the growth of a producing apparatus.

The idea of the self-ordering market (Adam Smith's "invisible hand") implies a unity of these two aspects of the classical theory. In particular, it suggests that the system of relations between independent property owners realizes as an unintended consequence its own reproduction and growth and therefore the reproduction and growth of the set of material/technical relations. A difficulty arises, however, in the attempt to unify the two aspects of the classical theory. This difficulty stems from the fact that when persons act according to their private interests they need not act in such a way as to encourage the reproduction of the material/technical order. Conversely, when we constrain agents to act so as to reproduce a system of material production we in effect require them to give up their private interests. One way of phrasing this paradox is to say that the classical theory requires that its agents act both as persons and as mere elements of an impersonal structure.

The difficulty arises insofar as agents acting as persons (i.e., in their private or self-interest) cannot be relied upon to act in a way that leads to systemic coherence. The market exists at the whim of its participants and is as ephemeral as their preferences. The core weakness of the Walrasian theory stems from the fact that it portrays the economy in just this way, and therefore says nothing genuinely determinate about economic relations. Classical theory develops a deterministic conception which allows for the analysis of economic processes without reference to preference, whim, and free choice. This is the great strength of the classical method when set against that of modern economics.

Classical political economy deploys two distinct notions of price to capture the two sides of its overall conception. These are the notions of natural and market price. Analysis of the relation between natural and market price reveals the underlying contradictions implied by the duality of the classical conception of the economy.

The classical theory intends the natural price to refer exclusively to conditions of production (or of material/technical reproduction) and the market price to refer exclusively to conditions within the market (property relations). This distinction initially leads to an identification of natural price with a notion of a quantity of labor time (assumed measurable without regard to the property system). This identification appeared to provide a firm rooting of price in the production process considered prior to and independent of market relations. However, the so-called labor theory of value led classical theory into serious and ultimately insoluble difficulties associated in particular with the calculation of labor value and the value of capital (Steedman, 1977; Levine, 1978, ch. 9). The methodological and analytical implications of the attempt to root exchange in production remain clear, however, when we leave aside problems specifically associated with the labor theory of value. The distinction between natural price and market price appears with equal force when we treat natural price as a production price, following that strain within classical theory recently emphasized in the work of Piero Sraffa.

In one sense, the idea behind the distinction between market and production price is to show how the circumstances of production govern the market and thus how the laws of the market simply express the conditions of production and reproduction. When the production price governs the market price so that commodities exchange at their production prices, then the price system makes possible the reproduction and expansion of the economy as a whole. When the production price fails to govern the market price the exchange of commodities need not assure and may even prevent the reproduction of the economy as a whole. The commitment of the classical theory to the idea of reproduction also commits it to establishing a mechanism that maintains the consistency of market price with reproduction. This mechanism treats the production price as a "center of gravity" which draws the market price toward a level consistent with reproduction.

Within the classical theory, production or natural price acts as a kind of ideal price implicit within the structure of production and the assumed pre-market determination of aggregate income distribution. The natural price, in this case, is determined by: (1) the technical conditions of production which enter into determination of costs of production, (2) the real wage (subsistence or cost of production of labor) which, together with the technical conditions, determines the rate of profit, and (3) the condition of equality of rates of return on capital advanced which assures that prices depend only on technical conditions and aggregate distribution. The natural price yields a revenue to the producer just adequate to repay the costs of labor, replace used up capital, and realize profit on capital at the normal rate.

The production price embodies an idea of allocation of capital and profit according to given (premarket) conditions of technology and distribution. When we make production price a part of the core of our idea of the market, we make the market (and market price) the result of determinants given from outside. When we do this, we significantly undermine any notion of the market as a determinant, treating it wholly as something determined. The classical economist designs the relation between market and natural price so as to treat the market in just this way.

In this respect, the classical method has something important in common with the method employed in Walrasian theory. We express this common quality when we treat both as instances of equilibrium theory (Walsh and Gram, 1980). The differences between classical and neoclassical theory have less to do with their conceptions of market price formation as a process executing nonmarket laws (realizing premarket determinants) and more to do with their specification of the premarket determinants of the market. The classical theory focuses on technology, reproduction, and aggregate distribution; the neoclassical theory focuses on scarce factors and individual preferences. While these differences are in their own way fundamental, both theories treat the market as a passive mechanism for realizing a predetermined result.

The distinction between market and production price originates in the idea that the condition of private ownership does not ultimately enter into the determination of the rates at which commodities exchange. Since the market is defined as the arena for the assertion of property right, the necessity that the market accomplish ends having nothing specifically to do with individual property ownership creates a genuine problem. Since market price directly expresses only the private decisions of individual property owners it cannot immediately be the production price. But, since the market and market price have no real purpose other than realizing conditions of production they must (at least tend to) become the production price.

While decisions made by individual property owners play no role in determining production price, they make up the whole basis of market price formation. This means that the specification of the agents (property owners) is crucial both in distinguishing market price from production price, and in establishing the ultimate determination of market price by natural price. The classical theory excludes social classes or corporate entities from acting as such within the market and identifies the market with confrontations between individuals pursuing their private interest. Forces not directly embodied within particular persons must act on the market indirectly. Within the market, systemic forces are aggregate forces which arise out of the summation of individual interests and endowments. The idea of supply and demand captures this notion of systemic forces as aggregates of individual facts. For this reason, the classical theory of the market begins with supply and demand.

In classical political economy, supply and demand take the form of fixed stocks of commodities brought to the market place at a given point in time. The object of the commodity owner is to sell his stock of commodities for as high a price as he can get. In practice, this amounts to the sale of commodities at whatever price the market "will bear". The classical and neoclassical theories look very similar at this point primarily because when they consider the market as such; they leave aside the processes outside the market that give rise to supply and demand. The market concerns itself only with the amounts and distribution of wants and endowments, not with their origin. The market price equates supply and demand, thereby clearing the market. In this sense, it is a market-clearing price.

In the first instance, the market-clearing price need bear no systematic relation to the natural price (since it does not take into account the conditions that stand behind endowments and wants). The market price may be inconsistent with both the reproduction of any given person and the reproduction of the economy as a whole. In order to avoid this result, the classical theory must place an agent into the market which, when acting in its private interest, brings about social reproduction and growth. The interaction between such agents links production price with market price. The agent is the capitalist, and the process of interaction is the competition of capitals.

The capitalist exchanges commodities in order to make profit. His rate of profit measures the revenue received from the sale of his products today against the cost incurred when he purchased the productive inputs in the past. Thus the calculation of profit correlates two market conjunctures and links market prices across time. The profit rates of individual producers resulting from the relation between market prices at different points in time determine whether market and production prices correspond. Equality of profit rates across producers and at a level consistent with the subsistence wage means equality of market price with production price. Inequality of profit rates requires an adjustment in the market price. Since the production price is a fixed ideal, it cannot meaningfully be said to be inappropriate nor required to adjust. By definition, the market price is the dynamic price. While the natural price changes with changes in technology and distribution, the actual price movement is one of market price now in the direction of an altered production price.

Price adjustment takes place through the movement of capital from less to more profitable lines of production. This shifts the relation of supply to demand, increasing supply in more profitable lines, reducing it in the less profitable. The movement of capital through its effect on supply and demand lowers prices and profit rates in the more profitable sectors while raising them in the less profitable. Ideally, this leads the market price toward the production price. Movement of capital and of prices ceases when profit rates are uniform.

In the classical theory, competition and the movement of capital eliminate, or at least tend to eliminate, all differences in profit rates between producers (or firms). Because of this the process of competition has no effect on its result: once production price rules no trace of competition remains. Since the theory defines the result of competiton independently of the process of competition, it eliminates any possible impact of the activities of firms on prices, distribution, and growth.

Firms do not enter explicitly into the classical theory but appear only in the guise of the individual capitalist or his unit of production. The firm is not considered an agent in its own right. The classical theory treats the firm as a creature of the capitalist, which comes into existence with a decision made at a point in time to embody capital into a particular form. This form exists at the discretion of the capitalist who gives it up as soon as conditions in the market require that the capital be moved to a different line of production. Without the implied mobility of capital, production price cannot dominate market price. This same mobility of capital makes the firm nothing more than a temporary agglomeration of capital for a specific purpose connected to a particular conjucture of prices.

At the same time that the classical theory treats competition and the firm as passive transmitting devices, its conception of natural price remains an empty ideal in the absence of competition; indeed, in the absence of a very special form of competition. Thus competition is both essential and ultimately irrelevant. This seeming contradiction leads the classical theory to a specific formulation of competition and the firm. In order to prevent the interaction of firms from having an effect on the outcome of market processes, the classical theory conceives competition in a specific way involving mobility of capital, supply and demand, and market-clearing price. But, when classical economics proceeds in this way it undermines the basis for a coherent reproduction process.

The dependence of price on conjunctures of supply and demand makes the valuation of capital contingent on a sequence of contingent price structures. The classical theory of the market reevaluates capital during each market period and on the basis of circumstances specific to particular market periods. Since the market price is a market-clearing price it can provide no assurance that the sequence of valuations will yield profit or even preserve the integrity of the capital and the firm from one period to the next. Because of this, the theory fails to establish the structural coherence of the market in principle.

A coherent theory of the market must identify mechanisms within the market which, at least under normal circumstances, assure its renewal. In the classical theory this mechanism is the capitalist or firm. But classical theory does not endow this agent with those qualities that would enable it to bring about either its own reproduction or that of the market as a whole. Indeed, the market-clearing price can deviate so sharply from the natural price as to make continued production impossible. When this happens, the process of price formation destroys the firm and the market, and for purely accidental reasons.

This conclusion has particularly important implications for the determination of the form of capital investment. Since each period brings with it a new regime of capital values, capital investment cannot provide a point of stability capable of providing coherence to the transition from past to future. Since investment in fixed capital requires stability of valuation across time, it necessitates a different method of market valuation than that required by the classical theory of markets. Because the classical theory ties market valuation to the mobility of invested capital and market-clearing price, it requires that capital investment take the form of circulating capital. It in effect treats all capital (including the formally fixed part) as circulating capital (Sraffa, 1960, p. 63; Levine, 1978, ch. 9). Clearly if we subject fixed capital to periodic reevaluation according to the rule of market-clearing price, we make the decision to invest in fixed capital problematic. The classical theory falls short of establishing the basis for a rational calculation of the relation between past and current costs on one side and the price of output in the present and future on the other. No theory which, in its conception of the dynamics of the market, fails to establish the basis for rational cost calculation in this sense can claim to provide an adequate theoretical account for the reproduction of the market system.

In the classical theory, market prices depend on supply and demand at the time of the relevant exchanges. Since supply and demand are not subject to any systematic determination and appear as the result of accidental circumstances, the prices of commodities in markets at points in time can fluctuate more or less without limit. This means that profit fluctuates with the contingent circumstances affecting supply and demand.

When prices and profits fluctuate in this way, they provide no basis for agents dependent upon the market to adopt the long-run view and to plan their economic activities upon the basis of the idea that the market provides them with a rational environment capable of securing their survival. The capitalist can only continue as such so long as the prices at which he sells his products exceed by a sufficient margin the prices he paid for the productive inputs. He expects this to be the case when he invests his capital in an industry on the basis of past profitability. But the past is a weak guide to the future in the classical model, which contains no mechanism to assure that the past has a determinate effect on the present and future. The fact that the conjuncture of prices has at one time provided adequate profit in a particular industry provides no basis for assuming that this will continue to be the case. The classical theory does not conceptualize the force within the market that makes the present sufficiently tied to the past and future so as to assure a basis for decision making consistent with the idea that the market secures the livelihood of the agents dependent upon it.

In economics, coherence presupposes a consistent transition between past, present, and future. Such a transition requires stability of the basic determinants of the market across time. Stability of structure supports the long-run standpoint. Neither stability nor the formation of long-period expectations exclude structural change. They do, however, limit and define a temporal framework for structural change consistent with a coherent transition between past, present, and future. Stability of structure across time means that at least certain elements of that structure must recur. Thus coherence of a market economy requires that it exhibit three interconnected attributes: stability, the long-run, and recurrence.

To see the importance of the concept of recurrence consider the way in which the classical model assures determinacy of prices. In the classical conception discussed above determinacy of prices stems from the condition that the system of commodities be reproduced through time. It is this condition of reproduction that limits prices. If we simply take the products of production in a particular period and exchange them without regard to the requirement that their exchange make possible their reproduction (as in the determination of market prices), then there are no limits to the rates of exchange (other than those having to do with the total supplies and their distribution among particular persons as in a Walrasian economy). But, once we require that the set of commodities reappear as the result of their own productive consumption, the set of viable price structures contracts. In this sense, the conditions of reproduction, and of expanded reproduction, determine the prices of commodities.

This is a very powerful idea; yet nowhere does the theory account for reproduction—the recurrence of the commodity system through time. Instead it simply assumes what it needs to establish. It does so precisely because its conception of economic agents does not include the notion of recurrence as an intrinsic objective of those agents and as an objective they can accomplish once they treat it as a goal. Thus while the theory requires recurrence, not only does it fail to account for recurrence, it constructs the economy in such a way as to make recurrence an accident.

Recurrence of the economic system as a whole requires that recurrence be a reasonable end for the particular agents. When this happens the system of agents will normally exhibit the kind of stability within which long-run decisions can be made, and reproduction will result from the inner workings of the economy rather than by accident.

Since the calculation of profit links the present, past, and future, the pursuit of profit provides one foundation for the kind of stability we associate with a consistent temporal flow. In the classical theory, the pursuit of profit appears as the motivation of particular persons and in this sense stems from a specification of self-interest. By introducing the profit motive, the classical theory directs a subset of agents toward the work of reproduction and growth. In classical theory the concept of profit always takes precedence over that of recurrence so that recurrence is at the mercy of profit seeking.

This happens because in its specification of agents, the classical theory includes only particular persons. These particular persons do not see beyond their private interests, nor do they subordinate their activities to any larger institutional entity in relation to which they can define their interests. The profit motive does not appear as a motive to create an enduring basis (of wealth) for a corporate entity that transcends the capitalist. Instead, the classical theory identifies profit seeking with self-aggrandizement. This obscures the relation of profit seeking to the work of creating and sustaining a (corporate) entity that goes beyond the particular person. Thus, the profit-seeking person seeks nothing more than mere profit.

This is the point in the structure of classical argument where its weaknesses with regard to the problems of coherence and reproduction are most sharply felt. And, indeed, a relatively small change in this element of the classical theory leads to substantial change in the overall meaning and theoretical import of the argument as a whole. In particular, once we assume that the profit motive has deeper roots in the desire of the agent to create an enduring structure two conclusions follow: First the pursuit of accumulation takes precedence over the pursuit of profit; and second, the agent subordinates current profit to the security of its capital. We commonly associate these two conclusions with the replacement of the self-interested person by the corporate entity or firm. Often the modern literature views this change as one of form or motive. And, given this standpoint it can be shown that the behavior of the economy depends relatively little on which specific motivation we consider. Pursuit of growth requires profit and generally will result in efforts to assure the highest profit consistent with the long-run survival of the firm. Similarly, survival over the long run requires profitability and so does not lead us away from the idea of profit seeking. All of this suggests that the three ends—profit, growth, and recurrence—work together.

There are, however, important implications connected to the way in which we organize our thinking regarding these three aspects of the ends of the capitalist or capitalist firm. In particular, the specific objective we take to be predominant or primary will determine the way in which the other two objectives assert themselves and the outcome of the efforts on the part of the agent to achieve the remaining goals. Thus, when we focus on profit making we tend to associate it with the ends of particular persons attempting to generate private wealth for private purposes. This leads to a conception of an economy made up of particular persons acting upon the basis of their own narrow views and special concerns. One result is that capital accumulation over time and the institutional stability of a structure of wealth production are contingent upon the whims of particular persons. This leads to the kind of problem evident in the classical theory when it attempts to make individual self-seeking assure the reproduction of a coherent and enduring institutional structure.

When the particular property owner enters the market with the purpose of acquiring some particular commodity which satisfies a particular well-defined need, the exchange orients itself to consumption outside of the market. Once completed, the act of consumption finishes the process and brings an end to the economic cycle. The orientation toward consumption does not lead directly to the recurrence of the market but requires a renewal of the need if the agent is to return to the market and renew the exchange. This makes recurrence of the market contingent on the recurrence of a particular need, or set of particular needs.

Keynes' theory also treats profit seeking as the goal of particular persons and subordinates profit making to decisions concerning the wealth positions of individuals. The profit motive determines the form in which individuals hold their wealth (which depends upon expected rates of return and riskiness of alternatives). Because Keynes treats profit seeking as the motive of an individual wealth holder he severs the link between profit and the creation of an enduring structure of production. He argues in a way analogous to classical political economy that the activity of the capitalist is that of moving wealth about in pursuit of its most profitable form. The capitalist has and makes no commitment to any particular form of wealth (e.g., investment in fixed capital) because to do so would impede the frenetic search for evermore profitable lines of investment. Thus Keynes shares the classical preoccupation with liquidity because he shares with classical economics the idea that profit is the motive of a class of individuals.

Keynes' argument differs from that of classical economics in the conclusion it draws concerning the implication of the pursuit of liquidity for wealth holding. The classical economist concludes that the logical form of capital investment is circulating capital and, in effect treats all capital as circulating capital. Keynes goes one step farther, arguing that the profit-seeking agent's preoccupation with mobility will lead him to invest in financial assets rather than means of production. The core of Keynes' theory is the argument that the profit motive undermines the reproduction and growth of the producing apparatus and leads to low levels of employment output and investment.

For Keynes the presence of a financial alternative leads wealth holders away from the work of building society's producing structure. The profit motive undermines the long-run standpoint. It does so, in part, because of its connection to the particular person rather then to an enduring (corporate) structure. He ignores those aspects of the motivation of the wealth holder that transcend the standpoint of private persons because he treats all wealth holders as private persons (Levine, 1984). The dominance of the profit motive over those of growth and recurrence follows.

When the profit-seeking agent differs from other agents only in the motive that drives its actions, even the making of profit itself becomes contingent. In order to overcome this contingency, we need to alter our conception of the agent to emphasize institutional endurance and growth through time. The individual capitalist of classical theory seeks his profit in temporary contingent circumstances within the market. The Keynesian wealth holder seeks his profit in speculative opportunities that arise outside of his control. For an agent to adopt a long-run view, the source of profit must endure through time and not be dependent on particular conjunctures of conditions at points in time. To endure through time is to structure the temporal flow so as to provide the necessary conditions for endurance. The agent must find itself within an environment structured to support recurrence and the long-run view, and it must actively form that environment to assure the possibility of its own endurance.

This process appears in various forms. In order to help clarify those ideas, we suggest the following elements or aspects of the process only as examples.

1. Fixed capital investment—Investment in fixed capital forces the firm to take a long run view. At the same time, for it to be rational for a firm to invest in fixed capital, that firm's market must have sufficient coherence to underwrite the idea that future revenues will pay for the equipment and yield profit. The presence of fixed capital forces the firm to rethink the way in which it calculates profit, building its survival into its concept of profit. We consider this calculation in the next section.

2. Financial reserves—The firm must maintain financial resources, or access thereto, adequate to allow it to survive those periods when receipts from the sale of commodities do not cover costs. The firm can view such periods (sometimes correctly, sometimes incorrectly) as the "short run" so long as it can view itself enduring beyond their limits. This work of seeing itself into the future depends upon the firm's ability to endure through good and bad times. It must cease to be dependent on particular sales, and on the market conjuncture in a given period.

3. Changes in the form of the product—For products that depreciate rapidly (due to spoilage, etc.), liberation from the dominance of the short-run depends upon the firm's ability to change the specification of its product. More generally, the firm seeks (on the one side through preservation of perishables, on the other through changes in style) to determine the rate of depreciation of the use value of its products. This is a good example of the way in which the firm alters the conditions of sale and consumption which govern profit making and growth.

4. Advertising and the sales effort—The firm seeks stability of demand in order to make reasonable its treatment of demand as part of an environment within which its own institutional coherence can be secured through time. Advertising can (when successful) increase the security of the firm's markets and support the long-run view. Other related aspects of advertising (associated with competition) can work to overthrow a stable division of the market (e.g., through the introduction of new products).[3]

One important implication of the change in the classical conception of the orientation of the firm to the market has to do with prices. Indeed, the literature focussing on this issue tends to look to price rigidity as that aspect of classical economics most important for the theory of economic growth (Kalecki, 1954; Steindl, 1952). When firms alter their environment in order to make it suitable for their reproduction over the long run, part of their intent is to make the price at which they sell their product independent, to a degree, of particular exchanges and particular conjunctures of supply and demand. This makes price an objective attribute of the commodity, of its production process, and of enduring aspects of its market.

Of course, price rigidity must be defined with reference to specific forces and a determinate time period. If we have a theory that defines price flexibility as the sensitivity of price to short-run fluctuations in supply and demand, then, if prices do not move in the face of excess or inadequate supplies, we term the resulting behavior "price rigidity". By so doing we make it appear that prices are absolutely less flexible and sensitive to circumstance than they would be were they responsive to current demand. Yet, there is nothing in the longer view of the agent as an enduring institution that makes prices absolutely less flexible. It only follows that prices may be sensitive to factors other than demand in the short run and the relation of supply to demand. Thus, in particular, prices may now be sensitive to long-run factors such as technology, market structure, and the structure of demand. Indeed, in the classical theory, the very sensitivity of prices to short-run fluctuations constituted a barrier to considering any systematic relation of market price to long-run factors and leads to the opposition between market and production price. Thus, the issue is not rigidity per se, but the nature of the forces in relation to which prices appear to be flexible, and especially whether those are of a long-run or short-run character.

A Model of the Expansion of Firms

The concept of a long-run price (or of price rigidity) referred to at the end of the preceding section needs to be made concrete through a specification of the long-run processes within a market economy which bring about the determination of prices. This is precisely the problem posed by the classical notion of a natural price. In order then to determine the long-run (or natural) price we must specify the fundamental process of a capitalist economy that binds together the series of points that constitute the temporal flow. The argument of the preceding section suggests a solution to this problem. This solution lies in the conception of the profit-seeking agent as a capitalist firm that subordinates profit making to the requirements of capital accumulation over the long run. A system of such firms constitutes the basis for a market governed by laws consistent with the survival and growth of its constituents. These are aggregate or systemic laws of economic growth.

The classical theory also includes laws of systemic growth but treats them in the way it treats production price, as independent of both the market and the survival and growth of firms. This is the most apparent for Ricardo who grounds the expansion of the capitalist economy in the natural fertility of the earth. In order to increase the social capital, which Ricardo assumes to consist exclusively of a wages fund, it is necessary to produce more of the subsistence required to hire and sustain the laborers. This requires either bringing more land into cultivation or more intensive cultivation of existing land. In either case, the result is a fall in the productivity of labor on the marginal unit of production, a decline in the rates of profit and investment, and eventually an end to the growth process due to exhaustion of natural fertility. Ricardo treats capital accumulation as a process by which persons work for an external end: realization of the innate productive potential of the earth. The ends and decisions of agents only play the role of realizing the potential productivity of nature.

Marx conceives of the problem in much the same way since he treats capital accumulation as a process that realizes a producing potential. The law of the process (the rising organic composition of capital) has nothing to do with the condition of property ownership and exists independently of the system of relations between property-owning agents (the market). In this respect, Marx advances a genuinely classical conception by analyzing the growth of the capitalist economy as a process of material/technical expansion. Once the structure of production has been conceptualized, it only remains for the classical theorist to establish how property owners act so as to assure the realization of the material-producing potential given to them as a natural/technical condition. This calls for the classical theory to show how the system of property relations, which appears to have its own purpose and outcome, has an implicit yet effective purpose in the realization of objective laws and of the development of an objective producing potential. In the classical theory, private agents act in their private interests and yet are driven to realize an historical mission, so to speak, which is that of realizing the producing potential of modern society.

This conception of the growth process is structurally analogous to the concept of natural price and reproduces the same dichotomy discussed above. It excludes any conception of the firm as an active and enduring agent and deprives the market of any capacity to bring about its own recurrence through time. The classical theory of growth in fact depicts a sequence of points along a development path without delineating a process to establish the way in which the configuration of today's prices and profit emerge from the past process of price determination. Since the particular configurations (of production price) are independent of market processes they do not lead from one to the next but depict the outcome once a transition has been fully accomplished. Thus the growth process, which in principle integrates a sequence of economic configurations, in the classical theory merely connects them externally one to another.

Evidently, the classical theory lacks an important element in its conception of growth. This element involves the way in which market growth constitutes an integrated process rather than a series of events. The missing element is precisely the conception of the market as a determinant. The Keynesian theory of ecomonic growth takes us an important step in the direction of recasting the idea of long-run growth to make it an integrated process. It does so precisely by focussing on the demand-creating effects of investment and on the part played by the market in determining the overall rate of economic growth.

The core idea of the Keynesian theory of economic growth is that the growth of a capitalist economy is a self-sustaining process which connects demand to investment in a cycle of mutual determination (Harrod, 1939; Robinson, 1962). Within this cycle, production and exchange reproduce the conditions necessary to continued production and exchange. In order to see the implications of this method we will present a formulation of the growth process based on this idea and then consider its implications for the reconstruction of the classical theory of markets. We begin by isolating the distinct premises of our reformulated theory with regard to the unit of analysis, price determination, distribution, and investment. In each case, we can see that the change from classical economics involves the way in which the idea of recurrence enters into the specification of the theory.

1. The unit of analysis—We will assume that the primary agent within a capitalist economy is the capitalist firm. The firm is irreducible to a particular person or set of particular persons; its needs and interests do not correspond to those of individuals (e.g., its owner or owners). We will assume that the primary objective of the firm is the preservation of its institutional integrity through the expansion of its capital (Penrose, 1959).

2. Price determination—We will assume that competition and market structure limit prices and profit margins. Since competition and market structure are attributes of the structure of the economy they change as part of the long-run process of economic development. In this sense prices depend on long-term factors rather than short-term configurations of supply and demand. The resulting price is not a market-clearing price and this means that short-run adjustments must be made in inventories and utilization of capital rather than prices.

3. Distribution—Since prices depend on structural conditions involving

the market, distribution cannot be determined independently of the market. Profits and the real wage depend upon the wage bargain (which determines the money wage) and upon the prices of commodities, which depend upon costs and profit margins.

4.   Investment—In the classical theory, capitalists automatically invest their profits (aside from a small part reserved for consumption) in new capital. They keep doing so until a point is reached at which the rate of return falls to zero (or below some minimum acceptable rate). The rate of return falls to zero when the productivity of new capital goes to zero. Aside from this point, no investment decisions (other than those having to do with the flow of capital across lines of production) need be made. By contrast, we will assume that investment depends upon expected profitability—which depends upon a number of factors including, but not limited to, productivity.

These conditions imply a relation of price to profit that differs from that underlying the classical formulation of production price. Rather than price depending upon cost and an independently given average profit rate, price and profit will be jointly determined. To see this clearly we will introduce the notion of a gross profit margin linking prices and distribution (Kalecki, 1954). Formally, the gross profit margin (e_i) is the ratio of gross revenue per unit of output to unit prime costs:

$$e_i = \frac{p_i}{w_i n_i + m_i} \qquad (2.1)$$

where p_i is the price, w_i the money wage rate, n_i unit labor requirements, and m_i the unit materials cost (all with reference to a particular firm producing a single product).

If we assume that some given part of gross profit is spent on distribution of earnings and the salaries of managerial personnel, then the remainder constitutes a pool of earnings R_i capable of financing gross investment:

$$R_i = [p_i X_i - (w_i L_i + m_i X_i)](1 - a_i) \qquad (2.2)$$

where X_i, L_i, and a_i represent output, employment, and the proportion of gross profit spent on salaries and distributed to shareholders. We will treat investment (I_i) as a share of earnings:

$$I_i = c_i R_i \qquad (2.3)$$

c_i, the capitalization rate, measures the relation between capital accumulation and profit, it links capital in the past to capital in the future. We consider it subject to a decision based upon expectations concerning future profitability. The theory of capital accumulation focusses on the structural conditions that determine the magnitude of c_i and e_i.

If we let α_i represent the rate of capital accumulation of the firm and K_i its capital investment, then

$$\alpha_i = \frac{I_i}{K_i}$$

which, together with expressions 2.1, 2.2, and 2.3, implies that

$$\alpha_i = \frac{c_i(1 - a_i)(e_i - 1)}{k_i} \tag{2.4}$$

where k_i is the ratio of capital to prime costs.

The market enters into the determination of the growth of the firm through its effect upon the growth of productive capacity. The net increase in productive capacity depends upon net investment (gross investment, I_i, less costs of replacing used-up equipment) and any change in the capital–output ratio implied by the introduction of new equipment. If we let z_i represent the ratio of depreciation costs to output then

$$z_i = v_i d_i$$

where v_i and d_i represent the capital–output ratio and the rate of depreciation (replacement costs measured as a proportion of capital invested). The rate of increase of output capacity (τ_i) will be

$$\tau_i = \alpha_i - \gamma_i$$

where γ_i is the proportional rate of change of z_i. The expression τ_i links the rate of growth of the capital of the firm to the growth of the market. By so doing it also connects (see expression 2.4) prices and profits to market growth. If we can establish the way in which the growth of the market limits the growth of the capital of the firm (α_i) we will have simultaneously established how market growth enters into the determination of prices and profits.

The market for the products of the firm depends on both aggregate factors and factors specific to the firm and its particular product. Formally, the growth of demand for the product of a particular firm is a function of the growth of the market as a whole and the change in the firm's market share:

$$\eta_i = \eta + \sigma_i$$

where η and η_i represent the rate of growth of the market as a whole and of the market for the products of the particular firm; σ_i represents the ratio of any change in the firm's (or product's) market share to the size of its market.

We can incorporate the idea that the growth of the market limits the growth of the firm by assuming that

$$\tau_i \leq \eta_i$$

This implies that

$$\tau_i \leq \eta + \sigma_i + \gamma_i$$

The Marxian theory assumes that γ_i governs this relationship over the long run. In the classical theory all particular rates of growth of firms are assumed equal (in equilibrium) so that the problem is directly one of aggregate growth. Equation 2.5 appears as

$$\alpha(t) - \alpha(t-1) = \gamma$$

where $\alpha(t)$ is the current rate of accumulation and $\alpha(t-1)$ is the rate of accumulation in the previous period (equals the rate of market growth η). Since $\gamma < 0$ due to an increase in the capital–output ratio, the rate of accumulation falls over time for reasons having nothing to do with the market.

We will assume, by contrast, that capital intensity does not exhibit any tendency to rise or fall with changes in technology and the growth of capital ($\gamma_i = 0$) so that

$$\alpha_i \leq \eta + \sigma_i \qquad (2.5)$$

This in effect reverses the classical method, emphasizing the factors it excludes and leaving out of account the factor to which it assigns the primary role. We will see further on, however, that while this difference is basic it also allows us to formulate an important classical theme in a more satisfactory way.

Equation 2.5 suggests that the growth of the market acts as a limit to the accumulation of capital. This conclusion is not, however, immediately implied. In particular, since the rate of growth of the market (η) depends upon the demand-creating effects of investment it must be assumed to rise and fall with the particular rates of accumulation of the particular firms. The more rapidly firms accumulate capital the higher the overall rate of market growth. Indeed, the overall rate of growth of the market adjusts to investment decisions and must, in principle, correspond to the investment decisions of firms. This is the sense in which growth is a self-justifying and self-sustaining process. It seems to imply that the market limitation expressed in equation 2.5 is purely formal. If the market adjusts to investment decisions, how can it also limit them?

If firms use all of their profits for the acquisition of new means of production (and if consumers do not save) then aggregate demand will just equal the value of current output. Since within the circular flow of income and output the revenues received by consumers in their capacity as suppliers of productive inputs exactly equal the demand they represent as consumers, the corresponding costs of production must equal demand for means of consumption. This implies that demand for means of production must equal the revenue of firms after these costs have been subtracted. In other words, demand for means of production must equal gross profit. Thus, the amount of profit received by the aggregate of firms will equal the amount they spend on investment goods. This makes the investment decisions of firms the immediate cause of their profits when those firms are taken as a whole (Kalecki 1954).

Firms generate revenues through production and sale of commodities. These revenues are the incomes of consumers (wages, salaries, and possibly revenue from ownership of capital). If consumers spend all of their incomes on means of consumption, then the demand they generate will fall short of the value of output by the amount of profit or retained earnings (if we consider income from capital). In order to maintain incomes at the current level, firms must invest the difference between the value of output and the incomes of consumers. Or alternatively, the amount of investment will determine the level of output that can be sustained and therefore consumer incomes and demand for means of consumption.

Investment decisions depend on the expected profitability of production with new plant and equipment. This is true insofar as the object of the firm is the expansion of its capital and its markets and therefore the orientation of current production toward providing the foundation for expanded reproduction in the future. Because of this orientation, investment and profit depend upon expectations about the future, and because of this the path of economic growth will depend upon the environment in which agents form expectations. Consistent with our earlier discussion, we will assume that the economy consists of agents which organize their environment in such a way as to make possible decisions oriented toward the future. In brief, this means that agents form and act on the basis of long-period expectations. If we assume that agents form such a view of the world, their expectations can be of two kinds: (1) the future will be exactly like the present and the past (aside from minor variations associated with contingent factors); and (2) the future, while in important ways similar to the past, will also differ from it in ways relevant to the investment decision.

If firm's expectations are of the first kind, they will act to transmit past experience directly into current decisions and to use the past as a model for the future. High current profits will stimulate high rates of growth since they will yield expectations of high profits in the future. When each firm accumulates at a rapid rate, then the market for firms as a whole will expand at a high rate and will justify individual decisions to maintain high rates of investment. Conversely, low current or recent profits will discourage investment, which will adversely affect demand and maintain profits and investment at a low level.

This circle of mutual determination of profit, investment, and demand means that the subjective factor we associate with expectations plays a primary role in determining the growth of the capitalist economy. In a sense, the capitalist economy grows as rapidly as it has the will to grow.

In Keynesian theories, the "will" to grow is more or less given; and this tends to imply that it has a contingent and subjective determination. Indeed, when we focus exclusively on the process of circular causation, it appears that within wide limits, this process can sustain itself at arbitrarily determined rates. The objective element arises directly out of the relation of the individual producer to the system as a whole. The aggregate results of individual decision making have an objective force for the individual firm and face that firm as an external coercive force. The level of output, investment, and profit becomes an objective fact simply because of its ability to sustain itself through time. Indeed, it becomes an impediment to growth by fixing expansion at a given rate.

This impediment takes on a new dimension when we introduce explicitly the firm as an active agent pursuing the expansion of its capital and increase of its markets. In order for the mutual causation implied in the two-sided relation between investment and demand to directly determine the growth process it is necessary for the agents (especially firms) to take the structure of the market to be given. This implies that firms must accept the limits to their growth implied by the system their growth creates.

This conclusion denies, however, the inherent dynamism of the capitalist firm, which views all limits to growth as a challenge to be overcome rather than as a signal to restrict its aspirations. Instead of acting as a passive transmitting device linking investment to demand in a process of self-replicating growth, the firm acts to break the circle of causation that limits the growth of its capital. This makes the firm the active agent responsible for transforming economic growth into a process of structural change.

A contradiction develops between the intent of the firm to expand its capital and markets as rapidly as possible consistent with its long-run survival, and the objective fact of a given ongoing aggregate rate of market expansion which coerces the firm to grow within the limit it defines. This contradiction forces the firm to translate its intent to grow in size into a drive to grow through structural change and thus to contribute to a process of economic development. This leads us to shift to the second assumption concerning expectations. Clearly, if the firm adheres to the first assumption regarding expectations, it cannot overcome the limit defined by the self-sustaining rate of aggregate expansion. If firms assume that the future, while limited by the past, need not replicate the past, then room exists for the firm to break the circular causation that binds its particular rate of growth to a given rate of aggregate expansion.

The only structural changes systematically incorporated into the classical theory are changes in productivity. For Ricardo, changes in productivity result from natural conditions. Because of this the economic agents play a purely passive part in structural change. Marx reverses the Ricardian idea, focussing on improvements in methods of production brought about by capitalists in an effort to increase profitability and accelerate the growth of their capitals.

The classical theory focuses on the way in which changes in productivity affect capital accumulation by pressing down the rate of profit. At the same time, it assumes that the object of the producer in introducing new technique is to increase profit and investment. These two ideas are reconciled through a specific formulation of the relation between the individual producer and the price system. While the new technique employed upon the basis of existing prices yields a higher rate of profit, the new technique employed within the framework of prices appropriate to it (the corresponding prices of production with a given real wage) yields a lower rate of profit. The adjustment of prices to a new equilibrium subsequent to the introduction of the new technique reconciles the motivation of the producer to raise his profit rate with the result of his action, which is a lower profit rate.

This way of reconciling individual decisions with their systemic context presumes price flexibility, capital mobility, and constancy of the real wage. It also assumes that technical change increases the capital output relation ($\gamma_i > 0$) and therefore presses down the rate of profit. We have elsewhere argued that this last assumption applies only to a limited (though significant) historical experience and does not have general applicability to the process of capitalist expansion (Levine, 1975). If we drop the assumption of rising capital intensity, the impact of changes in productivity on growth appears in a decidedly different light.

As productivity increases, unit labor and materials costs fall, and the gross profit margin increases. The increase in the gross profit margin implies a tendency toward accelerating accumulation of capital (equation 2.4). If firms increase their capitals upon the basis of the increase in profit, the growth of the market as a whole will accelerate. The initial increase in productivity raises the self-sustaining rate of accumulation to a new level. But, if firms take the growth of the market into consideration in determining their rates of accumulation, an opposition will result between their potential for accumulation and the perceived capacity of the market to absorb products at an increasing rate. While the market as a whole grows to accommodate accumulation of firms taken as a whole, the market of the particular firm does not expand to accommodate its particular rate of investment. The mutual determiniation of demand and investment holds for the system as a whole but not for the individual agent. This means that while the growth of the market results from individual investment decision it also limits accumulation since it confronts the individual producer as an external coercive force.

Thus, when changes in productivity tend to increase profit margins the potential for capital accumulation comes into conflict with the capacity of the market to absorb the output of new capital. In order to resolve this conflict, the firm must work to alter its particular relation to the market. Since it takes the aggregate rate of market growth (η) to be given, an increase in its rate of accumulation depends upon its ability to increase its market share ($\sigma_i > 0$). Equation 2.5 expresses this aspect of the accumulation process.

In order to take changes in market shares into account, we must drop the classical assumptions that force us to treat determination of the growth process as a corollary of the idea of an equilibrium state within which profit rates are equal across firms. Instead, we have suggested a formulation within which growth drives firms to attempt to differentiate their rates of profit and accumulation. As we will see, this differentiation constitutes the process of capitalist expansion.

Growth of the firm's market share results from two separate factors: (1) growth of the industry within which the firm produces relative to the economy as a whole, and (2) redistribution of market shares within an industry. The first factor involves new product development, the second involves adjustments in market structure during the course of the development of a given product. We will consider the second factor first.

If the firm assumes that the overall distribution of demand across products and the rate of aggregate market growth are given, it can only overcome the market limit to its growth by increasing its share of a given demand. So far as the classical theory considers competition at all, it assumes that competition has this limited objective and that it can only redistribute a given pool of demand (until the point is reached at which the distribution of demand yields equal profit on all capitals). However, the premise of this argument—that the struggle over market shares does not affect aggregate growth—requires closer scrutiny.

The object of the struggle over shares is to enhance the rates of accumulation of particular firms. Insofar as expectations of a change in market share justify firm investment at a rate that exceeds the overall market growth rate and insofar as these expectations do not directly affect investment plans of other firms, such expectations, if sufficiently widespread, can lead to a change in aggregate growth. We can divide firms into three groups on the basis of expectations:

Group 1: firms that expect their market shares to rise ($\sigma_i > 0$)
Group 2: firms that expect their market shares to fall ($\sigma_i < 0$)
Group 3: firms that expect their shares to remain constant ($\sigma_i = 0$)

The classical theory assumes that the magnitude of investment plans on the part of Group 1 firms equals that of Group 2. This need not be the case. If pessimistic expectations in Group 2 do not offset the optimistic expectations in Group 1, then the overall growth rate will increase. In the limit, if optimistic expectations in Group 1 do not imply pessimistic expectations elsewhere, the effort to increase market share translates into a commensurate increase in demand. The struggle over shares stimulates the market in such a way as to allow all firms to accumulate (albeit at different rates). It follows that the intensity of the struggle over market shares can enter into the determination of aggregate growth. This suggests a basic weakness in the classical method of treating competition which, as we have seen, requires that we consider the result of competition without regard to the process of competition.

It is clear, however, that the struggle over shares of the market for a given product proceeds within definite limits. The firm's expectation of an increase in its share stems from a judgment of the relative strength of its current position. If competition strengthens that position at the expense of other firms it will eventually eliminate the weaker competitors; and with their elimination the competitive process eliminates the basis for the expectations that fuel it. Thus the more competition goes on under conditions approximate to those assumed in the classical theory, the more it will become self-limiting in the long run. This condition leads firms to shift their attention from the effort to change market shares to the development of new products and new markets which do not involve the limitations associated with competition within an industry.

While the development of a new product may adversely affect the markets for existing products, the expectation under which the firm operates when it introduces the new product does not require that result. This increases the likelihood that, in association with the development of a new product, Group 1 firms will outweigh Group 2 firms so that the effort to increase market share through product innovation will have a positive net effect.

The magnitude of the impact of any given new product on aggregate growth will also depend on the nature and magnitude of the capital investment required for its development. The less appropriate the existing capital to producing and marketing the new product, the greater the net capital investment its development stimulates. The greater this net investment, the greater the demand created, and the greater the stimulus to aggregate market growth.

In the absence of opportunities to change the structure of the existing market by redistribution or new product development, firms can break the market limit to growth by penetrating external markets. We can define external markets by reference to the system of mutual determination of demand and investment. The demand created within this system constitutes the internal market. It includes demand directly generated by investment (for labor and means of production) and demand generated indirectly via the multiplier effects. The internal market is the self-generating system of capitalist commodity production taken as a whole. Demand originating outside of this system constitutes an external market. By definition, the external market arises out of noncapitalist relations of production and circulation. When noncapitalist producers produce for and depend upon exchange they constitute an external market for capitalist production. If capitalist producers can take over the markets of noncapitalist producers and make them markets for their own products, the markets for the products of those capitalist producers will grow at a rate in excess of the rate of growth of their internal market. This difference represents the rate of penetration of external markets and results from the competition between capitalist and noncapitalist systems of production and exchange.

The availability of external markets depends upon the presence of a common means of exchange between the capitalist and precapitalist systems. Only in the presence of a common means of exchange can the circulation of commodities in the noncapitalist sector constitute a market for capitalist commodity production. This condition tends to be self-terminating as the penetration of the external market leads to concentration of the means of payment into the capitalist sector. Unless the noncapitalist sector produces the means of exchange (e.g., gold), its relationship with the capitalist sector must ultimately destroy it.

Taking into account external markets and assuming that the firm accumulates capital at a rate determined by expected market limits, we can rewrite equation 2.5 as follows:[4]

$$\alpha_i = \eta + \sigma_i^1 + \sigma_i^2 \tag{2.6}$$

where σ_i^1 and σ_i^2 represent the firm's expectation of an increase in its market share and its ability to penetrate external markets. Equation 2.6 allows us to distinguish two distinct relationships between the particular firm and the market as a whole. In the first, we treat the firm as a transmitting device which sustains a given rate of aggregate market growth. Thus

$$\alpha_i = \alpha \qquad \text{for all firms, and} \qquad \alpha = \eta.$$

This relationship between the firm and the market characterizes the circular causation of the Keynesian theory and reproduces the classical idea of the firm as an adapting agent that takes the existing conditions to be given. The second relationship between the firm and the market focusses on the shares factors ($\sigma_i{}^1$ and $\sigma_i{}^2$) and emphasizes the way in which the firm works to distinguish its particular rate of growth from that of the market as a whole. In this case

$$\alpha_i - \eta = \sigma_i^1 + \sigma_i^2$$

The second relationship between the firm and the market, if sufficiently widespread, implies a change in the structure and growth rate of the market as a whole. It means that the new rate of overall market growth will differ by an amount determined by the net effect of structural change and this means that the rate of structural change as measured by the market shares factors enters into the determination of the pace of economic expansion. Under these conditions, growth takes place through structural change. Perception of and exploitation of opportunities for market development determine the rate of growth of the market. The unity of growth and development implied in the second relationship between firm and market challenges the classical method, which separates the process of structural change from the determination of the rate of growth viewing the rate of growth in equilibrium subsequent (in logical time) to the completion of the process of structural change.

This challenge to the classical method extends into the theory of the market and of price formation. The process of structural change is a process of the redistribution of the existing market and the opening up of new markets. Within this process, price determination must be understood as a mechanism of market development rather than as an equilibrating mechanism given technical conditions, income distribution, and, therefore, the distribution of output.

If we assume that the expected rate of market growth for the firm determines investment, then market growth together with technical conditions will determine the capitalization rate and profit margins. Combining expressions (2.4) and (2.6) we have

$$c_i(e_i - 1) = \frac{k_i(\eta + \sigma_i^1 + \sigma_i^2)}{1 - a_i}$$

If the capitalization rate is given, then the price and profit margin must adjust to the rate of market growth. If the capitalization rate is not given, it must be determined jointly with the profit margin. Such adjustments are impossible in the classical theory since the theory assumes (1) that all net profit is invested ($c_i = 1$) and (2) that the profit margin is determined either by market prices (supply and demand) or by the real wage (natural prices). This means that the determination must go from the profit margin to the rate of market growth rather than vice versa as suggested here.

The classical theory does not allow the firm to adjust the parameters of its relationship to the market in order to determine its particular rate of accumulation according to its perception of opportunities for market development appropriate to it. In the alternative theory outlined here, the firm treats its profit margin and capitalization rate as variables subject to determination within an accumulation strategy designed to take advantage of the ongoing process of market development.

The firm works to determine its particular market (its structure and growth rate) in accordance with its need to survive and grow. This does not mean that the firm possesses unlimited power to accomplish its particular ends. It does mean that the firm acts as the specific agent of change and because of this its particular ends and range of action in its environment must be taken into account in the analysis of the structure and growth of the market. Since the primary end of the firm is long-run accumulation, when we place the firm at the center of a process of development we must explicitly consider a structure and process that support reproduction and capital accumulation over the long run. And, we must treat the firm as in part responsible for bringing into existence a structure of long-run expansion which makes possible its own development into an enduring institution.

Towards a Rejuvenated Classical Economics

The classical theory conceives of the economy as a determinate system by treating the economic process as a material process. Our reconceptualization also focusses on reproduction or recurrence as the central concern of a deterministic theory. We have, however, relinquished the idea of equilibrium as material/technical renewal. In its place we propose to focus on the specification of the particular agent and that agent's relation to the system as a whole. We can draw conclusions about the nature of the determinacy of a market economy from a specification of this relation so long as the agents carry within them the drive toward renewal of the system as a whole, while the system generated out of the joint actions of agents limits and defines their activities.

As we have seen, the classical method incorporates a specific conception of the relation between the individual agent and the economy as a whole. This conception embodies a contradiction which undermines the development of a genuinely deterministic theory. The contradiction arises because of the opposition within the structure of classical theory between (1) the idea that determinacy is rooted in the recurrence through reproduction of the system of economic relations and (2) the specification of the agent and his relation to the system of agents in such a way as to make recurrence accidental. Our reconceptualization of classical theory accepts the validity of the first aspect of the classical argument while seeking to recast the conception of the agent in order to make it consistent with the idea of recurrence. This reconstruction allows us to conceptualize not only the implication of reproduction for a determinate price system but also the process through which the system regenerates and transforms itself through time.

The agent whose activities bind together the temporal flow and constitute a coherent process is the capitalist firm viewed as an entity sui generis. The firm organizes its world into a form consistent with its own sustenance and growth. This world, in turn, shapes the firm in accordance with its own intrinsic logic—the logic of a system of firms. This two-sided relationship constitutes capitalist development as a coherent, integrated process. The theory outlined above indicates the hidden potential of one aspect of classical methodology to articulate the logical structure of the development process of a capitalist economy.

Notes

[1] For a more detailed discussion, see Levine (1981).

[2] See in particular the work stemming from Sraffa (1960).

[3] Changes in the form of the product and advertising involve the consumer. They require a specification of rational decision making on the part of the consumer consistent with recurrence. See Levine (1981).

[4] Subscripts now refer to the weighted average over the set of products produced by a particular firm.

References

Harrod, R. 1939. An Essay in Dynamic Theory. *Economic Journal* 49.

Kalecki, Michal. 1954. *Theory of Economic Dynamics*. Reading MA: Allen & Unwin.

Levine, David. 1975. The Theory of the Growth of the Capitalist Economy. *Economic Development and Cultural Change* 24 (October). 114–136

Levine, David. 1978, 1981. *Economic Theory* (two volumes). London: Routledge and Kegan Paul.

Levine, David. 1980. Aspects of the Classical Theory of Markets. *Australian Economic Papers* (June). (19):1–15

Levine, David. 1982. Determinants of Capitalist Expansion. *Economic Development and Cultural Change* 3 (January):299–320

Levine, David. 1984. Long-period Expectations and Investment. *Social Concept* 1 (March):41–51

Penrose, E. 1959. *The Theory of Growth of the Firm*. New York: Wiley.

Robinson, J. 1962. *Essays in the Theory of Economic Growth*. London: Macmillan.

Sraffa, Piero. 1960. *Production of Commodities by Means of Commodities*. New York: Cambridge University Press.

Steedman, I. 1977. *Marx after Sraffa*. London: New Left Books.

Steindl, Josef. 1952. *Maturity and Stagnation in American Capitalism*. Oxford: Blackwell.

Walsh, Vivian, and Harvey, Gram. 1980. *Classical and Neo-classical Theories of General Equilibrium*. New York: Oxford University Press.

3 PROPERTY APPROPRIATION AND ECONOMIC THEORY

David P. Ellerman

Appropriation in Property Theory

The Distributive Shares Metaphor

There is a major logical gap in neoclassical economic theory. This gap has not been revealed in the debates between neoclassical value theory and alternative theories such as the neo-Ricardian, post-Keynesian, or Marxist value theories. The reason is simple; all these value theories ignore or misrepresent the structure of property appropriation in production. An accurate description of the structure of property rights and obligations in production requires not a new value theory, but a different type of theory, property theory.

Prior to the neoclassical marginalist revolution, the structure of property rights was considered part of political economy [e.g., J. S. Mill's *Principles of Political Economy*, especially Book II, Chapters I and II, "Of Property" and "The Same Subject Continued"]. There has been a recent revival of interest among economists in property rights—e.g., in the work of Coase, Alchian, Demsetz, Furubotn, Pejovich, and Williamson, which will be referred to as the *economics of property rights* literature.

The theory of property presented here differs markedly from the conventional economics of property rights because the latter has no rigorously specified theory of property appropriation in production. The literature is largely informal in its discussion of property rights. The question of appropriation in production is not sharply posed, much less adequately dealt with, in the economics of property rights literature.

The treatment of property appropriation given here is mathematically formulated (Ellerman, 1982) and is integrated with the existing description of the stocks and flows of value within the business firm, i.e., with accounting. But the conventional literature is informal and largely metaphorical; it uses the methodology of "as if". It is "as if" the factor suppliers each contracted for a share of the product and then the entrepreneur was the claimant of the remaining residual. It is "as if" piece workers were selling their product. It is "as if" employees with profit sharing joined the entrepreneur in getting a share of the residual profits.

The ruling metaphor is the *distributive shares metaphor* which pictures the factor owners as getting shares in the product. Income is pictured as being distributed within a firm "as if" each factor supplier had a contractual claim on a fixed or variable share of the product. In the usual treatment of marginal productivity theory, each factor is pictured "as if" it "produced" and then "received" a share of the product. It is "as if" all this were the case, but what is actually the case?

As a description of property rights, the distributive shares picture is quite misleading. The simple fact is that one legal party, such as the employer in a capitalist firm, owns all the product. For example, General Motors doesn't own just "capital's share" of the GM cars produced; it owns all of them. Orthodox economists are, of course, aware of this legalistic fact, but they feel called upon to metaphorically reinterpret the product as being "shared", or "distributed", in order to account for the income received by the input suppliers. How else can one account for the other factor incomes if one factor is pictured as owning all the product?

Economists should resist the temptation to improve upon the legal facts with the economic metaphor of distributive shares; the legal facts suffice to explain the factor incomes. Property can take either a positive or negative form as assets or liabilities, i.e., as property rights or obligations. By "product", economists mean only the positive product, the output assets produced in production. But there is also a negative product. To produce the output assets, it is necessary to incur the liabilities for using up the inputs. And one can 'own', or hold, liabilities just as one can own assets. The simple fact that accounts for the other factor incomes without the distributive shares metaphor is the fact that the one party who owns all the positive product also owns all the negative product, i.e., also holds all the liabilities for the used-up inputs. General Motors not only owns all the GM cars produced but also holds all the liabilities for the factors such as steel, rubber, glass, and labor used up in production. The money paid out to satisfy these liabilities represents the costs of production. The suppliers of the steel, labor, and other factors, instead of being joint claimants on the product, are only creditors of that one party who owns all the positive and negative product. One party owns all the outputs but that party does not receive its value in net terms since that party must also satisfy the liabilities for the inputs.

The Whole Product

We have seen that in order to accurately describe the structure of property rights in production without the "benefit" of the distributive shares metaphor, it is necessary to expand the usual concept of "product" to include the negative product (input liabilities) in addition to the usual positive product (output assets). This bundle of property rights and obligations will be called the *whole product*, i.e.,

$$\text{whole product} = \text{output assets} + \text{input liabilities}$$

A party can acquire the legal title to an asset in two ways: (1) by acquiring the legal right by transfer from a prior owner as in a market exchange, and (2) by being the first or initial owner of the asset. The first or inital acquisition of the legal right to an asset is called the *appropriation of the asset*. Similarly, there are two ways that a party can disacquire or give up the legal title to an asset: (1) by transferring the legal right to another party as in a market exchange, and (2) by being the last or terminal owner of the asset. In the second case, the owner surrenders legal right and claim to the asset but not by transferring it to another party (e.g., when the asset is consumed or used up in production). This termination of the legal title to an asset is called *appropriation of the liability* for the used-up assets.

In production, the outputs are produced and the inputs are used up. Prior to the productive activity, the output assets were not yet created and the legal right to the inputs had not been terminated. In production, a question arises. Who is to appropriate the liabilities for the used-up inputs and who is to appropriate the outputs? The output assets and the input liabilities are precisely the whole product. Hence the basic question about the structure of property rights and obligations in production is, "Who is to appropriate the whole product?"

This fundamental question has both a normative and a descriptive interpretation. Who ought to appropriate the whole product and who in fact does appropriate the whole product? We will first consider the descriptive question.

The Market Mechanism of Appropriation

It is interesting that the question of appropriation does not seem to be sharply posed in the economic, legal, or philosophical literature. When the question of appropriation is discussed, it concerns not day-to-day production and consumption but some original or primal distribution of property. Economists discuss the initial or original distribution of factor ownership in the models used in welfare economics but do not even recognize the occurrence of appropriation in any of the production that follows the initial distribution of factors. Jurists and philosophers contemplate the original appropriation of unowned or commonly owned objects in manner following Locke's example—which set the context as a mythical original state of society. Yet new property is created and old property is consumed in everyday production and consumption activities, not just in some mythical "original position." Moreover, when appropriation is discussed, it is limited to assets and neglects the symmetrical treatment of liabilities.

In the economic literature, production is sometimes described as "trading with nature." That is a metaphor, not a description of a legal mechanism of appropriation. Economists are well aware of the legal mechanism of contract used to acquire and disacquire property rights in market exchanges. But conventional economics has ignored the legal mechanism used to acquire and disacquire property rights in trades with nature. If one must use such a metaphor of appropriation as "trading with nature," then what is the legal mechanism—the "contract with nature"—by which one disacquires the inputs and acquires the outputs of production?

An appropriation, since it only involves one legal party such as a corporation, is not as public as a legal transfer between parties. Indeed, it is only the contested appropriations which involve two or more parties that come to the attention of the legal authorities. For example, a property damage suit arises out of a situation where one party, the plaintiff, has de facto appropriated certain liabilities that the plaintiff believes should be appropriated by another party. If the court agrees, then the resulting damage payments are an example of a legally enforced appropriation of liabilities by the defendent. But such examples are relatively rare, whereas the matter of appropriating liabilities arises whenever property is consumed, used up, or otherwise destroyed in all production or consumption activities. The matter of appropriating assets arises whenever new property is created, as in any production activities. If contract is the normal legal mechanism for transferring property, what is the normal legal mechanism for the appropriation of the assets and liabilities created in production and consumption?

When no law is broken so that the legal authorities do not intervene to hold a trial, then there is a laissez-faire or invisible-hand mechanism that automatically takes over. That is, when the law does not intervene to reassign the liability for a used-up asset, then that liability is automatically left in the hands of the last legal owner of the asset. If the last legal owner does not voluntarily appropriate the liability, the party can seek redress by trying to get the legal system to intervene and reassign the liability.

If appropriable new assets are produced as a result when certain commodities or assets are used up, then the legal party that voluntarily appropriated the liabilities for the used-up assets would naturally lay claim on the produced assets. In the absence of any reassignment of the liabilities, the legal authorities would consider that claim as being defensible. Hence we have the normal legal mechanism governing how assets and liabilities are in fact appropriated in normal day-to-day activities of production and consumption.

THE MARKET MECHANISM OF APPROPRIATION: When no law is broken, let the liabilities generated by an activity lie where they have fallen, and then let the party that assumed the liabilities claim any appropriable new assets resulting from the activity.

It is this laissez-faire mechanism that determines who in fact appropriates the whole product in normal production activities. One party purchases all the requisite inputs to production, including labor, and then that party bears those costs as the inputs are consumed in production. Hence that party has the legally defensible claim on the produced outputs. In this simple manner, one party legally appropriates the whole product of production (input liabilities and output assets).

The market mechanism of appropriation also shows how profits can co-exist with equal-valued market exchanges in a capitalist economy. Some exchanges are just exchanges, while some exchanges (e.g., the purchase of a complete set of inputs) set up the appropriation of the whole product via the market mechanism of appropriation. The profits are the value of that appropriated whole product.

The market mechanism of appropriation is quite independent of the various assumptions about market conditions and equilibrium usually made in economic models. The property theoretic mechanism has the same structure regardless of whether the markets are competitive or not or are in equilibrium or disequilibrium. One of the methodological techniques used in property theory (e.g., in our analysis of capital theory given below) is to first establish a property theoretic result in the context of a familiar competitive model, and then to note that the structure of property rights (properly formulated) is in fact independent of market conditions. That structure is concerned with the basic "rules of the game," a game that might be played under competitive or noncompetitive conditions and in states of equilibrium or disequilibrium.

Given a production activity, the legal party who legally appropriates the whole product of the production activity will be called the *firm*. Hence the question of who is to appropriate the whole product is really the question of who is to be the firm. There are three basic types of firms. In a capitalist firm, the whole product is appropriated by "capital", the suppliers of equity capital. In a socialist firm, it is "society" organized as the government that appropriates the whole product. In the type of firm called a worker cooperative or a self-managed firm it is the party herein called "labor", consisting of all those who work in the enterprise, who would appropriate the whole product (see the literature of the Industrial Cooperative Association such as Ellerman, 1981, 1984). Hence the basic question that differentiates capitalist production, socialist production, and self-managed production is the question: "Who is to be the firm?"—capital, the state, or labor?

The descriptive question of who is to be the firm is answered by the laissez–faire mechanism. The whole-product appropriator is the party who hired (or already owned) the inputs and assumed those costs as the inputs were used up in production and thus could lay claim to the produced outputs. Hence the determination of who is the firm, i.e., who appropriates the whole product, is based on how the input hiring contracts are made. If capital hires labor, then capital is the firm. If labor hires the capital, then labor is the firm. If some third party (such as an entrepreneur or even the state) hires both the capital and workers, then that third party is the firm. Hence the determination of who is to be the firm is decided in factor markets by who hires what or whom.

The determination of who is to be the firm is thus not decided by the ownership of the means of production or by any so-called "ownership of the firm". The ownership of capital does not legally determine who is to be the whole-product appropriator since capital can be hired out just as labor can be hired in. It is the *direction* of the hiring contracts that decides the matter. There is no property right called "the ownership of the firm" which legally determines the matter.

There is, of course, the legal form of the capitalist corporation that is owned by its shareholders. But prior to the hiring contracts, a corporation is only a capital owner. Capital owners meet labor in the market. Labor could hire capital just as the capital owners can hire labor. It is the direction of that hiring contract that determines whether the capital-owning corporation hires in labor and is thus the firm or whether the corporation is only a capital supplier whose business is hiring out its capital to another party who uses it in production and who is thus the firm (whole-product appropriator). There is no necessity for the other party such as labor to "buy the firm"; hiring the capital will suffice. The ownership of the means of production thus embodies no legal obligation for the owners of the capital to be the firm, to appropriate the whole product produced using that capital. However, the ownership of capital is quite relevant to the question of marketplace power, the question of which party has the power to make the hiring contracts in its favor.

Appropriation in Accounting

Property Accounting

The "firm," as it appears in price theory, is highly abstract and stylized. For a more realistic description of the fine structure of production inside a firm, e.g., the stocks and flows of value in a production process, one must turn to accounting. The development of property theory at the concrete level of business accounting has been introduced in more detail elsewhere (Ellerman, 1982, 1985, 1986). This new theory is called *property accounting*, and uses the formal machinery of double entry accounting with vectors to describe the subject matter of property theory. Property accounting provides a description of the fine structure of appropriation in production and shows where appropriation occurs beneath the transactions of conventional value accounting. Readers who do not wish to delve into this integrated treatment of property theory and accounting should go directly to the next section of this chapter.

In double entry property accounting, assets appear as property credits and liabilities appear as property debits in the equity or total-ownership property account called Total Assets and Liabilities. It is the property account underlying the value account of New Worth or Equity. Hence the appropriation of assets and liabilities is formulated in property accounting as the appropriation of property credits and property debits. The temporary property T-account which contains all the appropriated property credits and debits is called the Whole Product T-account since it represents all the assets and liabilities resulting from production.

In double entry property accounting, each property T-account consists of a pair of nonnegative vectors, the credit vector on the right-hand side of the T-account and the debit vector on the left-hand side:

property T-account = [debit vector // credit vector]

In the Whole Product T-account, the credit vector is called the *positive product* and represents the output assets appropriated in production. The debit vector is called the *negative product* and represents the input liabilities appropriated in production. The Whole Product is a right-hand side or credit balance T-account; so, as a vector with positive and negative components (rather than a pair of nonnegative vectors), the Whole Product is the difference between the positive product (credit vector) and the negative product (debit vector), i.e.,

whole product vector = positive product − negative product

Whole product vectors are not new in economic theory; they are the production vectors in the production set representation or productive opportunities inspired by the noncalculus mathematics of activity analysis (Koopmans, 1951). A feasible whole product vector is called a *production possibility vector* (Arrow and Debreu, 1954, p. 267), an *activity vector* (Arrow and Hahn, 1971, p. 59), a *production* (Debreu, 1959, p. 38) or *input-output vector* (Quirk and Saposnik, 1968, p. 27). Economists represent the outputs as positive components and the inputs as negative components but without any interpretation in terms of accounting (assets and liabilities).

How does property change? Property changes by

1. *transactions* between legal parties, and
2. *appropriations* (or, metaphorically, transactions with nature).

Transactions between legal parties can be divided into two types:

1. a.   *market transactions*, where there is an equal quid pro quo in market value, and
2. b.   *nonreciprocal transfers* between legal parties—e.g., dividends, taxes, and gifts.

It is convenient to further subdivide market transactions into

1. a. 1.   purchases, and
1. a. 2.   sales.

We have briefly catalogued the ways in which property changes. Any of these changes in property can be interpreted in either of two fundamental senses:

A. as a change in the legal property rights, i.e., as a *de jure* or *legal* change, and
B. as a change in the possession of the property, i.e., as a *de facto* or *factual* change.

For instance, in a market transaction, a legally valid contract constitutes the exchange of legal property rights. The actual delivery of the goods and the payment of the consideration constitute the factual exchange of property. The factual transfers are said to "fulfill" the contract. Both the legal transaction and the factual transaction must be recorded in property accounting. For a current cash market exchange, both the legal and factual transaction could be recorded with one accounting transaction.

For credit transactions, the legal and factual transfers are accounted for separately. In a credit purchase of inputs, there is the legal transaction wherein a present right to certain inputs is exchanged for the right to certain future-dated cash. Only one side of the factual transaction can occur at the time of the credit transaction, namely the delivery of the purchased inputs. The other side of the factual transaction, the payment of the future-dated cash, must await that future due date. In the mean time, the unfulfilled legal transfer sits on the balance sheet as a liability.

In order to express property accounting mathematically, it was first necessary to describe double entry bookkeeping in mathematical terms. Surprisingly, the modern mathematical treatment of double entry bookkeeping was not previously known in the accounting literature (see Ellerman, 1982, 1985). Double entry bookkeeping is mathematically based on the group of differences construction in group theory, which is used, for example, to construct the additive group of all the integers using ordered pairs of natural numbers (nonnegative integers). The ordered pairs are exactly the T-accounts of double entry bookkeeping. The extension to ordered pairs of nonnegative vectors gives the vector *T-accounts* or *T-terms* used in property accounting.

Let W, X, Y, and Z be nonnegative n-dimensional vectors. Given the two T-accounts $[W /\!/ X]$ and $[Y /\!/ Z]$, the *cross-sums* are the two vectors $W + Z$ and $X + Y$ obtained by adding the debit vector in one T-account with the credit vector in the other T-account. Two T-accounts are *equal* if their cross-sums are equal:

$$[W /\!/ X] = [Y /\!/ Z] \quad \text{if} \quad W + Z = X + Y$$

T-accounts add together by adding debit to debit and credit to credit:

$$[W /\!/ X] + [Y /\!/ Z] = [W + Y /\!/ X + Z]$$

The *zero T-account*, $[0 /\!/ 0]$ (where 0 stands for the n-dimensional zero vector), is the additive identity element:

$$[W /\!/ X] + [0 /\!/ 0] = [W /\!/ X]$$

The additive *inverse* of a T-account is obtained by reversing the debit and credit entries:

$$[W /\!/ X] + [X /\!/ W] = [W + X /\!/ X + W] = [0 /\!/ 0]$$

A T-account or T-term $[W /\!/ X]$ equal to the zero T-account will be called a *zero-term*.

Each T-account has a unique *reduced-form* representation where each component in the vectors is zero either on the debit side or the credit side of the T-account. A T-account, $[W /\!/ X]$ is put into reduced form by subtracting the minimum $\min(W, X)$ of the vectors (computed component-wise) from each side:

$$[W /\!/ X] = [W - \min(W, X) /\!/ X - \min(W, X)]$$

Given the T-account $[(100, 40, 18) /\!/ (120, 36, 20)]$, the minimum of the debit and credit vectors is $(100, 36, 18)$ so the reduced-form representation of the T-account is

$$\begin{aligned}
&[(100, 40, 18) - (100, 36, 18) /\!/ (120, 36, 20) - (100, 36, 18)] \\
&= [(0, 4, 0) /\!/ (20, 0, 2)]
\end{aligned}$$

"Putting a vector T-account into reduced form" is the vector accounting operation of "finding the balance in a T-account." The remaining vector accounting machinery will be developed in the context of the following concrete example.

A Property Accounting Example

Consider a simple manufacturing enterprise which utilizes the commodities of cash, outputs, and inputs so the quantity vectors are three dimensional:

$$(\text{cash}, \text{outputs}, \text{inputs})$$

There are no fixed assets. The cost of interest and taxes will be ignored. The initial *Assets* vector is $(2500, 10, 6)$ so there is \$2500 of cash on hand, the output inventory contains 10 physical units of outputs, and the input inventory contains 6 physical units of the inputs. In a later section, we will see how a property vector like the Assets (2500, 10, 6) might be multiplied by a cost vector such as (1, 2.5, 5) to yield the familiar valuation of Assets at cost: $(2500 \times 1) + (10 \times 2.5) + (6 \times 5) = \$2555$.

Debts are legal obligations for future-dated cash (or other asset) payments. We will represent debts in terms of the present cash which would pay off the debt. Debts are owed to other legal parties, so the vector representing that debt can be labeled with the name of that party. We assume that the firm owes a bank a debt with the present value of $1000, so it would be represented by the vector (1000, 0, 0). The remaining vector which completes the balance sheet identity will be called the Total Assets and Liabilities vector or just the Total A&L vector. The initial balance sheet vector equation is

$$\begin{array}{ccc} \textit{Assets} & \textit{Bank Debt} & \textit{Total A\&L} \\ (2500, 10, 6) = & (1000, 0, 0) + & (1500, 10, 6) \end{array}$$

The Total A&L property account records the total legal rights and obligations of the legal party. Temporary or flow accounts will be associated with it to record changes in legal rights and obligations. The summary flow account associated with the Total A&L will simply be called Changes in A&L or simply $dA\&L$. This summary flow account will be subdivided into other flow accounts which record the various specific ways that property rights change—e.g., market transactions, nonreciprocal transfers, and appropriations.The market transactions will be recorded in two accounts, Purchases and Sales. We will not consider any nonreciprocal transfers, so that account will not be needed. The appropriations will be recorded in the Whole Product account.

Debts owned by the firm and debts owed to the firm require personal accounts for the creditors (such as the Bank Debt account) and debtors. Since credit transactions create such debts, we require a personal account for each party involved in a credit transaction. In the economic activity being modeled in the example, we will assume a credit purchase of some inputs from suppliers so there will be a Suppliers account. With the flow accounts and the Suppliers account added in (all with zero balances), the initial balance sheet vector equation is

$$\begin{array}{ccccc} \textit{Assets} & \textit{Bank Debt} & \textit{Suppliers} & \textit{Total A\&L} \\ (2500, 10, 6) = & (1000, 0, 0) + & (0, 0, 0) & + (1500, 10, 6) \\ & \textit{Whole Prod.} & \textit{Purchases} & \textit{Sales} & dA\&L \\ & + \quad (0, 0, 0) & + \quad (0, 0, 0) & + (0, 0, 0) + & (0, 0, 0) \end{array}$$

An equation between nonnegative vectors, where each vector has a positive coeffficient, is *encoded* into a zero-term by encoding each left-hand-side (LHS) vector W as a debit balance or LHS T-account $[W /\!/ 0]$, and each right-hand-side (RHS) vector X as a credit balance or RHS T-account $[0 /\!/ X]$. Such a zero-term is called an *equational zero-term* since it represents an equation. The initial balance sheet equation is encoded as the following initial equational zero-term:

$$
\begin{array}{ccc}
\textit{Assets} & \textit{Bank Debt} & \textit{Suppliers} \\
[(2500, 10, 6) /\!/ (0, 0, 0)] \;+\; & [(0, 0, 0) /\!/ (100, 0, 0)] \;+\; & [(0, 0, 0) /\!/ (0, 0, 0)] \\
\textit{Total A\&L} & \textit{Whole Product} & \textit{Purchases} \\
+\; [(0, 0, 0) /\!/ (1500, 10, 6)] \;+\; & [(0, 0, 0) /\!/ (0, 0, 0)] \;+\; & [(0, 0, 0) /\!/ (0, 0, 0)] \\
& \textit{Sales} & \textit{dA\&L} \\
& +\; [(0, 0, 0) /\!/ (0, 0, 0)] \;+\; & [(0, 0, 0) /\!/ (0, 0, 0)]
\end{array}
$$

Since the T-accounts can only be added together, we can leave the plus signs implicit so that we have the set of property T-accounts called the *property ledger*.

The following is the list of the economic events we assume to take place:

1. 15 units of the inputs are purchased and delivered for $5 cash each.
2. Contract for credit purchase of 5 units of inputs at $5 each.
3. Suppliers deliver the 5 units purchased on credit.
4. 18 units of the inputs are used up in production.
5. 36 units of the outputs are produced.
6. 40 units of the outputs are sold and delivered for $3 cash each.

Each event will be encoded as a zero-term. These zero-terms will be called *transactional zero-terms* since they represent transactions. For instance, the transactional zero-term for the first transaction is

$$
\begin{array}{cc}
\textit{Assets} & \textit{Purchases} \\
[(0, 0, 15) /\!/ (75, 0, 0)] \;+\; & [(75, 0, 0) /\!/ (0, 0, 15)]
\end{array}
$$

The list of the transactional zero-terms with the affected T-accounts is the *property journal*.

Table 3-1:   Property Journal

	Accounts and Description	[Debit	//	Credit]
1	Assets	[(0, 0, 15)	//	(75, 0, 0)]
	Purchases	[(75, 0, 0)	//	(0, 0, 15)]
	Cash purchase of inputs			
2	Suppliers	[(0, 0, 5)	//	(25, 0, 0)]
	Purchases	[(25, 0, 0)	//	(0, 0, 5)]
	Contract to purchase inputs on credit			
3	Assets	[(0, 0, 5)	//	(0, 0, 0)]
	Suppliers	[(0, 0, 0)	//	(0, 0, 5)]
	Delivery of purchased inputs			
4	Whole Product	[(0, 0, 18)	//	(0, 0, 0)]
	Assets	[(0, 0, 0)	//	(0, 0, 18)]
	Inputs used up in production			
5	Assets	[(0, 36, 0)	//	(0, 0, 0)]
	Whole Product	[(0, 0, 0)	//	(0, 36, 0)]
	Outputs produced in production			
6	Assets	[(120, 0, 0)	//	(0, 40, 0)]
	Sales	[(0, 40, 0)	//	(120, 0, 0)]
	Cash sale of outputs			

The temporary or flow accounts—Whole Product, Purchases, and Sales are then closed into the summary flow account $dA\&L$, which is then closed into Total A&L.

Table 3-2:   Property Ledger

	Accounts and Description	[Debit	//	Credit]
C1	Whole Product	[(0, 36, 0)	//	(0, 0, 18)]
	$dA\&L$	[(0, 0, 18)	//	(0, 36, 0)]
	Close Whole Product into $dA\&L$			
C2	Purchases	[(0, 0, 20)	//	(100, 0, 0)]
	$dA\&L$	[(100, 0, 0)	//	(0, 0, 20)]
	Close Purchases into $dA\&L$			
C3	Sales	[(120, 0, 0)	//	(0, 40, 0)]
	$dA\&L$	[(0, 40, 0)	//	(120, 0, 0)]
	Close Sales into $dA\&L$			
C4	$dA\&L$	[(20, 0, 2)	//	(0, 4, 0)]
	Total A&L	[(0, 4, 0)	//	(20, 0, 2)]
	Close $dA\&L$ into Total A&L			

The list of the property T-accounts in the equational zero-term is the property ledger. "Posting the journal to the "ledger" means adding all the transactional zero-terms (the journal) to the equational zero-term (the ledger).

Table 3–3:   Posting the Journal to the Ledger

		Assets				*Bank Debt*	
	$[(2500, 10, 6)$	//	$(0, 0, 0)]$		$[(0, 0, 0)$	//	$(1000, 0, 0)]$
(1)	$[(0, 0, 15)$	//	$(75, 0, 0)]$				
(3)	$[(0, 0, 5)$	//	$(0, 0, 0)]$				
(4)	$[(0, 0, 0)$	//	$(0, 0, 18)]$				
(5)	$[(0, 36, 0)$	//	$(0, 0, 0)]$				
(6)	$[(120, 0, 0)$	//	$(0, 40, 0)]$				
	$[(2620, 46, 26)$	//	$(75, 40, 18)]$				
=	$[(2545, 6, 8)$	//	$(0, 0, 0)]$				

		Suppliers				*Total A&L*	
(2)	$[(0, 0, 5)$	//	$(25, 0, 0)]$		$[(0, 0, 0)$	//	$(1500, 10, 6)]$
(3)	$(0, 0, 0)$	//	$(0, 0, 5)]$	(C4)	$[(0, 4, 0)$	//	$(20, 0, 2)]$
	$[(0, 0, 5)$	//	$(25, 0, 5)]$		$[(0, 4, 0)$	//	$(1520, 10, 8)]$
=	$[(0, 0, 0)$	//	$(25, 0, 0)]$	=	$[(0, 0, 0)$	//	$(1520, 6, 8)]$

		Whole Product				*Purchases*	
(4)	$[(0, 0, 18)$	//	$(0, 0, 0)]$	(1)	$[(75, 0, 0)$	//	$(0, 0, 15)]$
(5)	$[(0, 0, 0)$	//	$(0, 36, 0)]$	(2)	$[(25, 0, 0)$	//	$(0, 0, 5)]$
(C1)	$[(0, 36, 0)$	//	$(0, 0, 18)]$	(C2)	$[(0, 0, 20)$	//	$(100, 0, 0)]$

		Sales				*dA&L*	
(6)	$[(0, 40, 0)$	//	$(120, 0, 0)]$	(C1)	$[(0, 0, 18)$	//	$(0, 26, 0)]$
(C3)	$[(120, 0, 0)$	//	$(0, 40, 0)]$	(C2)	$[(100, 0, 0)$	//	$(0, 0, 20)]$
				(C3)	$[(0, 40, 0)$	//	$(120, 0, 0)]$
					$[(100, 40, 18)$	//	$(120, 36, 20)]$
				=	$[(0, 4, 0)$	//	$(20, 0, 2)]$
				(C4)	$[(20, 0, 2)$	//	$(0, 4, 0)]$

The T-accounts are summed, put into reduced form, and those with a zero balance are closed (underscored twice). Dropping the closed flow accounts, we can reinsert the plus signs between the permanent or stock property T-accounts to obtain the ending equational zero-term.

$$
\begin{array}{cc}
Assets & Bank\ Debt \\
[(2545, 6, 8) /\!/ (0, 0, 0)] & + \quad [(0, 0, 0) /\!/ (1000, 0, 0)] \\
Suppliers & Total\ A\&L \\
+ [(0, 0, 0) /\!/ (25, 0, 0)] & + \quad [(0, 0, 0) /\!/ (1520, 6, 8)]
\end{array}
$$

The ending equational zero-term must be *decoded* to obtain the ending balance sheet equation. A LHS or debit-balance account $[W /\!/ X]$ is decoded as the vector $W - X$ on the LHS of the equation. A RHS or credit-balance account $[W /\!/ X]$ is decoded as the vector $X - W$ on the RHS of the equation. This yields the *final balance sheet vector equation*:

$$
\begin{array}{cccc}
Assets & Bank\ Debt & Suppliers & Total\ A\&L \\
(2545, 6, 8) = & (1000, 0, 0) + & (25, 0, 0) + & (1520, 6, 8)
\end{array}
$$

The income statement in value accounting could be defined as the statement that connects the Net Worth accounts in the beginning and ending balance sheet equations. In property accounting, the corresponding statement would be the *property flow statement* which connects the Total A&L accounts in the beginning and ending balance sheet vector equations. Since all those changes are channeled through the summary flow account, dA&L, the property flow statement is just a list of the activity in the dA&L account.

$$
\begin{array}{lccc}
\multicolumn{4}{c}{\textbf{Property Flow Statement}} \\
Whole\ Product & = [(0, 0, 18) & /\!/ & (0, 36, 0)] \\
Purchases & = [(100, 0, 0) & /\!/ & (0, 0, 20)] \\
Sales & = [(0, 40, 0) & /\!/ & (120, 0, 0)] \\
\hline
dA\&L & = [(100, 40, 18) & /\!/ & (120, 36, 20)] \\
& = [(0, 4, 0) & /\!/ & (20, 0, 2)]
\end{array}
$$

The dA&L account connects together the beginning and ending Total A&L accounts in the sense that

$$
\begin{array}{ccc}
Beginning\ Total\ A\&L & dA\&L & Ending\ Total\ A\&L \\
[(0, 0, 0) /\!/ (1500, 10, 6)] & + \ [(0, 4, 0) /\!/ (20, 0, 2)] & = \ [(0, 0, 0) /\!/ (1520, 6, 8)]
\end{array}
$$

The closing balance, $[(0, 0, 18) /\!/ (0, 36, 0)]$, in the Whole Product account shows that the liabilities for 18 units of inputs were appropriated in production and that 36 units of outputs were the assets appropriated in production. The Whole Product T-account is a RHS account so it decodes as the *whole product vector*, $(0, 36, -18)$. Whole product vectors are used without the cash component in the production-set representation of production opportunities.

A system of value accounting (balance sheet equation, journal, and ledger) can be derived from the above (highly simplified) property accounting system by multiplying each property vector by a vector of valuation coefficients such as prices or costs. Different rules for defining costs or recognizing revenue would lead to different value vectors and different derived systems of value accounting. But the property accounting system remains the same regardless of the values used. Thus property accounting allows one to sidestep the valuation controversies of accounting and to describe the underlying transactions in an objective manner.

Derivations of Value Accounting from Property Accounting

Given a price vector, a cost vector, or any vector of valuation coefficients, one can take the scalar product of the value vector times the property vector in a property accounting model to obtain a value accounting model. Different value vectors will yield different value accounting models from the same underlying valuation-free model of property accounting. Here the cost vector will be used to map the property accounting transactions into conventional value accounting transactions.

The market price vector is $P = (1, 3, 5)$. Since 36 units of output were produced by using up 18 units of input costing $5 each, the unit cost of the output is $2.50. Hence the cost vector is $C = (1, 2.50, 5)$.

The scalar product of the cost vector C times a vector T-term $[X /\!/ Y]$ is defined as the following scalar T-term:

$$C[X /\!/ Y] = [CX /\!/ CY]$$

For instance, $(1, 2.5, 5)[(80, 4, 0) /\!/ (0, 0, 2)] = [90 /\!/ 10]$. The value T-account $[CX /\!/ CY]$ is said to be the value T-account corresponding to the property T-account $[X /\!/ Y]$. A property T-account is said to "underlie" its corresponding value T-account. If the Whole Product property T-account is multiplied by the price vector, the corresponding value T-account would be called Production [Ellerman, 1982] or Economic Profit. If evaluated at the cost vector, the value T-account could just be called Cost of the Whole Product. Sometimes we will use the same name for a property account and the corresponding value account, when the valuation procedure is not important for the argument.

Much information is lost in the transition from property accounting to value accounting. Some transactions do not show up at the value level. Some transactions will wash out at the value level because of an equal-valued exchange. Other transactions will wash out because of the high level of aggregation. Any transaction that swaps one asset for an equal-valued asset will not show up in a model using an aggregated Assets account.

There are several ways that the same property accounting event can be analyzed as transactions. One way is to disaggregate or aggregate the accounts. A event recorded with one transaction might have to be recorded with two or three transactions if an account such as the Assets account is split up into several specific accounts. Another way to reformulate the property transactions is to split the flow accounts into positive and negative accounts. For example, a Net Income or Profit account can be split into the difference between a Revenue and an Expenses account, i.e., Profit – Revenue – Expenses. Or the Whole Product can be split into the Positive Product and the Negative Product.

If the Assets account is disaggregated into Cash, Output Inventory, and Input Inventory, then the initial balance sheet vector equation would be

$$\begin{array}{ccccc} \textit{Cash} & \textit{Output Inv.} & \textit{Input Inv.} & \textit{Bank Debt} & \textit{Total A\&L} \\ (2500, 0, 0) + & (0, 10, 0) & + \quad (0, 0, 6) & = (1000, 0, 0) + & (1500, 10, 6) \end{array}$$

Multiplying through by the cost vector yields the balance sheet equation for the conventional value accounting model:

$$\begin{array}{ccccc} \textit{Cash} & \textit{Output Inv.} & \textit{Input Inv.} & \textit{Bank Debt} & \textit{Net Worth} \\ 2500 + & 25 & + \quad 30 & = \quad 1000 & + \quad 1555 \end{array}$$

The equational zero-terms using scalars can be obtained either by directly encoding the scalar equation or by multiplying the value vectors times the vector equational zero-term.

The value accounting transactions can be obtained by multiplying the appropriate value vector times the transactional zero-terms involved in the property accounting transactions. Only selected transactions will be analyzed. The first transaction will be analyzed to show the separate legal and factual transfers. But the primary analysis is to show where the property appropriation of the whole product appears in conventional value accounting.

Consider the first property accounting transaction.

	Accounts and Description	[Debit // Credit]
	Assets	$[(0, 0, 15) \; // \; (75, 0, 0)]$
1	*Purchases*	$[(75, 0, 0) \; // \; (0, 0, 15)]$
	Cash purchase of inputs	

With the articulated asset accounts, this would be broken down into the following three transactions.

	Accounts and Description	[Debit	//	Credit]
	Suppliers	[(0, 0, 15)	//	(75, 0, 0)]
1a	*Purchases*	[(75, 0, 0)	//	(0, 0, 15)]
	Legal contract to purchase inputs			
	Input Inventory	[(0, 0, 15)	//	(0, 0, 0)]
1b	*Suppliers*	[(0, 0, 0)	//	(0, 0, 15)]
	Factual delivery of the inputs			
	Suppliers	[(75, 0, 0)	//	(0, 0, 0)]
1c	*Cash*	[(0, 0, 0)	//	(75, 0, 0)]
	Cash payment to suppliers			

This articulated presentation of the cash purchase of the inputs shows as separate transactions the legal exchange of rights in the contract (1a) and the factual deliveries (in fulfillment of the contract) of the inputs (1b) and the cash (1c). To see that these three transactional zero-terms can collapse back to the previous transactional zero-term, relabel Input Inventory and Cash as just Assets and add the three transactional zero-terms together. The net effect on Suppliers will cancel out, so we will end up with the previous transaction affecting only the accounts of Assets and Purchases.

If we multiply transaction 1, which uses the aggregated Assets account, by the cost vector, the transaction vanishes—because the input purchase is a swap of equal-valued assets. Use of the three transactions with the articulated assets accounts will elicit the information about the asset swap. The value transaction corresponding to property transaction 1a will be denoted by the asterisk—1a*, and so forth.

	Value Accounts and Description	[Debit	//	Credit]
	Suppliers	[75	//	75]
1a*	*Purchases (at cost)*	[75	//	75]
	Legal contract to purchase inputs			
	Input Inventory (at cost)	[75	//	0]
1b*	*Suppliers*	[0	//	75]
	Delivery of the inputs			
	Suppliers	[75	//	0]
1c*	*Cash*	[0	//	75]
	Cash payment to suppliers			

Each T-term in transaction 1a* vanishes. If we add the transactional zero-terms from 1b and 1c* together, the net effect on the suppliers cancels out, so we have the transaction:

Value Accounts and Description	[Debit	//	Credit]
1b* *Input Inventory (at cost)*	[75	//	0]
+ *Cash*	[0	//	75]
1c* Cash purchase of inputs			

This, at last, is the normal transaction recorded for transaction 1 in value accounting. The several underlying property accounting transactions show the legal and factual transfers of property behind this simple journal entry.

The whole phenomenon of appropriation is neglected in conventional accounting and economic theory. This is in part due to the fact that conventional accounting only records a transmittal of cost from inputs to outputs (often through an intermediary of "goods in process"). To see this, consider the two property transactions for the appropriation of the input liabilities and the appropriation of the output assets, where we have used the articulated asset accounts.

	Accounts and Description	[Debit	//	Credit]
	Whole Product	[(0, 0, 18)	//	(0, 0, 0)]
4	*Input Inventory*	[(0, 0, 0)	//	(0, 0, 18)]
	Inputs used up in production			
	Output Inventory	[(0, 36, 0)	//	(0, 0, 0)]
5	*Whole Product*	[(0, 0, 0)	//	(0, 36, 0)]
	Outputs produced in production			

Multiplying through by the cost vector $C = (1, 2.5, 5)$ yields the following:

	Value Accounts and Description	[Debit	//	Credit]
	Cost of Whole Product	[90	//	0]
4*	*Input Inventory (at cost)*	[0	//	90]
	Inputs used-up in production			
	Output Inventory (at cost)	[90	//	0]
5*	*Cost of Whole Product*	[0	//	90]
	Outputs produced in production			

If these two transactional zero-terms are then added together, the net effect on the Cost of Whole Product account will cancel out so we are left with the conventional transaction that transfers costs from the input inventory to the output inventory.

Value Accounts and Description	[Debit	//	Credit]
4* *Output Inventory (at cost)*	[90	//	0]
+ *Input Inventory (at cost)*	[0	//	90]
5* Production of outputs			

This shows that in conventional accounting the appropriation of the whole product lies behind the transactions that transmit costs from the input inventory to the output inventory (often through intermediate goods-in-process inventories). Thus we see at the level of accounting detail how the laissez-faire appropriation of the whole product occurs in production and is recorded in property accounting and in conventional value accounting.

Appropriation in Descriptive Economic Theory

A Logical Difficulty in Neoclassical Economic Theory

Property theory is not an alternative approach to price theory; it is concerned with a different subject matter, the structure of property rights and obligations—particularly in production. Hence property theory, unlike the alternative value theories, is not intended to displace neoclassical value theory or the other value theories. But it does have implications for descriptive economic theory, neoclassical or otherwise.

Neoclassical price theory neglects appropriation. There is one special case where appropriation can be safely ignored; and, accordingly, that special case has been the glory of neoclassical theory, general equilibrium theory under universal constant returns to scale. The logical gap is still there in that special case, but it is irrelevant for price-theoretic purposes. Outside of the special case of zero-profit equilibrium, the logical gap becomes a logical flaw in neoclassical economic theory.

One major casualty is the Arrow-Debreu model, which attempts to show that there can be a competitive equilibrium in a private enterprise capitalist economy, with decreasing returns to scale and positive pure profits. That model has withstood untold amounts of empirical criticism, but the property theoretic analysis shows the logical flaw in the Arrow-Debreu-type models. By misrepresenting the structure of property rights in production, these models exclude a variety of arbitrage that is perfectly possible in a private enterprise capitalist economy. The modeling error is fatal. Such arbitrage precludes a genuine competitive equilibrium with positive pure profits.

Other casualties are some of the basic concepts of capital theory such as the concepts of the "capitalized value of a capital asset" or the "marginal efficiency of a capital asset". These concepts misrepresent the structure of property rights by including in the bundle of rights associated with a capital asset certain rights which are appropriated and which thus cannot be pre-owned by the asset owner.

Appropriation Is Not a Return to a Factor

In a market economy, the whole product appropriator is not always the prior owner of some specific input. Usually owners of capital hire labor, but workers can borrow or hire capital, and an entrepreneur could hire both the labor and capital. The whole product appropriator is determined by the direction of the hiring contracts, by who hires what or whom. The whole product is a return to a contractual role, the role of being the hiring party (the last legal owner of the used-up inputs). Moreover, it is a return in terms of property; it is simply a value return. In the textbook model of perfectly competitive equilibrium under constant returns to scale, there are no pure or economic profits, so the net value of the whole product is zero. This does not mean that the hiring party gets "nothing". The hiring party gets no net value in that instance, but still gets the whole product in terms of property. Moreover, the property mechanism of laissez-faire appropriation operates regardless of whether the price mechanism is in equilibrium or disequilibrium and regardless of whether the markets are competitive or noncompetitive.

There is a widespread tendency, especially in economics, to "explain" any income as the return to some factor. The whole product is not a return to some factor. It is of no avail to postulate hidden or implicit factors. At best, some hidden factor might be priced so that the profits would be exactly zero when the factor is taken into account. Hidden factors do not change the structure of property rights involved in production. The whole product, even if of zero value, is still appropriated; it still accrues to the contractual role of being the hiring party.

The 'explanation" that profit is a return to risk bearing is quite tautologous when "risk bearing" means bearing the costs (appropriating the negative product). It is just the argument that appropriating the positive product is the "return" to appropriating the negative product. Of course, the party that appropriates the negative product also appropriates the positive product and thus nets the profits. But why in the first place did that party, rather than some other, appropriate the negative product and thus the whole product? Only by having the contractual role of being the last owner of the inputs.

The Imputation Fallacies of Capital Theory

Broadly speaking, economic resources have two types of uses, active and passive. A resource is used passively when it is sold or rented out in return for some market price or rental. A resource is used actively when, instead of being evaluated directly on the market, it is used up in production, usually along with other resources. Then the liabilities for the used-up resources and the rights to any produced assets are appropriated. Thus appropriation is involved in the active use, not in the passive use of resources.

Difficulties arise in the conventional treatment of the active case, since economics tends to ignore appropriation. The economic return in the active case is not just the value of the original resource but the extra value of the appropriated property. But the total return in the active case is mistakenly imputed only to the original resource, as if the ownership of the appropriated property were already included in ownership of the original resource. Property that is appropriated cannot be previously owned; otherwise it could not be appropriated. The extra value of the appropriated property (e.g., the whole product) is not a return to the original resource. In the context of the laissez-faire appropriation mechanism, it is a return to the contractual role of being the hiring party, the last legal owner of the used-up resources.

Appropriation is often neglected because the right to the whole product is treated as if it were part of a preexistent property right. This is the case in the Marxist view of the capitalist economic system where the preexistent property right is the "ownership of the means of production". This is also a common practice in neoclassical capital theory, where the preexistent right is the ownership of a capital asset. Property appropriated in the future can have a present value (which could be zero) but it cannot have a present owner, since otherwise it could not be appropriated in the future. The primary imputation fallacy in capital theory is the "capitalized value" definition.

The Capitalized Value of an Asset

One of the basic concepts of capital theory is the notion of the *capitalized value of an asset*. The definition is usually stated in a rather general fashion; owning the asset "yields" a future income stream and the discounted present value of the income stream is the capitalized value of the asset. But there are quite different ways in which owning an asset can yield an income stream. There are the active and the passive uses of capital. The capitalized value concept is unproblematic in the passive case where the income stream is the stream of rentals (net of maintenance) plus the scrap value. The capitalized value of that stream is, under competitive conditions, just the market cost of the asset. Bonds and annuities provide similar examples of income streams generated by renting out or loaning out capital assets, i.e., by the passive use of capital.

Capital theory would be somewhat less controversial if it stuck to such examples of hired-out capital. However, the capitalized value definition is also applied to the quite different active case where, instead of hiring out the capital, labor is hired in, a product is produced and sold. The present value of the stream of net proceeds is then called *the capitalized value of the capital asset* as if to impute the net proceeds to the capital asset. The net proceeds can, however, be analyzed into the stream of implicit rentals on the capital assets (including scrap value) *plus* the profits which are the value of the future appropriated whole products (Ellerman, 1982, ch. 12). The rentals are the return to the capital asset; the whole products are the return to the contractual role played by the capital owner (when the capital is used actively). The rights to the whole products are not part of the rights to the capital asset; whole products are appropriated.

The capitalized value definition overlooks appropriation. One might then think that by purchasing the asset or the *means of production*, one is thereby purchasing the outputs and the net proceeds—so there is no need to appropriate the outputs.

> When a man buys an investment or capital asset, he purchases the right to the series of prospective returns, which he expects to obtain from selling its output, after deducting the running expenses of obtaining that output, during the life of the asset. (Keynes, 1936, p. 135)

But in fact one thereby purchases only the asset. Any further return will depend on one's contracts. If one rents out the asset and sells the scrap, then one receives only the rental-plus-scrap income stream. If, instead, one hires in labor, bears the costs of the used-up labor and capital services, and claims and sells the outputs, *then* one receives the net proceeds mentioned by

Keynes. In each case, one owned the asset. The difference lies in the pattern of the subsequent contracts. By making the contracts so that one was the hiring party, one could additionally appropriate the whole product each time period with its positive or negative value. The capitalized value definition fallaciously imputes the value of the appropriated whole products to the capital assets rather than to the contractual role played by the capital owner.

The Yield Rate of a Capital Asset

Another example of assigning the whole product to the capital asset is involved in the notions of "marginal efficiency of capital" or "net productivity of capital." Under competitive conditions, the market interest rate would discount the stream of net rentals and scrap back to the market cost of a capital asset. When the capital asset is used actively then some discount rate will discount the stream of net proceeds back to the market cost of the asset. Such a discount rate is sometimes called an *internal rate of return* or *average rate of return over cost*. However, it is also presented as the *yield rate* of the capital asset and then it is called the *marginal efficiency of capital* (Keynes, 1936, p. 135) or the *net productivity of capital* (Samuelson, 1976, p. 600). This usage presents the value of future appropriated whole products as if it were part of the return to owning the capital asset when in fact it is the return to having the contractual role of being the hiring party. The real problem with the net productivity of capital is not that it can have multiple values (e.g., the reswitching controversy) but that it fallaciously imputes the return to the capital-owner's social role (being the hiring party) to the capital asset itself.

The Quasi-Rent of a Capital Asset

Yet another method of imputing the whole product and its value, the profits, to capital is the *quasi-rent doctrine*. In a genuinely competitive model, all factors including the services of plant and equipment would have a competitively determined price. Capital assets would have a competitive rental. In conventional microeconomics, it is held that capital assets might "earn" a short-run "quasi-rent' due to the short-run inelasticities of supply in capital assets. There is no merit in the argument that short-run inelasticities require a special notion of quasi-rents in addition to the usual competitive rentals. Short-term competitive rentals reflect such scarcities, and thus the short-run rental might be higher than the rental in the longer term. The quasi-rent doctrine is another example of the penchant in conventional economic theory to fallaciously impute the profits to capital. The value of the appropriated whole product, the profit, is added to the machine's competitive rental, and the result is dubbed the "quasi-rent earned by the machine" (Stonier and Hague, 1973, p. 328).

The Passive and Active Uses of Capital

There is a pattern here. Capital has a passive use and an active use. Thus capital theory will always have a pair of concepts associated with capital, one concept derived for the passive case and one concept for the active case (table 3.1). The value concept associated with the active case includes the concept for the passive case plus the value of the whole product (the profits) that is appropriated by the capital owner in the active case. The difference between the passive and active case is the appropriation of the whole product, which is the return to a contractual role, not a return to the capital. But conventional capital theory neglects appropriation, and imputes the whole product and its value, the profits, to capital.

Table 3.1

Concept	Passive Case	Active Case
Value of Capital Asset	Market cost	Capitalized Value
Yield of Capital Good	Marginal productivity	Net productivity
Yield of Money Capital	Marginal rate of return over cost	Marginal efficiency of capital
Capital Asset Rental	Market rental	Quasi-rent

The Retreat to the Zero-Profits Case

What is the neoclassical defense against the charge of fallacious imputations? It is retreat to the zero-profit case where the whole products will have zero value so the misimputation will not matter for price-theoretic purposes. In that instance, Professor Samuelson can claim to have demonstrated the *"Equality of capitalized value and reproduction cost"* (Samuelson, 1961, p. 42; 1966, p. 309). Similarly, a prominent capital theorist shows that the competitive "equilibrium price of a one-year-old machine in terms of 'costs'" is equal to the "present discounted value of the future *net* output which a one-year-old machine can produce" (Burmeister, 1974, p. 443).

In this special case, the fallacious imputation of the whole product to capital is a moot point from the price-theoretic viewpoint since the whole products then have zero value. In property terms, the imputation is as incorrect in that case as in general. And, of course, the capital theoretic definitions of capitalized value or net productivity are by no means restricted to the competitive model in the economics and finance literature. Professor Samuelson (1976, pp. 661 and 600) asserts that *"capital goods have a 'net' productivity"* (while the other factors have only a marginal productivity), as a "technological fact." It is a clear-cut case where the social role of capital as the hiring party in capitalist society is presented as a technical characteristic of capital goods.

The recent controversies in capital theory did not get to the root of the matter because they remained at the value-theoretic level (neoclassical versus neo-Ricardian/neo-Keynesian value theory). But capitalism is not a price system; capitalism is a property system. The root of the problem in capital theory is that it presents the return to capital's market role (being the hiring party) as resulting from the technical and legal characteristics of capital goods. The whole product is presented as part of the technological "net productivity of capital" and the legal rights to the whole product are presented as part of the "ownership of the means of production." One of the measures of the success and depth of capitalist ideology in economics is that even Marxian economics accepts the empirically false thesis that the right to the product is part of the ownership of capital assets.

Corporate Ownership Is Not the Ownership of the Firm

When the appropriation of the whole product is implicitly considered in conventional economics, the pattern, as in capital theory, is to construe the right to the whole product as being part of a preexistent property right. In its commonest form, this property right is called the *ownership of the firm*. We have defined the word "firm" to be the party who ends up appropriating the whole product:

firm = whole product appropriator

The identity of the firm (in this technical sense of whole product appropriator) is determined not by some preexistent property right such as the so-called "ownership of the firm," but by who hires what or whom. Firmhood is a contractual role, not a property right.

Economists sometimes use a rather abstract version of the "ownership of a firm". Technical production possibilities are represented by a production function, a production set, or a "production-opportunity locus" (Hirshleifer 1970, p. 124), and then economists speak of the "owners" of these technical possibilities, e.g., the "owners of the productive opportunity" [Hirchleifer, 1970, p. 125]. There is no such ownership right. Neoclassical economics' lack of attention to property-theoretic details is illustrated by the postulation of this peculiar "ownership" of a mathematical description of technically possible production opportunities such as a production function or production set. If one wishes to use the metaphor of appropriating the whole product as "trading with nature", then one should realize that there are no "owners" (Hirchleifer, 1970, p. 20) of the production set of possible trades with nature. There might be the ownership of certain specialized inputs, such as proprietory technical information, but that is only the ownership of inputs to the production opportunity, not the "ownership" of the productive opportunity itself. There is no such property right as the "ownership" of a production function, a production set, or a productive opportunity.

The notion of "ownership of a production set" is probably intended as an abstract version of the ownership of a corporation. But, as we have seen, a corporation is an owner of certain inputs such as physical and financial capital. The legal process of incorporation does not convert the ownership of a capital asset into the ownership of the production set of net product vectors that could be produced using that capital asset. Whether or not a corporate owner of inputs or any input owner appropriates the whole product produced using those inputs depends on whether the input owner hires in a complementary set of inputs and bears the costs of production or whether the input is hired out. The ownership of any input does not include within it the ownership of the whole product produced using the input; the whole product must be appropriated. Thus the ownership of a corporation (i.e., the indirect ownership of certain resources) is not the "ownership of the firm". Being the firm is a contractual role, not a property right.

The Failure of the Arrow-Debreu Model

In the early models of perfectly competitive equilibrium, constant returns to scale in production was assumed. This assured zero economic profits in equilibrium, so from the viewpoint of value theory, it was immaterial who was the firm, i.e., who appropriated the whole product vector (since it had zero net value). According to Professor Samuelson,

> it is precisely under strict constant returns to scale that the theory of the firm evaporates. (Samuelson, 1967, p. 114; 1972, p. 27)

In 1954, Professors Kenneth Arrow and Gerard Debreu published a paper (Arrow and Debreu, 1954) in which they claimed to show the existence of a competitive equilibrium under the general conditions of non-increasing returns to scale, i.e., decreasing or constant returns to scale. Under decreasing returns to scale, there would be positive economic or pure profits. Hence the Arrow-Debreu model alleges to show the existence of a perfectly competitive equilibrium with positive economic profits. In the following passage, Professor Arrow contrasts the Arrow-Debreu model with a model by Professor McKenzie (1959) which used constant returns to scale.

> The two models differ in their implications for income distribution. The Arrow-Debreu model creates a category of pure profits which are distributed to the owners of the firm; it is not assumed that the owners are necessarily the entrepreneurs or managers. . . .
> In the McKenzie model, on the other hand, the firm makes no pure profits (since it operates at constant returns); the equivalent of profits appears in the form of payments for the use of entrepreneurial resources, but there is no residual category of owners who receive profits without rendering either capital or entrepreneurial services. (Arrow, 1971, p. 70)

Since the whole product vectors can have a positive value in the Arrow-Debreu model, the model had to face the question as to how these vectors got assigned to people. The Arrow-Debreu model does *not* answer the question by postulating "hidden factors" (which would compromise the model in a number of ways (see Ellerman, 1982, ch. 13; or McKenzie, 1981). Arrow explicitly states that "pure profits" are distributed to "the owners of the firm," and that, in contrast, the McKenzie model does not have this "residual category of owners who receive profits without rendering either capital or entrepreneurial services."

The Arrow-Debreu model answers the question by assuming that there is a property right such as "ownership" of the production sets of technically feasible whole product vectors. The train of reasoning is that production sets represent the production possibilities of "firms" and "firms" are identified with corporations which, of course, are owned by their shareholders.

In a private enterprise capitalist economy, there is no such property right as the "ownership" of production sets of feasible whole product vectors. In the Arrow-Debreu model each consumer/resourceholder is endowed prior to any market exchanges with a certain set of resources and with shares in corporations. However, prior to any market activity, ownership of corporate shares is only an indirect form of ownership of resources, the corporate resources. It is the subsequent contracts in input markets that will determine whether a corporation, like any other resource owner, successfully exploits a production opportunity by purchasing the requisite inputs.

The Arrow-Debreu model mistakes the whole logic of appropriation. The question of who appropriates the whole product of a production opportunity is not settled by the initial endowment of property rights. It is only settled in the markets for inputs by who hires what or whom. In other words, the determination of who is to be the "firm" (the whole product appropriator) is not exogenous to the marketplace; it is a market-endogenous determination. This adds a whole new degree of freedom to the model, which can only be ignored in the special case of universal constant returns to scale when it does not matter (for income determination) who is the firm. This new degree of freedom eliminates the possibility of a competitive equilibrium with positive economic profits, e.g., with decreasing returns to scale in some production opportunity.

Production Arbitrage

There is no mathematical error in the Arrow-Debreu model; it (contrary to their claim) simply does not model a perfectly competitive free enterprise capitalist economy. By assuming that production possibilities are "owned," the Arrow-Debreu model does not allow anyone but the "owner" to demand the requisite inputs. But in a free enterprise capitalist economy, anyone can bid on the inputs necessary for some technically feasible production opportunity. In such an economy, production, the conversion of inputs into outputs, can be seen as a form of arbitrage, *production arbitrage*, between input markets and output markets. Traditionally, arbitrage is thought of as an exchange operation, e.g., in currency markets. But if the price of Chicago wheat exceeds the price of Kansas City wheat plus the transportation costs, then the operation of buying inputs (Kansas City wheat plus transportation services) and selling the outputs (Chicago wheat) would still be called arbitrage. If the price of a good one period hence exceeds the current price plus storage costs, then

> a sure profit could always be made by the time arbitrage, so to speak, of buying the commodity currently—borrowing, if necessary—and reselling one period later. (Fama and Miller, 1972, p. 62)

But in general equilibrium models, where commodities are differentiated by spatial and temporal location, transportation and storage are examples of production. As more characteristics of the inputs, besides spatial and temporal location, change in the production process, there is no magic dividing line that suddenly prevents the production arbitrage of buying all the requisite inputs and selling the outputs.

It is the concept of arbitrage applied to production itself, the concept of production arbitrage, that undermines the Arrow-Debreu model. When there is a sufficient price differential betwen input and output markets to allow positive profits, then a potential arbitrageur can attempt to reap those profits by purchasing the required inputs, bearing their costs as the inputs are consumed in production, claiming the produced outputs, and then selling the outputs. Naturally, such a grand arbitrage operation is difficult in the real-world economy, but it is quite possible in an idealized textbook model of perfect competition. Thus production profits can be viewed as arbitrage profits. A competitive equilibrium is not possible when there are profitable arbitrage opportunities, e.g., profitable production opportunities. Production arbitrageurs (i.e., entrepreneurs) would bid up input prices. Hence a competitive equilibrium is not possible in the situation that Professors Arrow and Debreu attempt to model, a competitive capitalist economy with some production opportunities exhibiting decreasing returns to scale.

This restores a certain symmetry betwen increasing and decreasing returns to scale. A competitive equilibrium is not possible at a point of increasing returns to scale because no one wants to be the firm (negative profits). A competitive equilibrium is not possible at the point of decreasing returns to scale because everyone wants to be the firm (positive profits). General equilibrium theory for a competitive capitalist economy only works in the special case of constant returns to scale where (by assumption) no one cares who acts as the firm (zero profits).

For the last several decades, the Arrow-Debreu model has been received doctrine in mathematical economics. Its failure is a major example of the impact on economic theory of an appreciation of the nature and structure of property appropriation. The reason for its failure, which was uncovered by the analysis of appropriation, was the market-endogenous determination of "firmhood", of who is to appropriate the whole product and thus be the firm. The whole product is assigned, by the laissez-faire mechanism, to a contractual role, not to a preexistent property right, and one's contractual role is determined by the contracts one makes or does not make in the marketplace.

The Breakdown of the Conventional Representation of Markets

The extra degree of freedom, the market-endogenous determination of firmhood, cuts much deeper into received doctrine that just the Arrow-Debreu model. It changes the very conception of how competitive markets operate, from an orderly process of equilibriation to a game-theoretically indeterminate struggle for positive profits. The conventional theory is that there are two basic types of economic agents, consumer/resourceholders and "firms". The consumer/resourceholders supply inputs to the input market and demand outputs on the output markets. The firms play the opposite role of demanding inputs on input markets and supplying outputs to output markets. The flow of commodities from the consumers as resource suppliers to the firms and the flow of products back to the consumers (with the money flows in the opposite direction) are represented in the familiar circular flow diagram (e.g., Samuelson, 1976, p. 46).

The conventional picture assumes that firmhood is determined prior to market activity. The resource owners are lined up on one side and the "firms" are supposedly lined up on the other side of the input markets. But this is not the case in a free enterprise capitalist economy. It is not legally predetermined that an input owner is a supplier of inputs rather than a demander of a complementary set of inputs. Prior to the market contracts, corporations are just other resourceholders. Any resource owner, corporate or otherwise, may aspire to be a "firm" in the technical sense of "whole product appropriator" by attempting to purchase the complete set of inputs to a productive opportunity. Hence the customary analytical machinery of resource owners having input supply schedules and "firms" having input demand schedules prior to market activity incorrectly represents the structure of the market process. The identity of the firms (parties who will appropriate the whole products) is only determined at the end of the game-theoretically indeterminate market process, not at the beginning. This is the breakdown, under the impact of production arbitrage, of the conventional representation of markets in a productive economy.

Appropriation in Normative Economic Theory

The Labor Theory of Value

The purpose of this section is to outline the modern treatment of the principal normative theory of property, the *labor theory of property* (see Ellerman, 1980a, or, for an earlier treatment, 1972, 1973), the theory that people have the right to the fruits of their labor. The labor theory of property has throughout its history been entwined with and often totally confused with the labor theory of value. Indeed, the two theories are sometimes almost identified when it is held that labor is the sole source of the value of produced property and that *therefore* labor should get the title to the property.

Various versions of the labor theory of value were used in the classical economic theories of Adam Smith and David Ricardo, without recognition of any property-theoretic implications. Smith used labor as a "measure of value" in the sense that price could be viewed in terms of the labor it commanded. Ricardo interpreted the price of a commodity, for the most part, in terms of the labor directly or indirectly embodied in the commodity. Property-theoretic implications of Ricardo's labor theory of value were developed by the small band of radical economic thinkers known as the "Ricardian socialists" or classical "laborists" (e.g., in Lichtheim, 1969, p. 135). Ricardo's labor theory of value was developed into a value-theoretic critique of capitalist production by Karl Marx, the "greatest of the Ricardian socialists" (Lichtheim, 1969, p. 139).

In England, the principal Ricardian socialists or classical laborists were Thomas Hodgskin, William Thompson, and John Francis Bray (see Menger, 1899). Historians of economic thought have viewed the Ricardian socialists less as thinkers in their own right and more as precursors to Marx. This has affected the parts in the Ricardian socialists' thought that are emphasized, namely the parts that were later developed by Marx. Indeed, many aspects of the Marxian labor theory of surplus value and exploitation can be found in the Ricardian socialists. But the Ricardian socialists or classical laborists also explicitly developed the labor theory of property, and this property-theoretic theme did not survive in the exclusively value-theoretic focus of Marx's thought.

Neoclassical Value Theory: The Response to the Labor Theory of Value

Marx explicitly developed the labor theory of value. The labor theory of property was thereafter eclipsed as debate focused on the labor theory of value. As the Ricardian socialists and Marx extracted radical conclusions from the Ricardian labor theory of value, orthodox economists became less and less satisfied with that approach to price theory. The full orthodox answer came with the marginalist revolution in the latter part of the nineteenth century. According to the neoclassical value theory that emerged from the marginalist revolution, price or market value was determined by considerations of marginal utility and marginal productivity that stand behind the supply and demand for commodities in the marketplace.

The labor theory of value was often represented by the slogan, "Only labor is productive." But neoclassical theorists quite correctly pointed out that other factors of production are also productive in the sense that the product will be reduced if these factors are removed. Even if one could in some meaningful sense reduce capital goods to labor, land, and time, that still left land, including all natural resources, and time as other factors necessary for production in addition to labor.

The Ricardian socialists often expressed the labor theory of property with the slogan, "Labor's right to the whole product." But neoclassical theorists quite correctly pointed out that labor cannot receive the value of all the outputs if there are other scarce productive inputs. The value of the outputs must be shared between all the productive factors. If labor is not the only productive factor, then how could labor expect to receive the "whole product"?

The neoclassical value theory aims not only to refute the labor theory of value but to appropriate some of the moral force of the labor theory of property. That is, the *marginal productivity theory of distribution* attempts to show that, under certain conditions, each factor gets what it produces in capitalist production. Each factor or input has a certain marginal productivity which can be considered as the increase or decrease in the amount of the product as one unit of the input is respectively added or substracted from production. For instance, a profit maximizing firm would not buy an extra man-hour of labor for a wage that exceeded the value of labor's marginal product—since that is the value of the extra product resulting from an extra man-hour. And, if the value of the marginal product exceeded the wage, more labor would be purchased until diminishing returns brought the marginal product down to the competitive wage level. Hence in competitive equilibrium, labor would be paid the value of its marginal productivity.

There is nothing in marginal productivity theory that is unique to labor. The same reasoning applies to any productive input. Capital and land also have a marginal productivity, and in competitive equilibrium each would be paid according to the value of its marginal productivity.

The marginal productivity theory of distribution is used not only as a descriptive theory to predict behavior in the competitive model, but as a normative theory to "answer" the labor theory of value. The idea is to interpret the marginal productivity of each factor as the amount of the product "produced" by that factor. For instance, since the product increases by the marginal productivity of, say, a shovel when an extra shovel is added as an input, it seems natural to view that extra product as being "produced" by the shovel. Since, in competitive equilibrium, the shovel or its owner would be paid the value of the shovel's marginal productivity, the shovel would "get what it produced". The same would hold for every other productive factor. Hence instead of imputing the whole product to labor as suggested by the classical laborists, the neoclassical theorists, such as John

Bates Clark, argued that the marginal productivity theory would impute to each factor what it produced; to labor the fruits of labor, to land the fruits of land, and to capital the fruits of capital.

The Labor Theory of Property

The modern treatment of the labor theory of property (Ellerman, 1980a) totally jettisons the labor theory of value (Ellerman, 1983a). The analysis and critique of capitalist production is constructed in a non-Marxist format and is strengthened by being based on the structure of property rights in production, not on value relations. The labor theory of property, being a property theory, is not intended to displace any value theory, including the neoclassical theory of value.

Any imagined moral force of the marginal productivity theory of distribution is defeated by refocusing on the actual structure of property rights in production. When marginal productivity theory attempts to "impute" shares of the product to the various factors, it is using the distributive shares metaphor: each factor is viewed as "producing" and then "getting" a share of the product. The normative use of marginal productivity theory then attempts to show that each factor "gets what it produces". But as a descriptive of property rights, we have seen that the distributive shares picture is quite misleading and false. The simple fact is that one legal party, such as the employer in a capitalist firm, appropriates the whole product of production. It is the actual structure of property rights in a capitalist firm that should be justified or criticized, not a metaphorical "as if" picture of property rights.

The labor theory of property addresses the normative question of who ought to appropriate the whole product of production. The labor theory of property holds that people have a natural right to the positive fruits of their labor and a natural obligation to bear the negative fruits of their labor. In any given productive enterprise, the production of the outputs and the using up of the inputs are, respectively, the positive and negative fruits of the joint labor performed by all the people working in the enterprise. The output assets are the positive fruits and the input liabilities are the negative fruits of the working community of the enterprise, i.e., of labor in the inclusive sense of the blue and white collar workers of the firm. Hence the labor theory of property implies that labor has the natural right to the outputs and the natural liability for the used up inputs, i.e., that labor should appropriate the whole product.

The labor theory of property is totally independent of the labor theory of value. In the statement "Labor produces *the value of* the outputs and therefore labor should appropriate the outputs," the words "the value of" should be deleted entirely—as should the labor theory of value itself. Labor produces commodities with certain characteristics. If those characteristics have a certain economic value, it is not because labor produced them but because they are useful elsewhere in production or are desirable to consumers.

Orthodox economists make no attempt to justify capital's appropriation of the whole product. Instead, they evade the matter entirely by looking at distributive shares. They use the distributive shares metaphor to "picture" capital and labor as each getting a "share of the product". Since the size of the pie shares in the functional distribution of income is partly a function of prices, orthodox economists base their "story" on a value theory, the neoclassical theory of prices. But the main point about the neoclassical value theory or even the Marxist labor theory of value is not whether it is true or false, but that it is quite irrelevant to the debate over capitalist production. Capitalism is not a particular type of price system or a particular set of value relations. Capitalism is a particular type of property system, the system that allows capital, by means of the employer-employee contract and the other input purchase contracts, to appropriate the whole product of production. The best of value theories would only determine the value of the assets and liabilities in the whole product, but would not determine who ought to appropriate that bundle of property rights and obligations in the first place.

The labor theory of property cuts beneath the value theories of the contending schools and directly addresses the structure of property rights in production. Production is a human activity carried out by the people involved in the production process. This human activity is called *labor* and, abstractly considered, it consists of using up various inputs in the process of producing certain outputs. The production of the outputs and the using up of the inputs are the positive and negative fruits of that human activity, the whole product of labor. According to the labor theory of property, the people carrying out this productive activity should appropriate the fruits of that human activity. This is only the case when the people who work in a firm are the legal members of the firm, i.e., when the enterprise is a worker coorperative or self-managed firm. Then the people working in the firm *are* the firm from the legal viewpoint so they jointly appropriate the positive fruits of their labor and are jointly liable for the negative fruits of their labor.

The development of the labor theory of property by the classical laborists such as Hodgskin, Thompson, and Bray suffered from several major deficiencies. While the use of the phrase "whole product" is borrowed from them, they failed to include the all-important negative product in their concept of the whole product. They just referred to the positive product, the produced outputs, as the "whole product." But the classical laborists' claim of "labor's right to the whole product" is incoherent without the inclusion of the negative product.

The Juridical Principle of Imputation

Another major deficiency in the classical laborists' development of the labor theory of property was their failure to interpret the theory in terms of the juridical norm of legal imputation in accordance with de facto responsibility. We are concerned with responsibility in the ex post sense of the question "Who did it?" not with "responsibilities" in the ex ante sense of one's duties or tasks in an organizational role. A person or group of people are said to be de facto or factually responsible for a certain result if it was the purposeful result of their intentional (joint) actions. The assignment of de jure or legal responsibility is called *imputation*. The basic juridical principle of imputation is that de jure or legal responsibility is to be imputed in accordance with de facto or factual responsibility. For example, the legal responsibility for a civil or criminal wrong should be assigned to the person or persons who intentionally committed the act, i.e., to the de facto responsible party.

Since, in the economic context, intentional human actions are called "labor", we have the following equivalence.

The Juridical Principle of Imputation: People should have the legal responsibility for the positive and negative results of their intentional actions.

The Labor Theory of Property: People should legally appropriate the positive and negative fruits of their labor.

In other words, the juridical principle of imputation *is* the labor theory of property applied in the context of civil and criminal trials. And the labor theory of property *is* just the standard juridical principle of imputation applied in the context of property appropriation. This equivalence was not evident in the classical treatment of the labor theory of property because that treatment ignored the negative product, and yet it is the negative side of the imputation principle that is applied explicitly in civil and criminal trials.

The lack of this juridical interpretation in the classical treatment led to the classical laborists' notorious failure to ever justify the slogans such as "Only labor is creative" or "Only labor is productive." Orthodox economists could correctly observe that all the factors of production, including land and capital, were "productive" in the sense that to add to or subtract from the employment of these factors would accordingly add to or subtract from the product. It is indeed true that land (including natural resources) and capital are "productive" in this sense of being causally efficacious in production. Otherwise there would be no occasion to use them. The reason that machine tools are used in metalworking and that good luck charms and magical incantations are not used is that the tools are much more efficacious.

Conventional economics has always been willing to admit certain peculiar characteristics of labor (e.g., Marshall 1920, p. 559), so long as they had no fundamental implications for capitalist production. But there is a fundamental difference between labor and the other productive factors, and its implications are profound. While all the factors are "productive" in the sense of being efficacious, *only labor is responsible*.

Capital goods and natural resources, no matter how useful they may be, cannot ever be responsible for anything. Guns and burglary tools, no matter how efficacious and "productive" they may be in the commission of a crime, will never be hauled into court and charged with the crime. Only human beings can be responsible for anything and thus only the humans involved in production can be responsible for the positive and negative results of production. In particular, the people working in an enterprise are factually responsible for using up the inputs and for producing the outputs. Hence the juridical principle of imputation (i.e., the labor theory of property) implies that the workers (in the inclusive sense) should have the legal liability for the used-up inputs and the legal ownership of the produced outputs.

Animism in Marginal Productivity Theory

The equivalence between the labor theory of property and the juridical principle of imputation pushes the roots of the labor theory back in history, far beyond Locke, to the time when "humanity" emerged from the world view of primative animism. Animism attributed the capacity for responsibility not just to persons but also to nonhuman entities and force. Accordingly, in order to escape the grasp of the imputation principle that imputes responsibility only to persons, orthodox economists have had to resurrect a metaphorical form of animism. This sophisticated animism views productivity in the sense of causal efficacy as if it were a responsible agency. All the inputs to production, both human and nonhuman, are viewed as "agents of production cooperating together to produce the product."

The attribution of responsible agency to natural entities and forces is a common literary and artistic metaphor that Ruskin called the *pathetic fallacy*. Examples are: "The wind angrily banged the shutters" and "The waves pounded furiously on the rocks." Examples in the literature of economics are: "Together, the man and shovel can dig my cellar" and "Land and labor *together* produce the corn harvest" (Samuelson, 1976, pp. 536–537). In spite of the romantic allure of the pathetic fallacy, it is still a fallacy. It confounds the distinction, well-grounded in jurisprudence (but virtually unheard of in economics), between the responsible actions of persons and the behavior of things. A shovel does not act together or "cooperate together" with a man to dig a cellar, because a shovel does not act at all. It is a thing. A person uses a shovel to dig a cellar, and the person is responsible both for using up the services of the shovel (the negative product) and for digging the cellar (the positive product).

To emphasize how the "agents" of production "cooperative together", Professor Samuelson says; "Factors usually do not work alone" (p. 536). The point is that, artistic metaphors aside, the nonhuman factors do not *work* at all. They are worked. The land is worked by the laborers to produce the corn harvest. Machines do not "cooperate" with workers; machines are operated by workers.

Marginal Productivity Theory

Orthodox economics is fond of two metaphors: (1) the pathetic fallacy wherein each factor is pictured as "producing" a share of the product, and (2) the distributive shares metaphor wherein each factor is pictured as "getting" a share of the product. Naturally, economists could not resist the temptation to put the two metaphors together and to co-opt the labor theory of property in defense of competitive capitalism by trying to show that each factors "gets" what it "produces" in competitive capitalism. The result is the ideological interpretation of marginal productivity (MP) theory.

Mimicry is the sincerest form of flattery. Since the labor theory of property can be expressed in two vocabularies, that of property appropriation and that of responsibility imputation, one would expect MP theory to imitate it by using the two vocabularies. And so it did. John Bates Clark (1899) developed MP theory using the vocabularly of property appropriation and Friedrich von Wieser (1889) developed MP theory using the vocabulary of reponsibility imputation.

The basic idea is to picture each factor as "producing" its marginal product. Is that what each factor "gets"?

When a workman leaves the mill, carrying his pay in his pocket, the civil law guarantees to him what he thus takes away; but before he leaves the mill he is the rightful owner of a part of the wealth that the day's industry has brought forth.

Does the economic law which, in some way that he does not understand, determines what his pay shall be, make it to correspond with the amount of his portion of the day's product, or does it force him to leave some of his rightful share behind him? A plan of living that should force men to leave in their employer's hands anything that by right of creation is theirs, would be an institutional robbery—a legally established violation of the principle on which property is supposed to rest. (Clark, 1899, pp. 8–9).

In competitive equilibrium, each factor price is the value of its marginal productivity. Hence, Clark concludes that each factor "gets" the share of the product it "produces" in competitive equilibrium; to labor the fruits of labor, to capital the fruits of capital, and to land the fruits of land. In this manner, Clark and later MP theorists have brilliantly attempted to co-opt the labor theory of property and to harness it in the defense of competitive capitalism.

Most orthodox economists, even those who loudly disagree with MP theory on empirical grounds, fully accept all the essentials of the ideological interpretation of MP theory. The essentials of the theory are that each factor "produces" its marginal product, and that each factor "gets" its marginal product in competitive equilibrium. Economists of both left and right persuasions, who criticize and refute the theory, in fact accept these essentials. The so-called criticism consists in pointing out that the real-world economy is hardly perfectly competitive, that marginal products are usually very difficult to measure, and that there is nothing sacred about the original distribution of ownership of the factors. None of this criticism touches the essentials of the theory.

Orthodox economists tend to accept as simple objective fact the essential points that each factor "produces" its marginal product, and that each factor would "get" its marginal product in competitive equilibrium. For example, Professor Milton Friedman takes it as fact that competitive capitalism, or a "free market society," operates according to the "capitalist ethic"; "To each according to what he and the instruments he owns produces." (Friedman, 1962, pp. 161–162). Most orthodox economists, like Professor Friedman, prefer to strike a posture of scientific objectivity and to refrain from any normative judgment as to the ethical status of the "objective fact" that a free market society allocates to "each according to what he and the instruments he owns produces." They are perfectly willing to let the reader supply the missing ethical postulate.

It is this widely acccepted "objective" interpretation of MP theory that is incorrect. It is only "as if" each factor "produced" and "received" its marginal product in competitive equilibrium. A nonhuman factor does not "produce" its marginal product because, metaphors aside, it does not produce at all. Each factor does not "get" any property right to a share in the product since, metaphors aside, the whole product is appropriated by one party.

The concept of marginal productivity can be understood in a manner consistent with the fact that persons act and things do not. Consider, for example, the so-called "marginal product of a shovel" in a simple production process wherein three workers use two shovels and a wheelbarrow to dig out a cellar. Two of the workers use two shovels to fill the wheelbarrow which the third worker pushes a certain distance to dump the dirt. The "marginal product of a shovel" is defined as the extra product produced when an extra shovel is added and the other factors, such as labor, are held constant. The labor is the human activity of carrying out this production process. If labor was held "constant" in the sense of carrying out the same human activity, then any third shovel would just lie unused and the extra product would be identically zero.

"Holding labor constant" really means reorganizing the human activity in a more capital intensive way so that the extra shovel will be optimally utilized. For instance, all three workers could use the three shovels to fill the wheelbarrow and then they could take turns emptying the wheelbarrow. In this manner, the workers would use the extra shovel and by so doing they would produce some extra product (additional earth moved during the same time period). This extra product would be called the "marginal product of the shovel", but in fact it is produced by the workers who are also using the additional shovel. In the workers' new whole product, the positive product is expanded by the extra output and the negative product is expanded by the utilization of the services of an extra shovel. The ratio of the *workers'* extra positive product to the *workers'* extra negative product is called the "marginal product of a shovel." In this manner, the concept of marginal productivity can be understood in a nonanimistic fashion.

The development of the ideological interpretation of MP theory using the vocabulary of responsibility and imputation was due to Friedrich von Wieser. Wieser's contribution is remarkable because he is one of the few capitalist economists who admitted in print that of all the factors of production, only labor is responsible.

> The judge, . . . , who, in his narrowly defined task, is only concerned with the *legal imputation*, confines, himself to the discovery of the legally responsible factor, —that person, in fact, who is threatened with the legal punishment. On him will rightly be laid the whole burden of the consequences, although he could never by himself alone—without instruments and all the other conditions—have committed the crime. The imputation takes for granted physical causality. . . .
>
> . . . If it is the moral imputation that is in question, then certainly no one but the

labourer could be named. Land and capital have no merit that they bring forth fruit; they are dead tools in the hand of man; and the man is responsible for the use he makes of them. (Wieser, 1889, pp. 76–79)

These are remarkable admissions. Wieser at last has in his hands the correct explanation of the old radical slogans "Only labor is creative" or "Only labor is productive," which even the classical laborists and Marxists could not explain clearly. Does Wieser resist his capitalist inclinations and develop a laborist critique of capitalist production?

Wieser's response to his insights exemplifies what passes for moral reasoning among many economists and social theorists in general. Any stable socioeconomic system will provide the conditions for its own reproduction. The bulk of the people born and raised under the system will be appropriately educated so that the superiority of the system will be intuitively obvious to them. They will not use some purported abstract moral principle to evaluate the system; the system is "obviously" correct. Instead the moral principle itself is judged according to whether or not it supports the system. If the principle does not agree with the system, then "obviously" the principle is incorrect, irrelevant, or inapplicable.

The fact that only labor could be legally or morally responsible did not lead Wieser to question capitalist appropriation. It only told him that the usual notions of responsibility and imputation were not relevant to capitalist appropriation. They applied to legal questions, whereas economists are concerned with economic questions. Capitalist apologetics would require a new notion of "economic imputation" in accordance with another new notion of "economic responsibility."

In the division of the return from production, we have to deal similarly . . . with an imputation, —save that it is from the economic, not the judicial point of view. [Wieser, 1889, p. 76]

By defining economic responsibility in terms of the animistic version of marginal productivity, Wieser could finally draw his desired conclusion that competitive capitalism "economically" imputes the product in accordance with "economic" responsibility.

Metaphors are like little white lies; one requires others to round out the picture. The Clark-Wieser theory uses one metaphor to justify another metaphor. Each factor's metaphorical responsibility for producing a share of the product is used to justify each factor's metaphorical property share in the product. By justifying one metaphor with another metaphor, capitalist apologetics can make a clean break with reality, the reality of the actual property relations of capitalist production and the actual juridical principle of imputation used in the legal system. It is the *actual* property relations of capitalist production, i.e., the employer's appropriation of the whole product, that need to be justified or condemned, and the notion of responsibility relevant to the structure of legal property rights is the normal nonmetaphorical juridical notion of responsibility that is used every day from "the judicial point of view".

The Employee as an Instrument in Capitalist Production

Symmetry is a powerful engine of human thought, but the implications are not always progressive. For example, the slavery system exhibited a certain symmetry between the slaves and beasts of burden. Capitalist economists exhibit an absolute passion for the symmetrical treatment of the human element in production, labor, and the nonhuman factors of production. There are two ways that labor can be treated as symmetrical with the inputs to production. One way, which we have already seen, is to animistically elevate the nonhuman inputs to the status of responsible agents of production cooperating with the workers. The other way is demote the human element to the level of the nonhuman factors as just another input to production. Thus the human activity of converting the inputs into the outputs is conceptualized as just another passive input to production.

Capitalist economists usually use one symmetrical picture or the other; either the active picture where all the factors are symmetrical active agents of production or the passive picture where all the factors are symmetrical passive inputs to production. The actual picture which recognizes the asymmetry between persons and things, which recognizes that persons act and things do not, is avoided. Since language itself deeply reflects the asymmetry between persons and things, economists use a variety of amusing linguistic contortions to describe the active picture or the passive picture of production. We have already described the use of the pathetic fallacy involved in the active picture which elevates the instruments of production into "agents of production cooperating" with the workers.

To describe the passive picture, economists have had to become masters in using the passive voice. The subjects who carry out the human activity of production have been reconceptualized as passive inputs to production, so the production process has no subject and can only be described in the passive voice. The outputs "are produced" and the inputs "are used up", but not by anyone. The production process is not an activity carried out by human beings, it is a "technological" process that just "takes place". A popular linguistic variation on the passive picture is to use some abstract noun, such as "technology," the "industry," or the "firm," as the putative subject or agent of the production process. Then the active voice can be used even though the human element is still treated as a passive input. "Technology" produces the outputs by using up the inputs. The "industry" or the "firm" produces such and such a product.

People are not, in fact, symmetrical with things. But the legal system of chattel slavery legally treated certain people as being symmetrical with beasts of burden. The present legal system of capitalism, and particularly the employer-employee contract, legally treats the *actions* of human beings symmetrically with the *services* of machines and the other nonhuman inputs as commodities that may be bought and sold. From the legal viewpoint, labor is a commodity. In the employment contract, labor services are bought and sold. When the services of a car or an apartment are bought and sold, the car or apartment is rented. When the labor of a person is bought and sold, the person is rented or hired. The employment contract is the rental contract applied to the rental of a person. It is no longer permitted to buy and sell workers; they may only be rented.

> Since slavery as abolished, human earning power is forbidden by law to be capitalized. A man is not even free to sell himself; he must *rent* himself at a wage. (Samuelson, 1976, p. 52 [emphasis in the original])

Thus the wage or salary payment is really the rental paid to "employ" a person, the "employee".

> One can even say that wages are the rentals paid for the use of a man's personal services for a day or a week or a year. This may seem a strange use of terms, but on second thought, one recognizes that every agreement to hire labor is really for some limited period of time. By outright purchase, you might avoid ever renting any kind of land. But in our society, labor is one of the few productive factors that cannot legally be bought outright. Labor can only be rented, and the wage rate is really a rental. (Samuelson, 1976, p. 569)

It is one of the magnificent conceits of liberalism that the institutionalized treatment of persons as things was eradicated with the abolition of slavery. Liberals and conservatives alike have so clouded their perception of social reality with a facade of metaphors that they cannot imagine how a civilization founded upon the voluntary renting of human beings could possibly be treating people as things. The property theoretic analysis of—not the metaphors—but the actual structure of rights in production reveals a different picture.

When a person rents himself or herself out in the employer-employee contract, the person takes on the legal role of an instrument. This can be verified by directly analyzing the structure of legal rights in the capitalist firm. Things lack the capacity for responsibility so they can bear no legal responsibility for the results of their services. As Wieser put it, "imputation takes for granted physical causality," so the legal responsibility is imputed through the instrument, as a conduit, back to the human user. That is the legal treatment of an instrument.

That is also the legal treatment of the employees in a capitalist firm. The employees have *none* of the legal responsibility for the produced outputs (i.e., no legal ownership of the outputs) and *none* of the legal responsibility for the used-up inputs (i.e., no legal claims against them for the used-up inputs). Instead, that legal responsibility for the positive and negative results of the employees' actions is imputed back through them, like a conduit, to the person or persons who use or employ them, the employer. The employer legally appropriates the whole product. Hence the employees in a capitalist firm have, within the scope of their employment, precisely the legal role of tools or instruments.

These facts about the actual legal responsibility of employees and the actual structure of property rights are, of course, quite obfuscated by the conventional metaphorical picture of labor and capital as each getting a share of the product. The following quotation from James Mill is remarkable in that it eschews the "as-if" picture of distributive shares in order to describe the fact that the employer owns 100% of the product (positive and negative). It makes it clear why so many modern economists prefer to hide behind a facade of shared-pie metaphors rather than deal with the actual structure of property rights in capitalist production.

> The great capitalist, the owner of a manufactory, if he operated with slaves instead of free labourers, like the West India planter, would be regarded as owner both of the capital, and of the labour. He would be owner, in short, of both instruments of production: and the whole of the produce, without participation, would be his own.
>
> What is the difference, in the case of the man, who operates by means of labourers receiving wages? The labourer, who receives wages sells his labour for a day, a week, a month, or a year, as the case may be. The manufacturer, who pays these wages, buys the labour, for the day, the year, or whatever period it may be. He is equally therefore the owner of the labour, with the manufacturer who operates with slaves. The only difference is, in the mode of purchasing. The owner of the slave purchases, at once, the whole of the labour, which the man can ever perform: he, who pays wages, purchases only so much of a man's labour as he can perform in a day, or any other stipulated time. Being equally, however, the owner of the labour, so purchased, as the owner of the slave is of that of the slave, the produce, which is the result of this labour, combined with his capital, is all equally his own. In the state of society, in which we at present exist, it is in these circumstances that almost all production is effected: the capitalist is the owner of both instruments of production: and the whole of the produce is his. (James Mill, 1826, ch. I, sec. II)

The employee in a capitalist firm and the slave both have the legal position of an instrument in their respective roles, but there are two major differences. The slave was owned on a full-time basis, whereas the employee is only hired or rented and thus only has the role of an instrument within the scope of the employment. Moreover the slave generally acquired the legal role of a chattel involuntarily whereas the employment contract is voluntary.

The employees in fact are, like the slaves were, responsible persons, not instruments. That is only their legal role. The employee is legally treated as an instrumentality only so long as the activities are lawful. When the employer and employees cooperate together to break the law, then the legal authorities step in, strip away the artificiality of the employees' role, and hold the employees coresponsible together with the employer for the results of the activities. The slaves, of course, enjoyed the same metamorphosis whenever they committed crimes. The "talking instrument" in work became the responsible person in crime. As one abolitionist observed in 1853;

> The slave, who is but "*a chattel*" on all *other* occasions, with not one solitary attribute of personality accorded to him, becomes "*a person*" whenever he is to be *punished*. (Goodell, 1853, p. 309)

We previously used a simple one-line definition of de facto responsibility because the analysis of capitalist production does not require analysis of grey-area borderline cases. Legal philosophers and jurisprudents write volumes upon volumes which dissect human actions to establish degrees of de facto responsibility under conditions of impaired mental competence, mistaken information, duress, and so forth in order that the appropriate degree of legal responsibility can be assigned in accordance with the juridical imputation principle. Now employees are fully capacitated; they are not children, they are not senile, they are not insane, and so forth. Yet one would scan the entire legal and philosophical literature in vain to find the simple observation that the actions of the employees in a normal capitalist firm are fully deliberate, intentional, voluntary, and responsible (no borderline case here)—but that the employees are assigned *zero* legal responsibility for the positive and negative results of these actions. Zero. It is the staggering power of social indoctrination which structures the perception of social reality so that certain aspects are seen very clearly while other aspects are quite invisible. Thus it is that lawyers and philosophers can spend a lifetime splitting hairs to properly apply the imputation principle to borderline cases and yet never even notice a direct one-hundred-percent violation of the imputation principle right in everyday economic life.

The Labor Contract as an Invalid Contract

The standard defense of capitalist production (the employment relation) is that it cannot be inherently unjust because it (unlike chattel slavery) is based on a voluntary contract, the employer-employee contract. The Marxist analysis of the wage labor contract is as superficial as the Marxist labor theory of value. Marxism enters a special plea that the contract is "really" involuntary. Firstly, this special plea is quite unconvincing. According to any workable juridical definition of voluntariness, the labor contract is quite voluntary, especially in these days of unions and collective bargaining. Indeed, the unionized worker's bargaining position compares quite favorably with the bargaining position of consumers (who usually must take prices as given). Secondly, the argument, that wage labor is exploitative because it is "forced" labor based on an "involuntary" contract, is superficial because it does not challenge the liberal premise that wage labor would be permissible if it were "really voluntary". It is that premise that is incorrect.

The employment contract is the key to the entire legal structure of capitalist production. It is the employment contract that legally packages the whole human activity of production as just another input commodity. By purchasing this peculiar commodity in the employment contract and by purchasing the other inputs, any legal party, no matter how absentee, can legally appropriate the whole product of production. Let us compare this contract for the renting of human beings with the normal input contracts.

Consider the contract for the renting of a machine or tool. The owner of an instrument or machine can use the instrument personally and be responsible for the results *or* the owner can turn the instrument over to be used independently by another person who would then be responsible for the results. If a person could similarly alienate and transfer the "use" of his or her own person, then the employment contract would be a bona fide contract—like the contract to hire out a genuine instrument. *If* the employees could alienate and transfer their labor services to the employer so that the employer could somehow use these services without the employees being inextricably coresponsible, then the employer would be solely de facto responsible for the whole product and then the employer's laissez-faire appropriation of the whole product would be jurisprudentially correct. But such a contractual performance on the part of the employees is not factually possible. Human labor is factually nontransferable. All the employees can do is to voluntarily cooperate, as responsible human agents, with their working employer, but then the employees are inextricably de facto coresponsible for the results of the joint activity.

The inexorable joint responsibility of all the people who participate in an activity is a matter of fact. Judicial decrees, legislative enactments, and philosophical pronouncements will not change those facts. For lawful activities, the law neither affirms nor denies those facts since the laissez-faire mechanism reigns. But when employees or, in legal jargon, servants commit civil or criminal wrongs at the direction of the employer, then the law sets aside the invisible-hand mechanism of imputation and steps in to render an explicit legal imputation based on the facts insofar as they are ascertained. Just as in an earlier age, the "talking instruments" in work became responsible persons in crime, so today the servants in work become the partners in crime.

> All who participate in a crime with a guilty intent are liable to punishment. A master and servant who so participate in a crime are liable criminally, not because they are master and servant, but because they jointly carried out a criminal venture and are both criminous. (Batt, 1967, p. 612)

It should be particularly noted that the employee is not guilty because an employment contract that involves a crime is null and void. Quite the opposite. The employee is guilty because the employee, together with the employer, committed a crime. It was their responsibility for the crime that invalidated the contract, not the invalidity of the contract that created the responsibility.

When the "venture" being "jointly carried out" is noncriminal, the employees do not suddenly become instruments (in fact). "All who participate in" the productive activity of a normal capitalist enterprise are similarly de facto responsible for the positive and negative results of the activity, i.e., for the whole product. The law does not suddenly decree that, as long as the employees' actions are lawful, the employees will be legally considered only as hired instruments being employed by the employer. It doesn't need to. The law achieves the very same results by now accepting the employment contract as "valid" and by accepting the same inextricably coresponsible cooperation on the part of the employees as fulfilling the employment contract. No explicit decree, judgment, or imputation is necessary since the laissez-faire mechanism has taken over again. The employer has borne all the costs of production, including the labor costs, so the employer has the legally defensible claim on all the outputs. That is the secret of capitalist appropriation.

The defense that the employment contract is voluntary is inadequate. Voluntariness is a necessary but not a sufficient condition for the validity of a contract. The hired criminal would certainly agree to voluntarily "transfer" his labor services and to voluntarily "transfer" the responsibility for the results of his actions. But this is not factually possible, as the law fully recognizes. It is as if one voluntarily agreed to be a beast of burden such as a horse. Why wouldn't such a contract be valid? It would be juridically invalid because it is impossible to voluntarily fulfill the contract to be a chattel. But the legal authorities could nevertheless accept such a contract to be a chattel as being "valid". If the person behaved appropriately like a chattel by doing as he or she is told, then the legal authorities would count that as "fulfulling" the contract to be a chattel, as least until a crime is committed. Then the legalized fraud would be set aside. Such a contract is not a concocted example. In the decade preceding the U.S. Civil War, general legislation was passed in six slave states to validate voluntary self-enslavement contracts "to permit a free Negro to become a slave voluntarily" (Gray, 1958, p. 527, quoted in Philmore, 1982, p. 47).

Today, the voluntary contract of self-enslavement, the contract to voluntarily sell oneself, is recognized as being invalid, but the contract to voluntarily rent oneself out is still recognized as "valid". Indeed, it is the basis for the capitalist system of production. However a person cannot voluntarily fulfill the contract to be an instrument or chattel for eight hours a day any more than the contract to be a permanent chattel. We have seen that the employee has the legal role of an instrument. Thus the employer-employee contract is a contract to play an instrumental role for eight or so hours a day. The worker cannot voluntarily fulfill that role any more than can the hired criminal. But the legal authorities nevertheless can and do say that if the person does as he or she is told within the scope of the contract, then that will count as "fulfilling" the contract, at least so long as no crime is committed. If a crime is committed, then the "contract" becomes a noncontract, the "transferred" labor becomes untransferred, and the "instrument" becomes a person, i.e., the whole fraud is set aside, so that the juridical principle of imputation (i.e., the labor theory of property) can be applied.

The voluntary contract to "transfer" labor, to play the role of a part-time "instrument", is *juridically invalid* because it is impossible to fulfill. The fault lies not in the laissez-faire mechanism of imputation, which is necessary in any system of private property. The fault lies in the invalid employment contract which causes the mechanism to misfire and misimpute the whole product. The capitalist legal system's acceptance of the workers' inescapably coresponsible actions as "fulfilling" the employment contract (outside of a crime) is only a legalized fraud, a massive fraud on an institutional scale. As always, a fraud allows a theft to parade about in the disguise of a voluntary contract. But this notion of the natural-law invalidity of the contract for renting human beings is absent from the utilitarian tradition of neoclassical economics. Indeed, utilitarian normative economics is unable to account for the invalidity of voluntary self-enslavement contracts (see Philmore, 1982; Callahan, 1985).

Self-Management: The Abolition of the Employment Relation

The employer-employee contract, being an inherently fraudulent and invalid contract, should be recognized as such by the legal system and abolished. Then it would no longer be permitted to rent people, so industry would be reorganized on the basis of people renting capital rather than vice versa. Such firms are called *self-managed firms* or *worker cooperatives*, and a market economy of such firms is referred to as the system of self management, worker cooperation, workplace democracy, or industrial democracy. In the words of John Stuart Mill:

> The form of association ... which if mankind continue to improve, must be expected in the end to predominate, is not that which can exist between a capitalist as chief, and workpeople without a voice in the management, but the association of the labourers themselves on terms of equality, collectively owning the capital with which they carry on their operations, and working under managers elected and removable by themselves. (J. S. Mill, 1848, bk IV, ch. VII, sec. 6)

In a worker cooperative corporation or self-managed firm, the membership rights are personal rights assigned to the functional role of working in the company. Hence all the people and only the people working in a worker cooperative hold the membership rights. This legal structure implements the labor theory of property. In legal terms, the corporation is legally liable for the used-up inputs and legally owns the produced outputs, i.e., the corporation appropriates the whole product. Hence when the people working in the company are the members of the corporation, then they, through their corporate embodiment, appropriate the positive and negative fruits of their labor—in accordance with the labor theory of property.

The eventual complete abolition of employer-employee relation, like the abolition of the master-slave relation, should be accompanied by positive legal guarantees of people's rights. This could be accomplished by a constitutional amendment which (1) legally recognized the employer-employee contract as being invalid, and (2) legally guaranteed people's membership rights in the firms where they work. Capitalist corporations could be directly converted into democratically self-managed cooperative corporations by internally reversing the contract between capital and labor. This is done by converting the equity capital into debt capital (e.g., convert shares into annuities or consols) and by reassigning the membership rights to the people who work in the firm (for more details, see the literature of the Industrial Cooperative Association such as Ellerman, 1981, 1983b, 1984; Ellerman and Pitegoff, 1983].

The economic system of self-managed worker cooperatives would bring the principle of democracy into the workplace where it can govern "what people do all day long". Instead of having people's daily work treated as a marketable commodity sold to a corporation, people would have an inalienable human right to the fruits of their labor by being guaranteed membership in the firm where they work.

References

Arrow, K. J. 1971. The Firm in General Equilibrium Theory. In *The Corporate Economy*. R. Marris and A. Wood eds. Cambridge: Harvard University Press.

Arrow, K. J., and Debreu, G. 1954. Existence of an Equilibrium for a Competitive Economy. *Econometrica* 22:265–290.

Arrow, K. J., and Hahn, F. H., 1971. *General Competitive Analysis*. San Francisco: Holden-Day.

Batt, Francis. 1967. *The Law of Master and Servant*. 5th ed. G. Webber (ed.). London: Pitman.

Burmeister, E. 1974. Neo-Austrian and Alternative Approaches to Capital Theory. *Journal of Economic Literature* 12:413–456.

Callahan, Joan C. 1985. Enforcing Slavery Contracts: A Liberal View. *Philosophical Forum* 16:223–236.

Clark, John Bates. 1899. *The Distribution of Wealth*. New York: Macmillan.

Debreu, G. 1959. *Theory of Value*. New York: Wiley.

Ellerman, David. 1972. Introduction to Normative Property Theory. *The Review of Radical Political Economics* 4(2):49–67.

Ellerman, David. 1973. Capitalism and Workers' Self-Management. Foreword to G. Hunnius and G. D. Garson (eds.), *Workers' Control: A Reader on Labor and Social Change*. New York: Random House. pp. 3–21.

Ellerman, David. 1980a. On Property Theory and Value Theory. *Economic Analysis and Workers' Management* 14(1):105–126.

Ellerman, David. 1980b. Property Theory and Orthodox Economics. E. J. Nell (ed.), *Growth, Profits and Property: Essays in the Revival of Political Economy*. Cambridge: Cambridge University Press.

Ellerman, David. 1981. Workers' Cooperatives: The Question of Legal Structure. Somerville, MA: Industrial Cooperative Association. 23 p. Also published in R. Jackall and H. Levin (eds.), *Worker Cooperatives in America*. Berkeley: University of California Press, 1984.

Ellerman, David. 1982. *Economics, Accounting, and Property Theory*. Lexington, MA: D. C. Heath.

Ellerman, David. 1983a. Marxian Exploitation Theory: A Brief Exposition, Analysis and Critique. *Philosophical Forum* 14 (3–4):315–333.

Ellerman, David. 1983b. A Model Structure for Cooperatives. *Review of Social Economy* 41(1):52–67.

Ellerman, David. 1984. Theory of Legal Structure: Worker Cooperatives. *Journal of Economic Issues* 18(3):861–891.

Ellerman, David. 1985. The Mathematics of Double Entry Bookkeeping. *Mathematics Magazine* 58(4):226–233.

Ellerman, David. 1986. Double Entry Multidimensional Accounting. *Omega* 14(1):13–22.

Ellerman, David, and Pitegoff, Peter. 1983. The Democratic Corporation. *Review of Law and Social Change* (New York University) 11(3):441–472.

Fama, E., and Miller, M. H. 1972. *The Theory of Finance*. New York: Holt, Rinehart and Winston.

Friedman, Milton. 1962. *Capitalism and Freedom*. Chicago: University of Chicago Press.

Furubotn, E., and Pejovich, S., eds. 1974. *The Economics of Property Rights*. Cambridge, MA: Ballinger.

Goodell, William. 1853. *The American Slave Code in Theory and Practice*. New York: New American Library, 1969 (reprint).

Gray, Lewis Cecil. 1958. *History of Agriculture in the Southern United States to 1860*. Vol. I. Gloucester: Peter Smith.

Hirshleifer, J. 1970. *Investment, Interest, and Capital*. Englewood Cliffs, NJ: Prentice-Hall.

Hodgskin, Thomas. 1832. *The Natural and Artificial Right of Property Contrasted*. Clifton, NJ: Kelley, 1973 (reprint).

Keynes, J. M. 1936. *The General Theory of Employment, Interest, and Money*. New York: Harcourt, Brace & World.

Koopmans, T. C., ed. 1951. *Activity Analysis of Production and Allocation*. New York: Wiley.

Lichtheim, George. 1969. *The Origins of Socialism*. New York: Praeger.

Marshall, Alfred. 1920. *Principles of Economics*. New York: Macmillan.

McKenzie, L. 1954. On Equilibrium in Graham's Model of World Trade and Other Competitive Systems. *Econometrica* 22(April):147–161.

McKenzie, L. 1959. On the Existence of a General Equilibrium in a Competitive Market. *Econometrica* 27:54–71.

McKenzie, L. 1981. The Classical Theorem on Existence of Competitive Equilibrium. *Econometrica* 49(4):819–841.

Menger, Anton. 1899. *The Right to the Whole Produce of Labour: The Origin and Development of the Theory of Labour's Claim to the Whole Product of Industry*. Clifton, NJ: Kelley, 1970 (reprint).

Mill, James. 1826. *Elements of Political Economy*. 3rd ed. Clifton, NJ: Kelley (reprint).

Mill, John Stuart. 1848. *Principles of Political Economy*. Donald Winch (ed.). Harmondsworth: Penguin Books, 1970.

Philmore, J. 1982. The Libertarian Case for Slavery: A Note on Nozick. *Philosophical Forum* 14(Fall):43–58.

Quirk, J., and Saposnik, R. 1968. *Introduction to General Equilibrium Theory and Welfare Economics*. New York: McGraw-Hill.

Samuelson, P. 1937. Some Aspects of The Pure Theory of Capital. *Quarterly Journal of Economics* 51(May):469–496. Reprinted in Samuelson (1966), 161–188.

Samuelson, P. 1957. Wages and Interest: A Modern Dissection of Marxian Economic Models. *The American Economic Review* 47(6):884–912. Reprinted in Samuelson (1966), 341–369.

Samuelson, P. 1961. The Evaluation of "Social Income": Capital Formation and Wealth. In F. A. Lutz and D. C. Hague (eds.), *The Theory of Capital*. Pp. 32–57. London: Macmillan. Reprinted in Samuelson (1966), 299–318.

Samuelson, P. 1966. *The Collected Scientific Papers of Paul A. Samuelson*. vol. I., J. Stiglitz, ed. Cambridge, MA: MIT Press.

Samuelson, P. 1967. The Monopolistic Competition Revolution. In R. E. Kuenne (ed.), *Monopolistic Competition Theory: Studies in Impact*. Pp. 105–138. New York: Wiley. Reprinted in Samuelson (1972), 18–51.

Samuelson, P. 1972. *The Collected Scientific Papers of Paul A. Samuelson*. vol. III. Robert C. Merton (ed.). Cambridge, MA: MIT Press.

Samuelson, P. 1976. *Economics*. 10th ed. New York: McGraw-Hill.

Stonier, A. W., and Hague, D. C. 1973. *A Textbook in Economic Theory*. 4th ed. New York: Wiley.

Wieser, Friedrich von. 1889. *Natural Value*. Trans. by C. A. Malloch. New York: Stechert, 1930.

4 TIME AND EQUILIBRIUM

Randall Bausor

All living things experience the fleeting caress of time. It brushes all our affairs as we grow, mature, age, and die. Living each moment, our days irretrievably pass away, and although everyone experiences time's flow, authentic analysis, or even speaking of it, remains difficult. Perceiving time only as we rush along with it, we can never step back to reflect upon it. Nevertheless, economists cannot proceed without addressing time's central role in volition, choice, and action. Just as time permeates our lives, it must permeate our discourse. By imposing a particular structure on us, it imposes an analogous structure on any truly dynamic economics.

The Nature of Time and the Logic of Analysis

The understanding of time begins with the present. We all live in the current moment, and spend all our hours within the eternal now. This durationless locus of sentience, what Shackle (1979) terms the "moment-in-being", encompasses the realization of self-existence, and contains both past and future. The present contains them epistemically and psychologically, for the past is a remembered image and the future is an imagined hypothetical.

93

Since both past memories and imagined futures arise within the present, they are its creatures and its products. They are both generated within the mind, and whatever we have of past and future is what the mind now concocts. Thus, our constructed internal images have no simple, reliable, or consistent relationship to any presumed external ontological existence. Whatever we think the past was, or imagine the future will be, both are of the mind's present. For human behavior, it is this epistemic experience that matters. Only in this sense can our intuitions about past and future, about the flow of time, and even about the direction of time be rendered comprehensible. Only in this sense can mortals come to a personal realization of time at all.

The present, the moment-in-being, masks an epistemic and evidentiary frontier between past and future. We denote past phenomena differently—in different tenses—from those belonging to the future, conceive of them differently, and accept assertions about them based on different evidence and argument. Indeed, the principal means of epistemically distinguishing past from future are the distinct devices establishing the soundness of images and impressions of them.

We may have sensory evidence and memory of the past, but only imagination of the future. Possessing memories of what was, our fundamental epistemic and cognitive distinction between one's past and one's future is that the former is knowable (although not necessarily known) and the latter is profoundly unknowable. Only through supernatural means can we claim to divine destinies, and then the source transcends the things of this universe.

This holds for both the extraordinary and the routine. We may be just as confident of victory in war as in the timely arrival of the bus to work, but we cannot *know* these things, for knowledge of events never precedes them. Indeed it is the acquisition of new perceptions amid fresh evidence that signals the passage of time, that convinces us that the present is something different from what it had been.

We perceive time as a flow because we are constantly reminded that the present continually evolves and changes. New information about that which had been of the future signals that what had been the object of speculative imagination has been transformed into a knowable component of the past. Knowledge of what had been unknowable renders it no longer the subject of expectation in the future, but of evidence and memory. Consequently, the present must have shifted, and we denote it by a new name; a new hour, day, or year. If, for example, I had expected to ride the bus to work at 8:00, and now notice that my clock records 8:15, and I remember having recently ridden the bus, I automatically accept that "now" is not 7:55. I realize that time passed because now I remember, and hence no longer anticipate, the journey. This transfer of the epistemic justification of propositions regarding an event establishes the apprehension of time's flow. Moreover, it assures us that time always moves forward. The future appears to slip into the past, which builds the illusion that the present is thrust into the future. The direction never changes. We can gain new objects of sensory perception, but what has once been accessible to recollection can never again be viewed solely as imagined anticipation. We may forget, but barring psychopathology, memory's decay emerges as the loss of knowledge, not the reversal of time. Forgetting one's wedding anniversary does not normally convince one that he or she has never been married. Thus, the accumulation of memory, or at least of the memorable, requires time to be conceived as unidirectional.

In the terminology of Georgescu-Roegen (1971) this renders time not only irreversible, but irrevocable. Our psyches can never return to exactly the same state as they had occupied. Having once achieved perception of an event as an object of perception and memory we cannot return to that relative innocence in which it had not yet happened. Even if we forget exactly what happened, we no longer consider it only a future possibility. We know that time has elapsed, and having elapsed we cannot return to precisely the same psychic state. No longer can we still hope and fear for it, as we had. Thus each succeeding moment necessarily possesses a unique past, delineates a unique future, and embodies an irrevocable present. Once today is gone, it is gone forever. There may be other days and other weeks, but no other morning will have the same sunrise. Today's ride on the bus is not the same as yesterday's, since now I remember yesterday's rain, and no longer wonder if it will snow yesterday afternoon.

This distinction between an unknowable future of imagined possibilities and a remembered past of perception and regret also governs our sense of causation. The experience of time as irrevocable conspires with the prestige of tangible evidence to persuade us that the past is ontologically immutable. We may continue to gain evidence about it and come to new knowledge of it, but do not ascribe the change to its ontological reality. It having established a direct evidentiary base within our minds, we no longer consider it malleable. We may attempt to learn more about it, or to persuade others to new interpretations of it, but we cannot undo it. Only God can now make the *Titanic* arrive in New York intact, and on schedule.

Conversely, the future is full of promise and opportunity. We know nothing of it, erect imagined possibilities for it, and hope to influence which possibilities ultimately appear. We each possess a talent for imagining what might be, and infer from our own experiences how behavior might affect which possibilities unfold. The future, being unknowable, is felt to be amorphous, and, to some degree, controllable.

Only through acceptance of this unknowable but fungible future do volition and choice matter. At any instant each individual possesses imagined possible futures and complex arrays of attitudes and emotions about them. Some may be considered desirable and others not; some may be considered chancy and others not. The individual considers and judges them, all the while knowing nothing of them. Choice, however, regards what is to be done now. It involves which imagined opportunities to pursue and how to achieve them. The present expectation of future realized consequence rules choice, so that choice always remains contingent upon a complete unknowable. Neither the ultimate consequences of our acts nor a complete set of potentialities is knowable.[1] Choice cannot be reduced to reason because, in the absence of knowledge, uncertainty and imagination dominate. The actual outcomes of a decision, as opposed to the anticipated outcomes, have nothing to do with it. For actual outcomes to influence decisions, they must be known. For them to be known they must be knowable. For them to be knowable they must be past. For them to be past renders the choice itself past and antiquated. If the expectation is past, then decisions dependent on it are forever foregone. Choice must be conceived as temporally, causally, and logically prior to consequences. Violation of this attribute of time contradicts its unidirectional flow and confuses past and future.

Each decision, moreover, is irrevocable and unrepeatable. Each act of choosing relates to collections and imagined possibilities uniquely embedded in time with a unique view forward. Every moment has its own past and its own future, so every decision has its own special epistemic and psychological antecedents that can be produced at no other instant. Every decision refers to opportunities, desires, and attitudes uniquely embedded in time, and not reproducible. Consequently, every choice is irrevocable: the act of choosing now forever demolishes the possibility of making the same choice again. Although I may have ridden the bus every day for years, each daily decision to attempt to do so is unique, for I cannot know, in advance, whether today it will fail to conclude its journey safely. Even when the act appears repetitive, the decision behind it is special. It is always unrepeatable. Attempting the trip today may or may not determine the attempt to make a similar journey tomorrow, but I can never again enjoy the opportunity of not making the journey at this time. Similarly, even if the vector of contracted ex post prices remains unchanged from period to period, the epistemic background guiding the acts leading toward such price vectors necessarily does change. Indeed the whole expectational foundation for all choices must have changed, even if the information about it distilled into prices has not. Similarly any economic process linked to social behavior through decision must also be irrevocable. Hence, any dynamic economics must incorporate a notion of time itself both irrevocable and irreversible.

From this discussion we can glean three structural attributes required of any authentically dynamic economic analysis. First, each moment, each decision, and each opportunity must be construed as irrevocable. Since time cannot reverse itself, no instant or period can be repeated. Each date has its own past and its own future, its own imagined possibilities, and its own anticipated opportunities. A truly historically dynamic economic analysis must incorporate an irrevocable conceptualization of time to assure that the system perpetually moves forward.

Second, each decision must be based upon *anticipated* outcomes. Since the future is unknowable, however, these must be explicitly distinct from ontologically *actual* outcomes. Causation extends forward from the present, but its channels cannot be known beforehand. They can only be imagined. To retain the historical structure of epistemic time, a model must logically render choice as contingent on current expectations which, in turn, refer to perceptions of past experiences and remain antecedent to their own ultimate consequences. The strict logical priority of all decisions to their own current and future consequences is the only way to retain within a model the cognitive and causal antecedence of choice to outcome. Violation of this property muddles the representation of time, denies time's one-way flow, and is incompatible with the epistemic distinction between past and future.

Third, since people act on the basis of individually compiled expectations, together they may not achieve systemically coherent plans. They may be at odds with each other, which can be reflected only in models capable of getting out of equilibrium. Historically dynamic processes can therefore be represented only when the outcomes of all possible combinations of choices, and not merely the equilibrated results, are specified. That is, historical-time economic models must be closed in the sense of Robinson (1980) and Shubik (1975).

Historical Time and the Time of Traditional Economic Analysis

Having long recognized the need to incorporate time into their analyses, economists' predominant formal representation of it focuses on the sequential pattern of events, and replicates it by the ordering of the real numbers. According to this scheme time can be introduced by a simple process of numerical dating. An additional variable, t, denotes the moment, and other variables can be phrased as functionally dependent upon it. This allows expansion of the model to discriminate between dates and automatically provides well-ordering sequences that symbolize earlier and later.

This conceptualization has enjoyed wide acceptance in economics. Hicks (1939) adopted it in the vision of sequentially active markets temporarily equilibrated each "week." Debreu (1959) invoked forward trading in commodities dated in the future to interpret the classical existence results in terms of time. Similarly, it lies at the foundation of the analysis of stability. Mathematically, in all of these modes, time assumes the attributes of another dimension.

To what extent does this tactic succeed in capturing the various properties of epistemically historical analysis outlined above? Clearly, the naming of dates is necessary to distinguishing events at different instants. It is, however, only a minimal condition without which explicit timelessness characterizes the model. Implicitly, time remains absent.

Conceptualizing the problem as equivalent to a geometrical dimension only provides a structured order to events. It does not generate a unidirectional flow of time, nor does it assure a causal antecedence to temporal precedence. In short, time, if it moves at all, may move backward. Examining the uses of this formalization more finely reveals its flaws.

Consider first Debreu's tactic of labeling commodities by date. This imposes an ordering on the discharge of obligations contracted forward, but all contracting for all deliveries at all dates must be concluded prior to the initiation of the first period. The process of coordinating economic activity is explicitly removed to a timeless epoch *prior* to the operation of the economy: to production, trade, and consumption. No dynamic process of learning and adaptation, of ongoing organization and planning enters this picture of economic evolution. Moreover, all decisions are undertaken simultaneously, and the trading outcomes of all expressed plans are simultaneous with their formation. That is, market-clearing equilibrium arises not through any adjustment and response to market conditions, but is imposed by the timeless efforts of the auctioneer. All demands are satisfied because their satisfaction is logically simultaneous with their expression. Quantities demanded are based on equilibrium market prices, which in turn depend on quantities demanded. Upon entering any market, the agent *knows* the competitive price which results, at least in part, from his or her own choices. This knowledge of the consequence (equilibrium prices) of one's acts as a prerequisite for those acts violates the epistemological structure of time. One must know in advance the consequences of one's attempts to trade. One can only know past events, however; mortals expect outcomes of current acts. To know them contradicts the unknowability of the future. Furthermore, in this model events are sequentially ordered, but there is no formal distinction between motion along time's dimension in one direction as opposed to the other. It is tempting to believe that high values for t should be associated with later dates (since we number later years with larger numbers), but this is only an unjustified illusion. One can shuttle back and forth between points on a line, and with this formalization one can shuttle back and forth in "time."[2]

Hicks (1939) introduced an alternative modeling method which not only dated commodities, but examined sequences of temporarily equilibrated outcomes. Plans are revised sequentially as well, so that behavior can be seen to evolve and develop. The process continues as sequences of spot markets open and close each "week"; all contracting need not occur in advance of time's commencement. This examination of sequences of temporarily equilibrated multimarket systems allows the economist to simultaneously address matters of coordination during each period, and of intertemporal coherence of plans (what Hicks called "Perfect Equilibrium"). Although Hicks (1979) now recognizes limits to this approach, an active literature has grown from his initial insight.[3]

First, coordination within the period, as opposed to between periods, transpires within an explicitly timeless environment. In *Causality in Economics* (1979) Hicks asserts that phenomena taken as temporally subsequent cannot be treated as causally antecedent. This leaves him scope for "contemporaneous causality," however, in which events of one period can be treated as causes of other events of the same period. The problem is that values of variables may change during the period. The initial stock of a commodity reflects the inheritance from the past whereas it can change with new production (p. 71). Since it becomes unclear which value of a variable may best characterize the period (the average over the period's duration may be compatible with infinitely many different paths during the period), this procedure may not prove satisfactory. Hicks suggests reverting to the ideal of equilibrium:

> One can construct a model in which expectations can be described as remaining unchanged, over a period, provided that *within the period* expectations are correct. . . . So expectations, which relate to the future, pass smoothly into experience of the past, without the figures that are set upon them having to be changed. Thus we can, in equilibrium (but only in equilibrium) speak of unchanged expectations, over the period; though admitting that during the period some of these expectations will have turned into realities. (Hicks, 1979, pp. 82–83)

This prohibition of change, however, requires a fundamental timelessness during the period. At the end of the period, what was to have been will have become what was, but no depiction of the economic process by which this happened—of production, consumption, marketing, and accumulation—can be had. In temporary competitive equilibrium each period is only a miniature version of static equilibrium in a multimarket system. People know, before entering the market, the equilibrium price vector. At the time they decide what tactics to pursue, the consequences of those tactics, that is prices, must be known already, not simply expected. Thus, these prices which themselves arise from the temporary coordinating process are already known prior to that process's initiation. Within any period, no matter how brief or long, real economic time does not exist. There is no process by which markets work. Literally, there is no time in which they can arrange deals, signal opportunities, or allocate commodities. The dynamics of market operation, per se, remain completely submerged. This later Hicksian sense of equilibrium still requires assured reconciliation prior to choice, which aligns only with knowledge of outcomes. The epistemic order of time must still be demolished within the period.

In competitive temporary equilibrium, for example, regardless of how long each period is, the business of coordinating market activity transpires within exactly the same timelessness that allows equilibration by the auctioneer in static analysis. Once equilibrated, the state might be interpretable as progressing through time, but that which assures equilibration requires foreknowledge, initial knowledge of what happens during the period, so that any characterization of market activity remains fundamentally atemporal.

Second, periods are numbered sequentially, but no other aspect of the system replicates authentic passage of time. In particular, since these models manifest time only as another geometrical dimension, nothing prevents it from slipping both ways—backward and forward—along that dimension. Only the mirage of associating high numbers with late dates permits the illusion that time is unidirectional. The formal structure cannot sustain the hope, for it is necessarily spatial and neglects other aspects of time.[4]

Careful examination of attempts in economic models to relate states in different periods reveals the limitation of their time-as-dimension approach. Consider Hicks' own analysis in *Value and Capital*. At that time he limited himself to discussion couched in terms of comparative statics. Periods are not linked by any explicit process, and only the relative position of them is specified. Thus, no mechanism within the model itself establishes how the state of one moment evolves into that of another. By looking only in the direction toward which you are pointed, one can rest assured neither that one reaches the presumed destination, nor, indeed, that the direction points to a later time. Only presumption that one moves forward rather than backward exists. Since what we really have is a spatial orientation, and a bias toward higher numbers, the comparative static properties might just as well point toward a 'previous' state as a later. Time exhibits symmetries in this conceptualization, and as long as the past and the future are merely opposite directions along a line, either direction can do just as well.

Problems of modeling the asymmetries of real time with the formal symmetries of the time-as-line approach are not overcome by replacing comparative statics with explicit rules establishing the ties between dates. Introduced into modern macroeconomics and general equilibrium analysis by Paul A. Samuelson (1939, 1941, 1947), this tactic has come to be known as *dynamics*. The model emerges as formally more integrated through this procedure, but it cannot overcome the conceptualization's inherent limitations. Whether proceeding with a system of difference equations and "discrete" time—as in Samuelson (1939)—or of differential equations and "continuous" time—as in Samuelson (1941)—matters little since the fundamental feature of each is that phenomena at one date are modeled as functionally dependent upon phenomena at another date. Customarily read to mean that later events explicitly depend upon earlier events, the opposite interpretation, that phenomena with smaller dates depend upon phenomena with larger dates, is, logically and formally, equally valid. A simple example from macroeconomics illustrates the point. One might wish to formalize the hypothesis that high levels of income in one period cause high levels of investment spending in the next. This might be accomplished by introducing a monotone increasing function where $I(t + 1) = f[Y(t)]$. If $f[\cdot]$ is a one-to-one mapping of the nonnegative real line onto itself, then we could interpret this as high income yielding high investment, but, since the inverse function provides $Y(t) = f^{-1}[I(t + 1)]$, we could interpret the mathematics as asserting that high investment causes high income in periods with smaller dates. As long as time's principal manifestation in an economic model remains isomorphic to a geometrical dimension, its most basic feature of an asymmetrically unknowable but maleable future distinct from a knowable but irrevocable past cannot be accommodated. Positions along a line appear symmetrically from any point on it; past and future events, however, never appear symmetrically at any instant.

The investigation of stability properties is yet another attempt to capture time's economic significance. In terms of general multimarket systems, this research program was propelled to prominence by Hicks (1939) and Samuelson (1941, 1947), and culminated in the elegant proofs of Arrow, Block, and Hurwicz (1959). At issue is the capacity of the model to converge upon, and remain at equilibrated states, even if disequilibrium characterizes the initial conditions. As all economists know, equilibria may be characterized by local stability or global stability, depending upon the model's evolutionary processes and initial conditions. Further, economists speak of the system as being stable if it converges to any equilibrium, regardless of initial conditions. All of these properties relate to convergence characteristics, and to the set of limit points toward which the system progresses. One typically investigates the price vector's approach to equilibrium, as guided by functional responses to excess demands. Arrow, Block, and Hurwicz proved the convergence of the price vector to the equilibrium price vector by showing that

$$\lim_{t \to \infty} (P_t - P) = 0$$

where P_t is the price vector at time t, and $\bar{P}$ is an equilibrium price vector. The argument uses the second method of Lyapounov to show that the distance between P_t and $\bar{P}$ is governed by a declining function of time. The system appears to naturally organize itself at an equilibrium if one is only sufficiently patient. This technique appears to introduce an intertemporal asymmetry corresponding to the authentic asymmetries of time since that which is "later" (with a higher date) must correspond to a state not "further" from an equilibrium than an earlier (lower date) state. Since, for a stable process, distances from equilibrium at one end of the time dimension are smaller than at the other, the system assumes an aspect of irreversibility.

This apparent asymmetry is not authentic, however, for it fails to emerge from an authentic image of the passage of time itself. Time remains nothing but a dimension, a line along which motion in either direction may occur. Stability proofs merely assert that toward one end of the line, the system's state must not be further from an equilibrium than in regions toward the other end. They do not forbid intertemporal backtracking. Nothing forbids interpreting the whole system as inexorably drifting away from equilibria, its order relentlessly decaying, running backward in time. Believing that time in these models flows unidirectionally toward the future is geometrically analogous to asserting that once a fly crawls into a trumpet's bell, it must always approach the mouthpiece. It need simply turn around, of course, to return whence it came.

Contrasting the analysis of general economic stability with classical thermodynamics provides helpful insights into the intellectual development of each. At the very least, it is notable that although they both employ the same convergence techniques, they achieve substantially different images of their respective phenomena. The economist sees a system that naturally and costlessly approaches a highly organized state whereas the classical physicist sees a system approaching an equilibrium of growing entropy and chaos. To the physicist differentiated structures decay with time, a process that can be reversed only with the expenditure of energy. To the economist differentiated structures emerge de novo as markets form and disseminate information.

Furthermore, in thermodynamics the "distance" from the current state to the equilibrium has achieved an immediate and intuitive interpretation in terms of entropy, whereas in economics it apparently has no natural meaning. Indeed, Arrow, Block, and Hurwicz note that construction of the Lyapounov function has no obvious economic antecedent, so that the particular metric employed is of no particular consequence. The long process of acquiring a clear understanding of entropy proved to be of some importance, and was one of the genuine problems in stating the Second Law. Prigogine notes that neither Lord Kelvin nor Clausius was able

> ... to express the entropy change in terms of observable quantities. This lack of clarity in its formulation was probably one of the reasons why the application of thermodynamics became rapidly restricted to equilibrium,... (Prigogine, 1980, p. 78)

That economics has developed so little interpretive clarity for such a fundamental concept, much less any empirical tie to it (how does one measure closeness to equilibrium while insisting that observed data reflect equilibrium states?), reflects an analogous difficulty with its conception of time and the ordering of preference, choice, act, and outcome. That the pure mathematics of convergence can be applied in such distinct paradigms attests to its flexibility. That its use in economics, as in physics, reveals conceptual imprecision attests to the difficulty with which it can be meaningfully applied.

That interesting alternatives to the orthodox economic treatment of time have been recently proposed suggests growing dissatisfaction with it. Gordon C. Winston (1982) recasts economic theory, especially of production, in terms of a dated activity analysis to extract insights regarding the critical performance of certain activities at certain times, and in certain orders. He emphasizes the need to combine inputs not merely in the correct combinations, but temporally at the correct stages. Time emerges as something vastly more important than just another input to production or commodity in consumption, for timing determines the outcome.

Innovative as this is, it is blemished, for he attempts to subject time itself to neoclassical maximization techniques. In this he continues to treat time as another variable, which neglects its fundamental asymmetries, conflicts with the arbitrariness of selecting a metric for it, and contradicts the irreducible uncertainty of all decisions and planning. He calculates an "optimum" capacity utilization, for example, without addressing the inevitable uncertainty faced by the planner in organizing production.

A second novel approach is that of Alvaro Cencini in *Time and the*

Macroeconomic Analysis of Income (1984). He identifies inconsistencies in the traditional definitions of income and expenditure arising from inappropriate notions of duration and of the instantaneous. His solution treats expenditure as the defining criterion of an instant in economic time so that the durationless moment at which an expenditure is made defines a quantum of economic time. Cencini argues that conceptualizing the economic process as governed by these time quanta, each generated by instantaneous acts of expenditure, leads back to the authentic insights about income and expenditure of John Maynard Keynes. His case is not always compelling, however, for his application of the quantum-mechanical metaphor frequently seems strained and unnatural.

Perhaps the deepest treatment of time in economic analysis, however, lies in the work of G. L. S. Shackle (1968, 1972, 1974, 1979). He has been the most thorough to unravel the consequences of recognizing that the present separates an unknowable future from an irrevocable past. More articulately than any other economist, he has shown that people create the future from imagination. Further, choice arises in human affairs as the selection of what to do now in order to help achieve certain imagined possibilities. We never choose between ontological phenomena, but only between what imagination provides as a sense of the possible.

Different individuals have different experiences, and come to distinct images of past and future. Consequently, each achieves his or her own idiosyncratic collection of imagined possible futures to guide behavior. Since uncertain expectations rather than knowable alternative "states" govern behavior, choice is not properly seen as reducible to certainty equivalents by probabilistic calculation. Nobody ever *knows* that his or her imagined futures exhaust possibility, so that sets of expected possibilities cannot rightly be treated as sample spaces. Shackle offers an alternative to probability, that of potential surprise. This measures a person's currently anticipated surprise if a currently imagined possibility were to be revealed as having occurred at some point in the future.

This foundation leads to a profoundly creative economic analysis. People construe their own expectations, and since these expectations result from unreasoned hopes and fears, they may yield incompatible acts. Individuals may pursue quite different strategies simply because their hopes and fears are necessarily idiosyncratic. Consequently, economic affairs need never be coordinated, nor need the economic system ever approach the equilibrated ideal. Rather, it may perpetually vibrate, being thrust forward by a complex process of mutual adaptation and response which Shackle calls *kaleidics*. Therein individuals form uncertain expectations which yield attempted acts. In the future they perceive the success or failure of their past attempts, which in turn influences their new expectations. Each situation is unique, however, so that past experience is never a certain guide for current behavior, and no one can ever avoid facing new possibilities with new acts. This helical process of forming expectations, and choosing strategies which lead to future outcomes, and ultimately back to future perceptions and expectations, rules the economics of time. Equilibrium concepts compatible with it can be derived, but the substantive content of its spirit pleads for an intellectual approach transcending any notion of equilibrium. This is the point of kaleidics: to model nonequilibrium processes in the full richness of possibility.

An Economic Model in Historical Time

As we have seen, formal economic models traditionally analyze systemic performance with an analytico-logical concept of time, which violates intuitive notions of time's flow and duration spontaneously arising from human epistemics. Attempts to incorporate this historical sense of time into formal models require new techniques and approaches. The model developed here provides a dynamic depiction of decentralized choice and strategic interaction, and is designed to focus attention on problems of truly dynamic coordination. The model is cast in terms of discrete "periods", which facilitates the discussion. Our general tactic is to present an aspect first in greatest generality, subsequently introducing additional properties useful in discussing problems of economic coordination. The chapter appendix provides a glossary of notation.

During each period agents anticipate, but do not know, current and future outcomes of their actions. They act on the basis of those expectations. Each period's ex post trades, and the prices implicit in them, are revealed only after its decisions are made. Within this context, ideas of temporary market-clearing equilibrium, and of historical continuity of plans and expectations across periods are investigated. Under familiar information assumptions, e.g., that agents are rational in the sense of Muth (1961), it is shown that historical continuity is necessary but not sufficient for the existence of ex ante temporarily coordinated equilibria. Even with historical continuity of plans and temporary competitive equilibrium, moreover, the system need neither achieve nor converge upon a set of Pareto-optimal states.

We consider a model of an economy consisting of n persons and m commodities temporally progressing through discrete time. It contains three functions connecting sets respectively representing expectations, strategies, and outcomes. Current expectations depend upon past experience, mold current actions, and indirectly influence outcomes.[5] The following notation is adopted throughout.

Strategies

Strategies embody intended transactions; they are sequences of planned trades. Each element in the sequence is an m-dimensional vector indicating the quantities of the various goods an individual plans to trade during a period. If t_0 is the initial date and $i = 1, 2, \ldots, n$, then person i's strategy at $t \geq t_0$ is

$$S_i(t) = [s_i(t), s_i(t+1), \ldots] \qquad (4.1)$$

where each $s_i(t+k)$ is a vector of planned exchanges, and is person i's plan at time t for period $t + k$ (where k is a nonnegative integer). Each of these vectors is contained by $\hat{B}$, a compact convex subset of m-dimensional euclidean space. Letting $s(t+k)$ be the $n \times m$ matrix whose row vectors are individual marketing plans for period $(t + k)$,

$$S(t) = [s(t), s(t+1), s(t+2), \ldots] \qquad (4.2)$$

indicates the combined strategies undertaken at t. $\hat{S}(t)$ is the set of all sequences of this form possible at t, and

$$\hat{S} \equiv \bigcup_{\forall t \geq t_0} s(t)$$

is the set of all possible configurations of strategies.

Outcomes

For each integer $t \geq t_0$, the $n \times m$ matrix $B(t)$ indicates all commodity exchanges contracted at time t. Each $b_{ij}(t)$ is the quantity of good j person i received during t. Each row of $B(t)$ is an element of $\hat{B}$, the set of all feasible trades. Thus, $B(t)$ is an element of $\hat{\hat{B}}$, the set of all possible outcomes, where

$$\hat{\hat{B}} \equiv \prod_n \hat{B}: \quad B(t) \ \epsilon \, \hat{\hat{B}} \text{ for all } t \geq t_0$$

Moreover, the historical sequence of outcomes at any time t,

$$\mathscr{B}(t) = [B(t_0), B(t_0 + 1), B(t_0 + 2), \ldots, B(t - 1)] \qquad (4.3)$$

represents the system's "real" trading history at time t, and is a subset of $\hat{\hat{B}}$. The set of all possible sequences $\mathscr{B}(t)$ is $\hat{\mathscr{B}}(t)$, and

$$\mathscr{B} = \bigcup_{\forall t \geq t_0} \mathscr{B}(t)$$

contains all possible histories. Obviously, it must contain, but is not limited to each instant's actual past; that is, the ultimately unfolding history of the whole system.

Strategies to Outcomes

The exchanges achieved at any time depend on the exchanges attempted. Thus the function M: $\hat{S} \rightarrow \hat{B}$, where $B(t) = M[S(t)]$ represents the process by which motivated behavior is transformed into realized activity. It is the social mechanism by which ex ante plans become manifest in ex post events, and transpires at a level of disaggregation logically antecedent to the organization of markets as economists normally conceive them.

Additional insights about each period's matrices $S(t)$ and $B(t)$ inform recognition of how profoundly historical-time analysis diverges from analytic-time economics. Although these two have the same dimensionality they generally are unequal, indicating that what we actually achieve typically diverges from what we had intended. When $S(t)$ was selected $B(t)$ was unknown, so that its representation of the choice's consequences cannot affect the choice itself. Ignorance of what actually will occur, however, violates any guaranty that plans are actualized [$S(t) = B(t)$] or that plans of different agents are sufficiently compatible that coordinated outcomes may emerge.

For example if quantities of commodities are conserved across exchange, as is traditionally presumed, then the sum of the elements of every column of $B(t)$ must equal zero:

$$\sum_{i=1}^{n} b_{ij}(t) = 0, \quad \text{for all } j = 1, \ldots, m. \tag{4.4}$$

What one person receives in trade must have been relinquished by someone else. Even this most basic feature of ex post trades need not apply to $S(t)$, however $S(t)$ represents plans contingent upon expectation, not realization of outcomes. True decentralization of action means that individuals independently reach their respective rows in $S(t)$. That independence provides the freedom to pursue mutually incompatible aims. Everyone, by illustration, may want to purchase oranges, in which case the sum of elements in the "orange" column of $S(t)$ must be positive. Clearly not all (perhaps none) of these plans can be satisfied: if everyone wants to buy, then there is no one from whom to buy. The means by which society achieves

$$\sum_{i=1}^{n} s_{ij}(t) \neq \sum_{i=1}^{n} b_{ij}(t) = 0 \qquad (4.5)$$

constitutes a central coordinating issue, yet remains explicitly suppressed within the logical-time framework which imposes logical simultaneity between plans (here the $s_{ij}(t)$'s) and outcomes (here the $b_{ij}(t)$'s). Only within historical-time models can questions of the mechanisms by which plans yield outcomes through the function $M(\cdot)$ be phrased.

Expectations

Each individual contemplates a variety of possible exchanges, not only in the current period, but in the future as well. In judging the ability to achieve trades, however, people recognize the dependence of attainment upon plans and attempts. Thus, define $E_i(t)$ as a sequence of anticipated exchanges contemplated by individual i at time t:

$$E_i(t) = [e_i(t), e_i(t+1), e_i(t+2), \ldots] \qquad (4.6)$$

where each $e_i(\cdot)$ is an m-dimensional vector of feasible trades, i.e., $e_i(\cdot) \in \hat{B}$. Further $E(t)$ is the set of all conceivable future exchange trajectories at time t, and

$$\hat{E} = \bigcup_{\forall t \geq t_0} \hat{E}(t)$$

is the set of all possible sequences of trades. Obviously, if person i is not considering any trades during $t + r$ according to scenario $E_i(t)$, then $e_i(t + r) = 0$. Similarly, not every person need think about the infinite number of possible scenarios. Indeed, typically a person would consciously imagine only a relatively small subset of them. The rest would be imaginable, but unimagined.

Associated with each such potential sequence of trades is a strategy so that the duple $[E_i(t), S_i(t)]$ formally articulates the conjunction of a planned strategy with a possible consequence of pursuing it. Each one forms an imagined hypothesis concerning the ultimate consequence, $E_i(t)$, given that $S_i(t)$ is pursued. An indication of the agent's attitude about $[E_i(t), S_i(t)]$ is also necessary, for it is the emotions, the hopes, fears, and ontological imputation concerning an imagined result that renders the possibility relevant to choice. For this purpose we adopt G. L. S. Shackle's measure of potential surprise (1968). This associates with every imagined possible outcome a measure of the person's currently anticipated surprise should that possibility be revealed in the future to have happened. The more confident one now feels, the less surprised he or she might expect to be, and the lower the potential surprise. If one feels certain about an outcome, then the measure of potential surprise attached to that outcome is zero, and all rival possibilities must carry positive potential surprise. Thus, for each duple, $[E_i(t), S_i(t)]$, i's measure of potential surprise assigns a nonnegative real number, and maps elements of $\hat{E} \times \hat{S}$ into the nonnegative reals. From this we define an expectation as the triple $\{E_i(t), S_i(t), PS_i[E_i(t), S_i(t)]\}$ where $PS_i[E_i(t), S_i(t)]$ is the value of i's potential surprise concerning the denoted scenario. $\mathscr{E}_i(t)$ is i's set of expectations at t, a subset of $\hat{\mathscr{E}}(t)$ (and a point in its power set $2^{\hat{\mathscr{E}}(t)}$), the set of his or her possible expectations at t, which, in turn, is a subset of $\hat{\mathscr{E}} = \bigcup_{\forall t \geq t_0} \hat{\mathscr{E}}(t)$ set of all possible expectations.

Only actually imagined possibilities enter the calculus of surprise, so that its measure is, unlike probability, nondistributional. Similarly, nothing in the nature of its construction, nor in historical time, suggests that what is imagined describes what ultimately will be revealed. What will be seen to have transpired may prove to be so profoundly startling that we had not even previously imagined its possibility.

People are different. Thus, the imagined possibilities they consider, and their reactions to them remain persistently idiosyncratic and distinct. Thus, for any $i \neq j$, $\mathscr{E}_i(t)$ may vary radically from $\mathscr{E}_j(t)$, reflecting their conflicting pictures of what is yet to be. Similarly, at any t, the configuration of different people's expectations is a set $[\mathscr{E}_1(t), \mathscr{E}_2(t), \ldots, \mathscr{E}_n(t)]$ of n points in $2^{\hat{\mathscr{E}}(t)}$, or a point $\hat{\mathscr{E}}(t)$ in the n-fold cartesian product of $2^{\hat{\mathscr{E}}(t)}$,

$$\hat{\hat{\mathscr{E}}}(t) = \prod_{\pi}^{n} 2^{\hat{\mathscr{E}}(t)}$$

The corresponding vector of each person's expectations we label $\hat{\mathscr{E}}(t)$. For completeness we define the set of all possible social patterns of expectations as

$$\hat{\hat{\mathscr{E}}} = \bigcup_{\forall t \geq t_0} \hat{\hat{\mathscr{E}}}(t)$$

Outcomes to Expectations

Every agent in the model bases his or her current expectations upon past experience. This link from past performance to current anticipation can be represented for each individual j by the function I_j: $\hat{\mathscr{B}} \to 2^{\hat{\mathscr{E}}}$ where $\mathscr{E}_j(t) = I_j[\mathscr{B}(t)]$. The function I_j incorporates the myriad processes of information availability, private perception of the past, and inductive projection of that knowledge onto imaginative expectation of the future. It represents the highly personalized reactions to the past in forming images of the future, as well as the more public channels by which information regarding past events is signalled. Analogously we can incorporate the system-wide distribution of information and response to it within the function $I: \; \mathscr{B} \to \hat{\mathscr{E}}$ where $\mathscr{E}(t) = I[\,\mathscr{B}(t)]$. It represents society's allocation of information combined with each person's extrapolation from it into the uncertain future.

Significantly, expectations are based only on past experience. Current outcomes remain unknowable and unknown. Unlike analytical-time models, today's consequences of today's behavior remain beyond cognition, which abolishes the temporal disarrangement within the period generated by the logical simultaneity of its components.

Expectations to Strategies

Strategy selection, the decision to pursue a particular plan, depends upon the expectation of reward. Within the model, this dependence of an individual's choice upon his or her expectations is expressed by the functions $D_j: \; 2^{\mathscr{E}} \to \hat{B}$ where $S_j(t) = D_j[\; \mathscr{E}_j(t)]$, which leads naturally to the function $D: \; \hat{\mathscr{E}} \to \hat{S}$ where $S(t) = D[\; \mathscr{E}(t)]$. $D(\cdot)$ reflects the melding of preferences and anticipations into choice and action.

This structure completes the general outline of the model. During each period expectations form only from past experiences, and guide current choices. Current actions contrive, through the processes of social action, to determine this period's ontological outcomes. Thus, current results depend directly upon current intentions and indirectly on current expectations. Since the latter of these form only on the basis of past outcomes, choices are independent of, and logically antecedent to their own results, a basic feature of any authentically dynamic system.

The model consists of its three functions,

$$\mathscr{E}(t) = I[\,\mathscr{B}(t)]$$
$$S(t) = D[\; \mathscr{E}(t)]$$
$$B(t) = M[S(t)] \tag{4.7}$$

which are indicated schematically in figure 4–1. Precedence evolves from $\mathscr{B}(t)$, to $\mathscr{E}(t)$, and from $\mathscr{E}(t)$ through $S(t)$ to $B(t)$, and hence to $\mathscr{B}(t+1)$ which sets the stage for next period's activity. Much of the initially cumbersome detail in defining the system's sets arises from the need to replicate time's asymmetry, and to specify sufficient generality that behavior both in and out of equilibrium can be analyzed. That is, the system's sets and functions are defined sufficiently broadly for any state of the system, as well as its

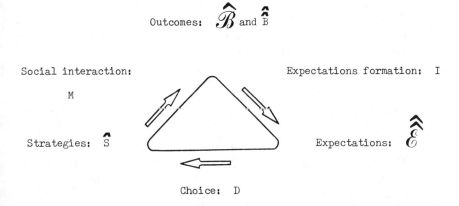

Figure 4–1.   Structure of the Model.

consequences, to be considered. We are not, from the outset, constrained to particular results, to special inferences, or to equilibrium. Ex ante is defined separately from ex post, and it is always unambiguous in which sphere a component resides. Significantly for the analysis of time, planned intention and accomplished result may, therefore, diverge. The system is open.

Similarly, time must run only forward. Functions tether the present to the past and the future to the present. These functions introduce intertemporal asymmetries, however, and functions reversing the logic are not implicitly derivable within the model.

Articulating the structure of such a model develops insights into the analytical consequences of seriously incorporating historical time into economics. It shows, for example, the fundamental separation of intentions from achievements, so that properties of the former may not be inadvertently ascribed to the latter. Moreover, this basic potential for failure of coincidence between plan and result requires casting the model in terms as general as possible so that no implicit presumptions of coordination implicitly enter unexpectedly. Only in such a scheme, where it is authentically possible to be out of equilibrium, can the problem of coordinating economic activity in a dynamic context be fully explored. Only in such a setting, where agents' surprised reactions to past outcomes can reverberate throughout the system in Shackle's "kaleidics," can the significance of equilibrium assumptions be appreciated. Within either static or logical-time models the truly extraordinary incongruity of equilibration through prereconciled planning remains suppressed.

In the next section we introduce notions of both intertemporal consistency and intraperiod coordination. Subsequently, we critically consider the various additional assumptions employed to demonstrate their existence, and then show that historical continuity is necessary but not sufficient for the existence of ex ante temporary equilibrium when agents are rational in the sense of Muth.

Coordination and Continuity

Our model can be used to analyze two basic questions of economic organization: (1) Can a system in which choice is decentralized achieve systemically coordinated results? and (2) Do the processes of economic dynamics permit intertemporal coherence of both individual behavior and aggregate performance? These are both classic economic problems, and have received considerable attention within the orthodox tradition. Arguments about static coordination typically relate to the existence of competitive equilibrium, which is shown to exist with familiar fixed-point theorems. These analytical-time results, however, achieve coordination of plans through their prereconciliation by the auctioneer. When people contract they do so with knowledge of the equilibrium price vector. Since prices are determined by offers communicated to markets, however, the actual contracted prices cannot be known, in authentically historical-time models, until after the offers have been expressed. Consequently the knowledge provided by the auctioneer results only from a convenient but misleading conceit. Coordination in such models occurs not because "markets" efficiently express desires and trading opportunities, but because the auctioneer dispenses with time's forward flow. He knows the consequences of ex ante plans, and can, by inserting himself or herself into the process, stop time and run it backwards, repeatedly, until markets are made to get it right. Historical-time models, such as ours, must dispense with this little fiction. As we shall see, only in special cases will historical time achieve the great successes of competitive equilibrium.

Historical consistency of plans and outcomes is similarly crucial to the successful operation of any economy. Although adaptation and evolution remain basic features of life, suddenly capricious changes and unprecedentedly surprising alterations in behavior startle people from the complacency of habit, and force them to adjust to alien and unfamiliar situations. These continual jolts occupy the heart of processes Shackle describes as "kaleidic." Here people constantly face uncertain opportunities and surprising outcomes. Their reactions may further startle others so that the whole economy may perpetually buzz with the tension of disequilibrium adjustment. This continual historical vibration may have nothing to do with equilibration, and may prevent the economy from ever fully settling into periods of intertemporal consistency and calm. Such a possibility, however, is not the only one. An important heuristic task before us is to isolate conditions under which historical continuity of expectations, plans, and outcomes emerge. Not unexpectedly, these conditions prove to relate closely to the acquisition of knowledge of the past, and its projection onto our imagined futures. They also prove to be remarkably restrictive. Similar issues are attacked within the logical-time framework of sequences of temporary equilibria, but we shall now be in a position to critically evaluate assumptions leading toward epistemic intertemporal coherence in historical time. From our new viewpoint those conditions seem artificial and obscure.

By traditional nomenclature, a market is temporarily equilibrated if and only if the quantity demanded in it equals the quantity supplied to it during the same period. Distinguishing between intentions and outcomes introduces unfamiliar twists to this notion of equilibration, however. In terms of outcomes, this means that a market clears ex post if and only if the sum of all elements in the relevant column of $B(t)$ equals zero:

$$\sum_{i=1}^{n} b_{ij}(t) = 0 \qquad \forall_j = 1, \ldots, m \qquad (4.8)$$

Obviously, condition (4.8) implies that the rank of $B(t)$ is not greater than $(n-1)$ since each person's vector of trades equals (-1) times the sum of the trade vectors of all other people. That is, somebody acquires what somebody else relinquishes (barring philanthropy, theft and fraud). Since this happens whenever commodity quantities survive exchange, ex post market clearing, per se, is independent of Walras' Law, and offers few insights into the nature of the coordination of intentions.[6] At a sufficiently disaggregated level, such as ours, however, we see that even this is something rather different from traditional ideas of markets and trading. In particular, it does not mean that the pattern of trades was contracted at consistent bargains (and values) across individuals. This possibility can be illustrated with a simple case of trades involving two goods and four people, where $B(t)$ is given as

Goods

		A	B
	1	-3	2
persons	2	3	-2
	3	-2	2
	4	2	-2

(1) purchases two units of B from (2) in exchange for 3 units of A while (3) purchases 2 units of B from (4) in exchange for only two units of A. Clearly (2) and (3) reached more advantageous trades than did, respectively, (4) and (1). The terms of trade are different for different components of the economy, which may have resulted from errors, blunders, ignorance, habit, or lassitude. Nevertheless, even within these temporarily equilibrated markets remarkably different bargains have been accepted at different ex post relative prices.[7] Since we are concerned with the coalitions which form at a level of aggregation more decentralized than economy-encompassing markets, and since no one can turn time around and recontract once ex post outcomes have been revealed, nothing—not even ex post temporary market-clearing—eliminates the chance for conflicting and incompatible bargains. Nothing assures that any agent or group of agents will voluntarily "make the market" for any or all commodities, since that could prove a costly activity (unlike the auctioneer who somehow generates consistency without expense), and so nothing, even in this case of ex post market clearing guarantees that the economy succeeds in spontaneously organizing itself into coherent markets. Rather, the system may be decomposed into separate orbits of differentiated trading cells. The Law of One Price is no "law" at all, and in historical time may be chronically violated. In particular, it cannot be derived from ex post market clearing. The two concepts are independent of each other. Once I agree to buy two apples for three tomatoes from my neighbor, I cannot revoke the contract simply because you bought two apples for two tomatoes from your neighbor. Without the auctioneer pushing time backwards, my neighbor may already have eaten one of her new tomatoes.

Alternatively, the pattern of trade need not reveal a unique nontrivial vector of prices. Mathematically, we have

$$\underset{n \times m \;\; m \times 1}{B(t) \, P(t) = 0} \qquad\qquad (4.9)$$

which solves for unique, but trivial nominal prices if and only if $B(t)$ is nonsingular, and unique nontrivial relative prices if and only if the rank of $B(t)$ equals $(m-1)$. Neither case is general, and the capacity to interpret past trades as having occurred at nontrivial systemic prices need not arise. The lustre of prices which unambiguously signal opportunities rapidly tranishes in this climate. If n is greater than m, and the rows of $B(t)$ span m-space, then no consistent positive prices exist, and if the variety of different trades is such that the rows of $B(t)$ span fewer dimensions than $(m-1)$, then relative prices cannot be uniquely inferred. The bargains at which people traded carry too little information to determine value.

These problems with pricing and evaluation grow more severe when we address notions of ex ante market clearing as well. Ex ante, markets temporarily clear if and only if the total planned quantity demanded in every market equals the total planned quantity supplied:

$$\sum_{i=1}^{n} s_{ij}(t) = 0 \qquad \forall_j = 1, \ldots, m \qquad (4.10)$$

Satisfaction of equation 4.10 suggests that it ought to be possible to achieve ex post cleared markets and apparent coordination. This, however, is far weaker than the assertion that any planned trades can be undertaken. In particular, it fails to assure that I find a trading partner, even though a potential willingness to trade with me exists. Moreover, it is insufficient to assure that all plans embody the same price vector. Indeed, there may be no unique nontrivial ex ante price vector compatible with all planned trades. Clearly, therefore, Walras' Law need not hold, even though markets clear, ex ante. The economy may not be sufficiently well organized to support consistent evaluation.

In addition, cleared markets in this overall sense need not impose the more stringent case that person i successfully communicates his or her $s_{ij}(t)$ to some potential trading partner k where

$$s_{ij}(t) + s_{kj}(t) = 0 \qquad (4.11)$$

It is not enough to want to buy, even if others want to sell. In addition, one must express one's intentions to someone else who wants to sell. Time will not stop for those whose search for trading partners proves frustrating, even though potential trading partners exist. They may fail to contract as time proceeds, and no auctioneer halts its progress while they sort their opportunities. Precisely at this step of aggregation we see why organized markets are so convenient; they facilitate the search for trading partners. They are not free, however, as any merchant, realtor, or bond broker knows. Continued expenditure of effort and resources are required to maintain and tend them; and in historical time, neighboring grocers may sell corn flakes at different prices.

Condition 4.10 assures only that it is possible for markets to clear. It does not assure that all planned trades are contracted, that $S(t) = B(t)$. Thus, it reflects only the potential for coordination.

Slips may enter whenever one must actively search for trading partners. We can, therefore, consider a more exacting criterion for temporary equilibrium. In addition to market-clearing of plans (condition 4.10), and outcomes (condition 4.8), we require that trading plans be accomplished:

$$S(t) = B(t) \qquad (4.12)$$

This captures the essence of temporary social equilibration, and we shall use it, rather than the market-clearing conceptualization.[8] That which individuals had privately decided they would try to do, they subsequently have done. Here we have the basic idea behind most notions of coordination: satisfaction of all market demands and market supplies. There should be no particular surprise or disappointment.

This condition is obviously restrictive. In static analyses the auctioneer stops the clock to arrange for prereconciliation of marketing plans. In historical time, however, no such agent exists. If plans are reconciled, it may result from accident or luck, but cannot be assured in general, for how people read the past and imagine the future is always subject to wild variation and emotional disguise. Only after special rules about cognitive individuality have been (somewhat arbitrarily and artificially) imposed, can sufficient regularity of expectations across time and people guarantee $S(t) = B(t)$.

To examine further difficulties of reaching coherent organization of society, we must now examine the processes of pricing and evaluation more closely. One would like to reconstruct both ex ante prices (implicit in plans), and ex post prices (from the pattern of contracted trades), but even this poses thorny problems. As we have seen ex post prices may be unknowable from the configuration of contracted trades. In addition, different people may undertake plans revealing contradictory notions of prices, so that selected strategies may implicitly embody no overall price vector. Selecting a strategy prior to the subsequent determination of prices severs the connection back from contracted prices to quantities demanded so familiar in logical-time models. No one need plan to contract at the prices that ultimately emerge. Moreover, different coalitions may prove to have traded at different ex post prices so that distinct agents may be trading at distinct price vectors; and third, even if the economy somehow organizes itself into a coherent pattern of markets with single prices, the resulting pattern of trades need not unambiguously signal prices, either nominal or relative. The key to deriving both anticipated prices from an individual's planned trades, and actual prices from contracted trades lies in assuming that exchange conserves value. In terms of planned strategies and expected prices, this gives

$$\sum_{i=1}^{m} s_{ij}(t)P_i(t) = 0 \qquad (4.13)$$

Condition 4.13 amounts to Walras' Law applied to intentions, and $P_i(t)$ is the expected price vector tacitly generated by person i's plans. Clearly, in general, no vector $P_i(t)$ can be uniquely inferred from $s_i(t)$. The null vector always solves, and so long as $m > 1$ (trade is conceivable), an infinite number of nontrivial nominal-price solutions work as well. Further, relative prices may not be uniquely determinable. The significance of Walras' law erodes in the absence of unambiguous prices at which consistent evaluation can be made. That the net value of all demands should cancel means little if one cannot confidently infer the prices at which such evaluations are made.

Equation 4.13 also implies that if an individual intends to purchase anything, he or she must simultaneously plan to sell something (unless, of course, everything one plans to trade is expected to be free). Exchange requires a *quid pro quo*.[9]

In addition, nothing suggests that $P_i(t) = P_j(t)$ when $i \neq j$, since different people achieve their own idiosyncratic imagined outcomes. Different individuals need not adopt plans based on the same prices. They may simply try to do different things. I may, for example, plan to buy ten oranges for two apples at the same time you plan to sell eight oranges for two apples. We have reached incompatible plans through disparate anticipations of prices. Such coordination failures may occur, even though market-clearing conditions, both ex ante and ex post are satisfied. They may, but need not, actually lead toward disappointment of plans, and toward violation of condition 4.11, however, depending upon the rank of $S(t)$. Different people may select compatible strategies based on distinct price expectations even if they both expect a relative price vector that solves $S(t)P(t) = 0$, i.e., if the rank of $S(t)$ is less than $m - 1$. Here, more than one nontrivial vector of relative prices solves. As we saw before, without the mythical auctioneer society may possess no agent who makes it his or her personal business to organize economy-wide markets. The ex post opportunity for arbitrage, in historical time, cannot entail its own ex ante elimination: that which must come later cannot govern that which comes earlier. In logical time, an opportunity opening signals its own closing, but only by running in temporal circles. In historical time, no such circles exist.

In sum, a temporarily coordinated equilibrium is a state in which all trading intentions are satisfied. Formally, $S(t) = B(t)$, where total commodity quantities survive exchange. This is a stronger condition than the familiar notion of market clearing, but is still not so strong as a perfectly competitive temporary equilibrium with its flawlessly informed plans. As we shall see, that still more special state requires considerable additional structure, and perfect knowledge of all future opportunities. It is still true that outcomes depend on plans guided only by expectations. Gloomy readings of the past may yield gloomy anticipated opportunities, so that a temporary equilibrium of despair and hardship may arise. It may be both inefficient in the sense of squandered resources, and Pareto suboptimal.

We now turn to a notion of historical equilibrium. This is intertemporal consistency of expectations, strategies, and outcomes. It addresses the perseverance of plans, the survival of expectations consistent with what they had been, and the accomplishment of outcomes not perfidiously varying through time. The issue is not with the momentary coordination of decentralized plans, but with the working of a system in which phenomena at different times resemble one another. At stake in historical equilibrium is the dynamic continuity of the economic process, and the capacity for that process to provide a stable basis for economic organization and coordination. As we shall see, under many circumstances, historical equilibrium is necessary but not sufficient for temporary equilibrium.

Precise definition of historical consistency requires considerable care in a model of historical time, for each moment is necessarily unique. Tuesday morning must be something different from Monday afternoon, if only in that Monday evening may no longer be expected and planned, but must now be remembered.

Historical persistence of outcomes can be seen most easily since the trades contracted at different dates can be the same. Although the ultimate significance of trading two apples for a tomato may be different on Monday from Sunday, the terms of trade are the same. Thus we say that outcomes at $(t + 1)$ are in historical equilibrium with respect to outcomes at t if and only if $B(t + 1) = B(t)$. Analogous trades are made by everybody. Even if this condition holds, the history of the system at $(t + 1)$ is not the same as at t, for there is "more of it"; another date. Thus $\mathscr{B}(t + 1) \neq \mathscr{B}(t)$. Although $B(t + 1) = B(t)$, the ontological history of the system at the beginning of $t + 1$, the sequence of past trades, $\mathscr{B}(t + 1)$, is not the same as the history $[\mathscr{B}(t)]$ had been one period earlier. Even though the same trades have been contracted, their historical significance is not the same. In this deeper sense that recognizes historical embedding of trades, no steady state exists.

Since $S(t + 1)$ never equals $S(t)$, we say strategies are historically equilibrated at a period $(t + 1)$ if and only if each person continues to pursue the successor stages of the plans they adopted at time t. That is, strategies at $(t + 1)$ are historically consistent with strategies at t if and only if $S(t) = [s^*(t), \ s^*(t + 1), \ s^*(t + 2), \ldots]$, and $S(t + 1) = [s^*(t + 1), \ s^*(t + 2), \ldots]$. At $t + 1$ everyone continues with the later stages of plans previously pursued. Nobody has had a change of heart regarding what to do now based on the outcomes at t, even though their plans at $t + 1$ are necessarily not what they had been at t.

Historical consistency of expectations is expressed with even more difficulty. An expectation is a triple consisting of an anticipated scenario, a strategy, and the measure of potential surprise at the imagined possibility's occurrence if the strategy is pursued. Since both trajectories $E_i(t)$ and $S_i(t)$ range over the uniquely defined future characteristics of instant t,

$\hat{E}(t) \cap \hat{E}(t') \neq \phi$ whenever $t \neq t'$, which entails $\mathcal{E}_i(t) \neq \mathcal{E}_i(t')$ whenever $t \neq t'$. Expectations constantly change, which is the very essence of time's flux. Consequently, any definition of historical consistency of expectations must not rely on constancy, but on similarity and continuity. Thus, we say a person's expectations at $(t + 1)$ are historically consistent with respect to his or her expectations at t if and only if, for each expectation, he or she assigns the same potential surprise to the continuation of strategy and anticipated outcome sequences as he or she had assigned to some ancestor of those sequences at t. One will feel much the same about the remainder of one's expectations tomorrow as one feels about all of them today. Accordingly, no revelation during the period will jolt anyone with a surprise that forces future expectations away from the grounds for today's expectations.

With these three notions of historical persistence and consistency of phenomena we understand that historical equilibrium represents the dynamic continuation through time of analogous expectations and plans which each period yield the same exchange outcomes. If people are surprised, that surprise never gets translated into either intentions or ontological outcomes. Business as usual proceeds from date to date without disruption, people persist in old and familiar strategies (whether or not they are satisfied each date), and people adhere to familiar ways of thinking and evaluating.

This tedious fate sharply contrasts with the full richness of historical possibility that is kaleidics. Only out of equilibrium does the hustle and bustle of economic activity truly thrive. Only there do new ideas yield novel attempts. Only there do surprises provoke adjustments and reactions to unsuspected opportunities. Only there do enterprise and entrepreneurship genuinely matter. Kaleidics is the full spectacle of collision and adaptation, of hope and anxiety, of pursuit and attainment.

Its sheer generality and wealth of possibilities inhibit formal analysis since each particular situation may yield amazing, unprecedented, and surprising results. Merely to describe the abstraction needed to articulate it has proven complex and detailed. To precisely specify the actual path followed, and to offer specific predictions of future behavior violates the spirit of an unknowable future emerging from a present bursting with imagined possibilities. We can no more hope to completely track along time into the future than we can hope to know it. All we can do is specify the behavior of various analytical cases and investigate the consequences of differing algorithms and rules. In this way we may ultimately achieve a taxonomy of different behavior patterns, as has been suggested in Vickers (1984), and Bausor (1984).

Equilibrium Properties

We begin this project with analysis of equilibria, not because of descriptive superiority, but for three pedagogical purposes. First, it provides the closest bond with the familiar economics of logical time, and an obvious basis for comparing images of the economic process resulting from logical-time and historical-time models. Second, it reveals what very special and peculiar things equilibria are. In developing conditions leading toward equilibration we encounter conceptual restrictions at every turn, and realize how truly extraordinary events must be to attain and sustain equilibrated states. Third, it provides a basis for investigating the relationship between historical tenacity and temporary coordination.

Development of equilibrium analysis proceeds at the expense of generality. Conditions and assumptions sufficient for focusing on equilibrium must be introduced, and compromises with the tremendous scope of historical possibility must be made. These assumptions will address issues of information distribution, expectation formation, preferences, rationality, and market structure. Indeed, one of the greatest insights to be achieved from confining the model to equilibria is to discover how intellectually restricting that can be. The catalogue of conditions collectively guaranteeing the existence of equilibrium bears witness to how very special phenomena equilibria are. With these conditions in place, we shall be able to show that in many circumstances, historical continuity is necessary, but not sufficient for the existence of temporary competitive equilibrium. Moreover, in historical time, even competitive equilibrium is not sufficient for the welfare properties normally associated with it in logical-time analysis.

Of our several asumptions, we begin with those directly related to the formation of expectations from the system's ontological history, i.e., with the function $I(\cdot)$ from possible histories to possible expectations. These involve both the distribution of information about past performance, and its use to form expectations of the future.

Consider first:

- All markets are sufficiently well organized so that it is possible to infer a unique vector of relative prices for each period. Accordingly the rank of $B(t) = m - 1$ for all $t \geq t_0$.   (A.1)

This asserts that the economy is adequately coherent to be organized as a market system. Although it may not be necessary for coordinated results, it is necessary to characterize the economy as governed by a system of prices. One cannot speak of markets as providing the informational basis for efficient management of a decentralized economy if markets are themselves so poorly organized that prices cannot be inferred from trades. Without condition (A.1), all the information about preferences and cost conditions allegedly signalled by prices cannot be so communicated. Although our previous discussion suggests that satisfaction of (A.1) is unlikely, it remains necessary if a decentralized economy can be characterized as a "price system."

Next, we have:

- Every individual knows $\mathscr{B}(t)$, at time t, and not earlier, for all $t > t_0$.

$$\text{(A.I.1)}$$

(A.I.1) means that everybody has complete and accurate information of the economy's trading history. Obviously more of an ideal than a realistic description of actual economies, it is important in the background to equilibrium in that it banishes blunders resulting from deceit. (A.I.1) together with (A.1) means that at any $t > t' \geq t_0$, everybody knows the past history of the system, and can therefore infer from each $B(t')$ the ex post price vector at t'. Consequently, the information available to all n persons is sufficient to generate the sequence $[P(t_0), P(t_0 + 1), \ldots, P(t - 1)]$ at time t.

Our third assumption marks perhaps the single greatest retreat from the spirit of historical-time economics. For analysis of historically consistent sequences at competitive equilibria, however, it is nearly indispensable, for at a stroke it eliminates the quirks of authentically innovative imaginations, and the behavioral havoc they produce in derailing equilibrium into kaleidics. Although explicitly invalid, it provides the monumental knowledge without which the existence of sequences of temporary equilibria becomes profoundly problematic. Thus, in much of the following we will invoke the following condition:

- Expectations are probabilistic. $\qquad\qquad$ (A.I.2)

This powerful presumption means that imagined possibility must be known to contain all possibilities so that its distributional character is justified. Similarly, the "true" possibility must have been imagined and contemplated so that genuine surprise is automatically banished. All of this requires knowledge of the future, knowledge that sample spaces contain all possibilities, knowledge that can be revealed only in the future. Historical-time analysis can never be comfortable with assumption (A.I.2), but it is a familiar and straightforward device by which an unruly kaleidics can be disciplined into equilibration. In no epistemic sense is it ever valid. We introduce it not for descriptive richness, but to insure the analytical simplification from which coordinated equilibration is derived.

To understand how (A.I.2) affects the particulars of the model, we return to the duple $[E_i(t), S_i(t)]$ which formally articulates the conjunction of a planned strategy with a possible consequence of pursuing it. (A.I.2) allows this combination of a plan and a possible result of it to be interpreted as an element in a sample space. To see this, first consider $\hat{E}(t)$, the set of all possible sequences of the form given by $E_i(t)$, i.e., the set of all possible sequences of the form given by $E_i(t)$, i.e., whose first element is $e_i(t)$. The set

$$\mathscr{E}(t) = \hat{E}(t) \times \hat{S}(t) \qquad (4.14)$$

is the set of all possible combinations $[E_i(t), S_i(t)]$, and is the sample space of the probability space given by the triple $\mathscr{E}_i(t) = [\ \mathscr{E}(t), 2^{\mathscr{E}(t)}, \mathscr{P}_{it}(\cdot)]$ where $2^{\mathscr{E}(t)}$ is the power set of $\mathscr{E}(t)$, and $\mathscr{P}_{it}(\cdot)$ is a real-valued function defined over domain $2^{\mathscr{E}(t)}$ satisfying the axioms of a probability measure. The state of each individual's expectations at time t is symbolized by $\mathscr{E}_i(t)$ where $\mathscr{P}_{it}(t)$ is the particular probability measure indicating i's subjective probability at time t.[10]

Recognizing that, in general, different people may simultaneously adopt different probability measures motivates construction of the set $\mathscr{P}(t)$ of all probability measures over $2^{\mathscr{E}(t)}$. With this in mind, we see that the individual's problem of generating expectations at time t reduces $\hat{\mathscr{E}}(t)$ to

$$\{[\ \mathscr{E}(t), 2^{\mathscr{E}(t)}, \mathscr{P}_{it}(\cdot)]\ |\ \mathscr{P}_{it}(\cdot) \in \hat{\mathscr{P}}(t)\} \qquad (4.15)$$

and permits phrasing the problem as selecting a probability space at time t from the set of all possible probability spaces at t. Again, it cannot be overemphasized that (A.I.2) involves powerful information assumptions that eradicate the potential for surprise. Its appeal in equilibrium analysis directly follows from these information assumptions, for they provide a spectacular cognitive control over the future.

Turning to other assumptions about expectations we next have the conditions of Muthian rationality (Muth, 1961):

• Every individual adopts, as his or her subjectively expected price, the mathematically expected price, given $B(t)$, for all goods. That is, the

   expected price vector $P^e(t) = [1/(t - t_0)][\sum_{t'=t_0}^{t} P(t')]$. (A.I.3)

• Every individual is at a rational steady-state in the sense not only that he or she identifies and adopts the mathematically expected price vector as his or her own subjectively expected price vector, but also recognizes that deviations from it are orthogonally distributed.

$$(A.I.4)$$

As with the previous conditions, these are truly special, reflecting an advanced state of comprehension of the past, and recognition that the future will be governed by the stochastic properties isolated from that past. The conjunction of (A.1), (A.I.1), (A.I.2), (A.I.3), and (A.I.4) entails that everybody will have identified the systematic determinants of past price vectors, and so can decompose variation of price into permanent and random components. In addition, all of the n persons adopt the permanent component as their subjective estimate of prices for all $t'' \geq t$. That is, its perceived permanence allows it to be projected indefinitely into the future.

- People anticipate participating in perfectly competitive markets at their expected equilibrium prices in those markets. (A.I.5)

Assumption (A.I.5) implies that everybody believes that, given equilibrium prices, he or she will be able to trade any finite quantity of any good at those prices. Also, everyone believes that the extent to which one enters the market neither changes price nor diminishes the ability to contract at equilibrium prices. Note that this is not the same as assuming that ontologically markets are perfectly competitive. It may be, for example, that some individuals could objectively influence prices but fail to recognize their own market power. (A.I.5) is clearly restrictive, but is a familiar depiction of an ideal of how markets work. Together, the foregoing six assumptions mean that all individuals expect the same price vector, that they expect it to persist into the future, and that they expect to be able to contract their desired quantities at that price vector.

Developing a characterization of choice, we include the following properties from the familiar mechanics of constrained utility maximization.

- Person i has a complete, reflexive, and transitive preference ordering defined over $\hat{\mathscr{E}}$. In addition, these preferences are representable by a finitely real-valued continuous function U_i: $\hat{\mathscr{E}} \to [0,\infty)$ for all $i = 1, \ldots, n$, and all $t \geq t_0$. (A.D.1)

Such a utility function imposes a random variable defined over the sample space, $\mathscr{E}(t)$, for each individual and period. Its expected value at time t, assuming the integral exists, is given by

$$\int_{\mathscr{E}(t)} U_i([E_i(t), S_i(t)]) \, \mathscr{P}_{it}\{d([E_i(t), S_i(t)])\} \qquad (4.16)$$

More importantly for strategy selection at time t, the expected value of the random variable, conditional upon the selection of a strategy $S_i'(t)$ is given by

$$\frac{1}{\mathcal{P}_{it}\{{}^{\wedge}S_i'(t)\}} \int_{{}^{\wedge}S_i(t)} U_i([E_i(t), S_i(t)]) \, \mathcal{P}_{it}\{d\Theta\} \qquad (4.17)$$

where

$$\Theta = [E_i(t), S_i(t)],$$
$${}^{\wedge}S_i(t) = \{[E_i(t), S_i(t)] \mid S_i(t) = S_i'(t) \in S(t)\} \qquad (4.18)$$

and

$$\mathcal{P}_{it}\{{}^{\wedge}S_i'(t)\} > 0.$$

This integral is assumed to exist for all $s_i'(t) \in \hat{S}$. If

$$\mathcal{P}_{it}\{{}^{\wedge}s_i'(t)\} = 0,$$

then the conditional expected value of the random variable also equals zero. This leads naturally into the following condition: there exists a unique $s_i^*(t) \in \hat{S}(t)$ such that

$$\frac{1}{\mathcal{P}_{it}\{{}^{\wedge}s_i^*(t)\}} \int_{{}^{\wedge}s_i^*(t)} U_i(\Theta)\mathcal{P}_{it}\{d\Theta\} > \frac{1}{\mathcal{P}_{it}\{{}^{\wedge}s_i'(t)\}} \int_{{}^{\wedge}s_i'(t)} U_i(\Theta)\,\mathcal{P}_{it}\{d\Theta\}$$

for all $s_i'(t) \neq s_i^*(t)$.

$$(A.D.2)$$

and

At all $t \geq t_0$, all individuals make decisions so as to maximize the expected value of their utility functions, i.e., they select $s_i^*(t)$.   (A.D.3)

(A.D.1) through (A.D.3) guarantee that for each $t \geq t_0$, and for all $i = 1, 2, \ldots, n$, a unique strategy, $S_i^*(t)$, which maximizes the expected utility of i at t, exists and is chosen by i at t. Thus, if $D(\cdot)$ obeys (A.D.1)–(A.D.3),

$$S(t) = \begin{pmatrix} S_1^*(t) \\ S_2^*(t) \\ \ldots \\ S_n^*(t) \end{pmatrix}$$

$$(4.19)$$

Intertemporal consistency needs still another assumption on preferences, that they be historically stable. If desires capriciously change with the passage of time, then so will behavior; and equilibration remains problematic. Thus we have: preferences at $(t + 1)$ are historically consistent with respect to preferences at t if and only if,

$$\{U_i([E_i(t), S_i(t)]) > U_i([E_i'(t), S_i'(t)])\}$$
$$\rightarrow \{U_i([E_i(t+1), S_i(t+1)]) > U_i([E_i'(t+1), S_i'(t+1)])\} \quad (A.U.1)$$

where

$$E_i(t) = [e_i(t), e_i(t+1), e_i(t+2), \ldots],$$
$$E_i'(t+1) = [e_i'(t+1), e_i'(t+2), \ldots],$$
$$E_i(t+1) = [e_i(t+1), e_i(t+2), \ldots],$$
$$S_i(t) = [s_i(t), s_i(t+1), s_i(t+2), \ldots],$$
$$S_i(t+1) = [s_i(t+1), s_i(t+2), \ldots],$$
$$S_i'(t) = [s_i'(t), s_i'(t+1), s_i'(t+2), \ldots], \text{ and}$$
$$S_i'(t+1) = [s_i'(t+1), s_i'(t+2), \ldots] \tag{4.20}$$

for all $t \geq t_0$, and all $i = 1, \ldots, n$.

(A.U.1) requires that if, at time t, an individual prefers one point in the sample space to a second, then he or she also prefers the direct successor of the first to the direct successor of the second.

These various conditions all relate to the manner in which individuals form expectations and select strategies, to the manner in which epistemics and volition combine to govern individual behavior. Now we introduce conditions on the performance of markets. Specifically, we assume that markets allocate goods in a way such that each person actually buys (sells) the quantity of any good he or she choses unless total supply (demand) expressed in the market is less than the total demand (supply) communicated to it. In that case, the available supply (demand) is proportionally rationed to purchasers (sellers). Formally, this assumes that $M(\cdot)$ obeys

$$b_{ij}(t) = a_j s_{ij}(t), \quad \text{for all } i = 1, 2, \ldots, n;$$
$$\text{all } j = 1, 2, \ldots, m; \text{ and}$$
$$\text{all } t \geq t_0 \tag{A.M.1}$$

where a_j is defined by

$$a_j = 1 \quad \text{if and only if} \quad \sum_{i=1}^{n} s_{ij}(t) = 0 \quad \text{or} \quad \sum_{i=1}^{n} s_{ij}(t) > 0 (<0), \quad \text{and}$$
$$s_{ij}(t) < 0 (>0)$$

$$0 \leq a_j < 1 \quad \text{if and only if} \quad \sum_{i=1}^{n} s_{ij}(t) > 0 (<0), \quad \text{and}$$
$$s_{ij}(t) > 0 (<0) \quad \text{where} \quad \sum_{i=1}^{n} a_j s_{ij}(t) = 0 \tag{4.21}$$

According to (A.M.1) if total ex ante excess demands in a market equal zero (it clears), then everybody trades his or her planned quantity in that market. Otherwise, the available quantity is rationed on the short side of the market.

Under this assumption, the period is analogous to the "market run" in which quantities of commodities are fixed.

Questions regarding the relationship between temporary equilibrium and historical consistency can now be directly addressed in:

> Theorem 1: If (i) conditions (A.1), (A.I.1), (A.I.2), (A.I.3), (A.I.4), (A.I.5), (A.D.1), (A.D.2), (A.D.3), (A.U.1), and (A.M.1) are satisfied; and (ii) markets are temporarily equilbrated at all $t \geq t_0$; then expectations, and strategies are historically consistent over all $t \geq t_0$.

Proof: Temporary equilibration of all markets means that for every $t \geq t_0$, $\sum_{i=1}^{n} s_{ij}(t) = 0$ for all $j = 1, \ldots, m$. Consequently (by (A.1) and (A.M.1)), $B(t) = S(t)$, $B(t)P(t) = S(t)P(t)$, and the ex post price vector equals the ex ante price vector in every period. By (A.I.1), (A.I.2), and (A.I.3), every agent knows $\mathscr{B}(t)$ at t, and adopts the mean of the historical distribution of the price vector, $P^e(t) = (1/(t - t_0)) [\sum_{t_0 \leq t' < t} P(t')]$, as his or her subjective expectation of prices throughout the period $t'' \geq t$. Moreover, by (A.I.4) they identify these prices as the rationally expected permanent components of actual prices. By (A.I.5) they each consider themselves to be price takers in perfectly competitive equilibrium, and so interpret these expected prices as the equilibrium competitive prices at which they will trade for all $t'' \geq t$. With this we can look more closely at the probability measure each agent adopts.

If $s_i(t + k)P^e(t) = 0$ for all $k \geq 0$ (an agent's plan satisfies his or her expected budget constraint), and since everybody expects markets to be competitive, if $e_i(t + k) = s_i(t + k)$, then

$$\mathscr{P}_{it}\{[E_i(t), S_i(t)] \mid S_i(t)\} = \frac{\mathscr{P}_{it}\{[E_i(t), S_i(t)] \cap {}^{\wedge}s_i(t)\}}{\mathscr{P}_{it}\{{}^{\wedge}s_i(t)\}} = 1 \qquad (i)$$

If $s_i(t + K)P^e(t) = 0$ for all $k \geq 0$, and if $e_i(t + k) \neq s_i(t + k)$ for any $k > 0$, then $\mathscr{P}_{it}\{[E_i(t), S_i(t)] \mid S_i(t)\} = 0$. Each person believes that he or she can achieve an expected sequence of trades if and only if that expected sequence satisfies the budget constraint generated by expected prices. Furthermore, if $s_i'(t + k)P^e(t) \neq 0$ for any $k \geq 0$ and $S_i'(t) = [s_i(t), s_i(t + 1), \ldots, s_i'(t + k), \ldots]$ then the strategy contains an attempt to trade at prices other than the rationally expected prices, and—by (A.I.5)—the perfectly competitive price taker anticipates being unable to trade at these other prices. No agent simultaneously acts as a price taker and a price setter. Consequently, $\mathscr{P}_{it}\{{}^{\wedge}s_i(t)\} = 0$. Therefore, $\mathscr{P}_{it}\{[E_i(t), S_i'(t)]\} = 0$ for all $E_i(t) \in E(t)$. In summary, if $S_i(t) = [s_i(t), s_i(t + 1), \ldots]$, $E_i(t) = [e_i(t), e_i(t + 1), \ldots]$,

$S_i(t + k)P^e(t) = 0$, and $e_i(t + k) = s_i(t + k)$ for all $k \geq 0$, then

$$\mathcal{P}_{it}\{[E_i(t), S_i(t)] \,|\, S_i(t)\} = 1, \quad \text{otherwise} \quad \mathcal{P}_{it}\{[E_i(t), S_i(t)] \,|\, S_i(t)\} = 0 \tag{ii}$$

for all $i = 1, \ldots, n, t \geq t_0$. If a strategy satisfies the expected budget constraint throughout its future, then the probability of achieving it if it is attempted equals one. Every other case is viewed as impossible. This implies that the particular $S_i^*(t)$ that maximizes

$$\frac{1}{\mathcal{P}_{it}\{[{}^{\wedge}s_i(t)]\}} \int_{{}^{\wedge}s_i(t)} U_i([E_i(t), S_i(t)]) \, \mathcal{P}_{it}\{d[E_i(t), S_i(t)]\} \tag{iii}$$

over $S(t)$ satisfies $s_i^*(t)P^e(t) = 0$, for all $i = 1, \ldots, n$, and $S_i^*(t)P^e(t) = 0$. Therefore, by the condition of temporary equilibrium,

$$S^*(t) = B(t) \tag{iv}$$

but $B(t)P(t) = 0$, which yields

$$P^e(t) = P(t) \tag{v}$$

That is, at any $t > t_0$, the rationally expected price is self-fulfilling. Consequently, when, at $(t + 1)$ agents examine $\mathcal{B}(t + 1)$, and again derive new price expectations, their new datum, $P(t)$, cannot disturb their old price expectations:

$$P^e(t + 1) = P(t) = P^e(t) \tag{vi}$$

Since expectations at $(t + 1)$ obey (ii) for all $i = 1, \ldots, n$, however, expectations at $(t + 1)$ are historically consistent with expectations at t, and expectations at any later date, $(t + k)$ are also historically consistent with expectations at t. Without loss of generality, set t equal to $(t_0 + 1)$. Therefore, expectations are historically consistent.

The historical consistency of strategies is also related to constancy of the expected price vector. Let $S_i^*(t)$ be the strategy chosen at t. Thus

$$\frac{1}{\mathcal{P}_{it}\{[{}^{\wedge}s_i^*(t)]\}} \int_{{}^{\wedge}s_i^*(t)} U_i[E_i(t), S_i(t)] \, \mathcal{P}_{it}\{d[E_i(t), S_i(t)]\} >$$

$$\frac{1}{\mathcal{P}_{it}\{[{}^{\wedge}s_i'(t)]\}} \int_{{}^{\wedge}s_i'(t)} U_i[E_i(t), S_i(t)] \, \mathcal{P}_{it}\{d[E_i(t), S_i(t)]\} \tag{vii}$$

where $S_i^*(t) \neq S_i'(t) \in \hat{S}(t)$. ${}^{\wedge}s_i^*(t)$ can be partitioned into two sets, $\{[E_i^*(t), S_i^*(t)]\}$ and ${}^{\wedge}s_i^*(t) \,|\, \{[E_i^*(t), S_i^*(t)]\}$, so that by the countable additivity of $\mathcal{P}_{it}(\cdot)$, and the impossibility of ${}^{\wedge}s_i^*(t) \,|\, [E_i^*(t), S_i^*(t)]$,

$$\mathcal{P}_{it}\{{}^{\wedge}s_i^*(t)\} = \mathcal{P}_{it}\{[E_i^*(t), S_i^*(t)]\} \tag{viii}$$

Similarly, $\mathscr{P}_{it}\{\Lambda s_i'(t)\} = \mathscr{P}_{it}\{[E_i'(t), S_i'(t)]\}$. We also know that the two integrals above reduce, respectively, to

$$U_i([E_i^*(t), S_i^*(t)]) \; \mathscr{P}_{it}\{[E_i^*(t), S_i^*(t)]\} \quad \text{and}$$

$$U_i([E_i'(t), S_i'(t)]) \; \mathscr{P}_{it}\{[E_i'(t), S_i'(t)]\} \tag{ix}$$

Substituting (viii) and (ix) into (vii) provides

$$U_i([E_i^*(t), S_i^*(t)]) > U_i([E_i'(t), S_i'(t)]) \tag{x}$$

That is, given this expectations-generating mechanism, the strategy that maximizes the expected value of utility also maximizes the value of utility. Conditions (x) and (A.U.1) imply that

$$U_i([E_i^*(t+1), S_i^*(t+1)]) > U_i([E_i'(t+1), S_i'(t+1)]) \tag{xi}$$

where $[E_i^*(t+1), S_i^*(t+1)]$ is a direct descendant of $[E_i^*(t), S_i^*(t)]$ and $[E_i'(t+1), S_i'(t+1)]$ is a direct descendant of $[E_i'(t), S_i'(t)]$. Since expected prices are constant and expectations are historically consistent, however, the expected value of $[E_i^*(t+1), S_i^*(t+1)]$ must be greater than the expected value of any $[E_i'(t+1), S_i'(t+1)]$ in $\hat{\mathscr{E}}(t+1)$ where $S_i^*(t+1) \neq S_i'(t+1)$. Therefore, if $S_i^*(t)$ is chosen, $S_i^*(t+1)$ is chosen also. Since t can be assigned arbitrarily to any value greater than t_0, strategies are historically consistent.

$$\text{Q.E.D.}$$

The conclusion of Theorem 1, that a "rational" system of temporarily equilibrated markets contains historically consistent expectations and strategies, suggests how wonderfully remarkable equilibrium is. It is that blissful condition in which people are not surprised, and so persist with their usual ways. Without distress or surprise they can successfully anticipate future prices. Since they are all using the same algorithms to extrapolate into the future, self-fulfilling price expectations should be no very great surprise. Everybody simply expects prices to be what they were, satisfies a budget contraint, and thereby finds a strategy from which the same prices can later be inferred. Interestingly, although temporary equilibrium provides $S(t) = B(t)$, and constant ex post prices, it is not strong enough for constant outcomes, i.e., $B(t) = B(t+1)$ is not established. People are merely trading at the same prices. They may all know, for example, that markets are closed on the Sabbath, and so make no attempts. Prices will persist onto the next business day although quantities traded may be different.

Further, the assumption in (i) of the antecedent conditions suggest ways in which plans may be disrupted by intervening events. Without (A.1) markets may be disorderly and fractured. It assures ex post satisfaction of Walras' Law. Without (A.M.1), bids and offers may not be effectively communicated to all persons, and opportunities thereby inadvertently lost. Without identifying a trading partner, mutually agreeable trades may not be contracted. The conditions on $I(\cdot)$ tightly limit an individual's scope for imagination and self-deception. (A.I.1) guarantees that everybody is fully informed of past activity. Without it, intrigue and deception may replace historical consistency. (A.I.2) enables the critical leap from genuine uncertainty and kaleidics to risk, certainty equivalents, and equilibrium. (A.I.3) and (A.I.4) permit the key leap from past prices to a constant expected price vector projected throughout the future. The rationality of these conditions endows intentions with a consistency upon which plans can be based. Otherwise, chaos and incoherence may replace intertemporally systematic anticipation. (A.I.5) provides an interpretation of prices as perfectly competitive equilibria, which permits the identification of the expected price vector with actual anticipated trading opportunities. Without condition (A.I.5), the association of successful strategies with satisfaction of the expected budget constraint collapses. The three conditions on $D(\cdot)$ depict choice as selecting that unique strategy which maximizes the mathematically expected value of a random variable representing preference over points in the sample space. They are analogous to the familiar analyses of constrained utility maximization, except that preferences are defined over neither commodities nor exchange sequences.

Consider now

Theorem 2: If (i) conditions (A.1), (A.I.1), (A.I.2), (A.I.3), (A.I.4), (A.I.5), (A.D.1), (A.D.2), (A.D.3), (A.U.1), and (A.M.1) are satisfied; and (ii) expectations and strategies are historically consistent; then the system need not be temporarily equilibrated for all $t \geq t_0$.

Proof: All that is needed is to show that historical consistency of expectations, and historical consistency of strategies are not sufficient for the existence of temporary equilibrium. Consider a case in which contracted prices are historically consistent: $P(t_0) = P(t_0 + 1) = P(t_0 + 2) = \cdots = P(t)\ldots$. Must knowledge of past ex post prices adequately signal actual current and future trading opportunities? According to (A.I.1), (A.I.2), (A.I.3), (A.I.4), and (A.I.5), individuals identify the vectors of past prices, rationally anticipate that future prices will be the same, and interpret these prices as perfectly competitive equilibria. Thereby conceiving of oneself as a price taker, each individual's expectations obey the following:

$$\text{if } e_i(t+k) = S_i(t+k) \quad \text{and if } \quad S_i(t+k)P^e(t) = 0$$
$$\text{for all } t \geq 0, \quad \text{and}$$

$$\mathscr{P}_{it}\{[E_i(t), S_i(t)] \mid S_i(t)\} = 1;$$
otherwise, $\mathscr{P}_{it}\{[E_i(t), S_i(t)] \mid S_i(t)\} = 0.$ (i)

Therefore, in the presence of constant prices, expectations are historically consistent. In addition, each individual selects that strategy, $S_i^*(t)$, which maximizes

$$\frac{1}{\mathscr{P}_{it}\{\Lambda S_i^*(t)\}} \int_{\Lambda S_i^*(t)} U_i(\Theta)\mathscr{P}_{it}\{d\Theta\}$$ (ii)

With the expectations derived from constant prices, this reduces to selecting the $S_i^*(t)$ that maximizes $U_i([E_i^*(t), S_i^*(t)])$. In conjunction with (A.U.1), this implies that $S_i^*(t+1)$ is a direct descendant of $S_i(t)$ for all $i = 1, \ldots, n$, and all $t \geq t_0$. Therefore, strategies are historically consistent.

In addition,

$$S^*(t)P^e(t) = S^*(t)P(t)$$ (iii)

since the expected price equals the actual price. Therefore,

$$S^*(t) = B(t)P(t) = 0$$ (iv)

This does not, however, imply that

$$S^*(t) = B(t)$$ (v)

When $S^*(t) \neq B(t)$, however, $S^*(t) \neq S^*(t)a(t)$, where $a(t) = [a_i(t), a_2(t), \ldots, a_m(t)]$, and $a(t) \neq 1$. Therefore, $S^*(t)$ is not a temporary equilibrium.

Q.E.D.

This surprising result asserts that even if all individuals are "rational," and are historically consistent in their plans and expectations, they may incorrectly anticipate their own opportunities, and in basing plans on those expectations may perpetuate mistakes and consistently miss the mark of temporary equilibrium. They do this primarily because they rely on only price information, and neglect quantity information. Consequently they recognize no distinction between the ex post results of prior periods, and the ex ante offers provoking those trades. Effectively forgetting any possible distinction between the volume of these ex ante offers and the size of actually traded bundles—a lapse entailed by the rational-expectations concentration on prices only—they persist in the (erroneous) belief that they are trading at equilibrium prices. They discard information by focusing only on the sequence of past price vectors so they may consistently fail to select strategies compatible with ex ante market clearing. That markets clear ex post, leads people to wrongfully believe that they must have cleared ex ante as well.

Such a fundamental delusion, that past actualities signal either past plans or future intentions, permeates economic thinking. It flows from the auctioneer's efforts in logical time but cannot guarantee coordination in historical time. Rather, the blunder of concentrating on price encourages neglect of other aspects of the bargain, particularly quantity conditions, and may thus perpetually fail to establish a temporary equilibrium of trading intentions.

Together, theorems one and two imply that, given their assumptions, historical consistency of plans is necessary, but not sufficient, for markets to clear during each period. This arises from the nature of strategy choice, and from the manner of interpreting prices. Everybody assumes that the currently perceived sequence of past prices signals ex ante equilibrium at those prices. Consequently they plan according to those signals. In doing so, they have neglected the detailed quantity information at their disposal, and may thus misinterpret prices. In this way they may base their plans on expectations that treat prices as unambiguous indicators of past phenomena, when those prices may also be capable of supporting other stories. The plans they achieve will all be compatible with their expected ex ante prices and ultimately with the ex post prices as well, but the actual quantities they trade need not match their intentions. That actual future prices coincide with currently anticipated prices does not mean that the expected price vector must be a market-clearing equilibrium price vector.

By similar reasoning, even when the system achieves temporary equilibrium, it may not achieve a Pareto optimum. Since each agent maximizes expected welfare at the anticipated prices in temporary equilibrium, no other allocation *at those prices* is Pareto superior to the equilibrium allocation. Each price vector, however, has different opportunities and different welfare properties. Consequently, different histories of equilibrated markets at intertemporally constant but different prices will all generate different welfare properties. Nothing in the nature of the system assures that the particular equilibrium path followed is Pareto superior to all the others. For example, if everyone thinks chocolate is exorbitantly dear, then it may be universally shunned for strawberry sundaes, whereas an alternative equilibrated history may have it cheap and plentifully consumed. It is conceivable that this alternative history may be Pareto superior, but nothing in the prices these markets generate will aim toward it.

Given Muthian rationality and constrained welfare maximization, the realization of everybody's trading plans occurs only when the historical consistency of those plans and the expectations generating them is assured. Only then is the system's behavior sufficiently regular and reliable that past performance is a sure enough guide to planning and organization for coordinated results to emerge. In historical time no mythical agent stops time to permit recontracting. Only when that is assured, and people feel justified in ignoring the potential for altered prices, is it possible for reconciled intention to occur. Without this stable, but unreal, historical background, in which price flexibility is meaningless, the planning, confidence, and courage needed to undertake, organize, and govern any economic activity may be thwarted and disappointed. Such stability is necessary for, but never acts as guarantor of, equilibrium, much less optimality.

Neither can such stability be seen as normal or even plausible. Returning to the true generality of historical time, we recall how narrow are the assumptions on information and inference from past to the future upon which historical consistency of expectations rests. Everybody must *know* the complete history of the system, and everybody must be willing to accept the contention that the future will be governed by the same stochastic process as the past. Everybody must *know* the entire range of all future possibility, and never doubt that an unimagined contingency might erupt into their peace. The future must be known, at least in part, so that deep uncertainty about it never shadows the mind. To know the future demolishes time, however.

These conditions, and the equilibrium they sustain, mock an authentically dynamic economics. The alluring coordinations of temporary equilibrium should by now have been revealed to be an illusory concoction of logical-time relics. Prereconciliation of strategies is not impossible, but it is profoundly implausible without knowledge of future outcomes. Ultimately, we simply do not know what will happen, and are always subject to blundering into surprises. Knowledge of the future, even probabilistic knowledge, calms anxiety as it eliminates uncertainty. In eliminating uncertainty, however, its stabilizing powers derange time.

This stability, this quiet, this complacently presumed knowledge of the future is not, and never was, the stuff of which mortal humans make their existence. The future is never ours to know, but ours to imagine. We nurture hopes and poison our present with fears, but never, never *know* what will be. We attempt guesses, sometimes succeeding, sometimes not, but the courage to try never fully abandons us. We are forced to act without knowing the consequences, and make the best of what we can. We can no more assure ourselves an equilibrated economy, however, than we can assure ourselves that no one will ever err in judgment or blunder in deed. Since action often results from unreasoned imaginations and hopes; however, our economic lives are constantly subject to surprise and disappointment, to amazement and delight. These are not the properties of equilibrium, but of kaleidics.

Here lies the conceptual foundation for an economics of historical time, a reformulated analysis in which time and timing matter in ways inconceivable to logical-time thinking. The model presented in this chapter provides the basis for such an economics. We utilized it to examine two notions of equilibrium, but its employment can be extended to cases with more natural information and expectational conditions. It can lead the way from traditional notions of equilibration to kaleidic social interaction. With it, we can investigate the full range of possibilities opened by imagination.

Appendix: A Glossary of Notation

$b_{ij}(t)$: the quantity of good j person i received in trade at time t.

$B(t)$: the $n \times m$ matrix of all contracted commodity trades at t.

$\hat{B}$: the compact convex subset of m-dimensional euclidean space containing all vectors $s_i(t+k)$.

$\hat{B}$: the set of all possible outcomes.

$\mathcal{B}(t)$: the historical sequences of outcomes at time $t > t_0$.

$\mathcal{B}(t)$: the set of all possible sequences $\mathcal{E}(t)$.

$\hat{\mathcal{B}}$: $\underset{\forall t \geq t_0}{\cup} \mathcal{B}(t)$; contains all possible histories.

D: the economy's choice function, where $S(t) = D[\mathcal{E}(t)]$.

D_j: individual j's choice function linking strategy selection to expectations according to $S_j(t) = D_j[\mathcal{E}_j(t)]$.

e_i: an m-dimensional vector of feasible trades.

$E_i(t)$: a sequence of anticipated exchanges contemplated by individual i at time t.

$\hat{E}(t)$: the set of all conceivable future exchange trajectories at time t.

$\hat{E}$: the set of all possible expected sequences of trades.

$\mathcal{E}(t)$: the configuration of different people's expectations at time t; a point in $2^{\mathcal{E}(t)}$.

$\hat{\mathcal{E}}_i(t)$: person i's set of expectations at time t.

$\mathcal{E}(t)$: the set of all expectations possible at time t.

$\hat{\mathcal{E}}$: the set of all possible expectations.

$\hat{\hat{\mathcal{E}}}(t)$: $\overset{n}{\Pi} 2^{\hat{\mathcal{E}}(t)}$

$\hat{\hat{\mathcal{E}}} = \underset{\forall t \geq t_0}{\cup} \hat{\hat{\mathcal{E}}}(t)$

I: the function representing system-wide distribution and use of information, where $\mathcal{E}(t) = I[\mathcal{B}(t)]$.

I_j: person j's expectations-formation function, where $\mathcal{E}_j(t) = I_j[\mathcal{B}(t)]$.

m: the number of commodities.

M: the function mapping $\hat{S}$ into $\hat{B}$ where $B(t) = M[S(t)]$.

n: the number of persons.

$P(t)$: price vector at time t.

$PS_i\{[E_i(t), S_i(t)]\}$: person i's potential surprise that $E_i(t)$ will occur given that strategy $S_i(t)$ is pursued.

$s_i(t + k)$:   the vector of trades person i plans at time t to trade at time $t + k$.

$s(t + k)$:   the $n \times m$ matrix whose row vectors are the $s_i(t + k)$ where $i = 1, \ldots, n$.

$S_i(t)$:   person i's strategy at time t.

$S(t)$:   the strategies undertaken at t.

$\hat{S}(t)$:   the set of all strategies possible at t.

$\hat{S}$:   the set of all possible configurations of strategies.

t_0:   the initial period's date.

$s_{ij}(t)$:   the quantity of good j individual i plans to purchase at time t. The element in the ith row and jth column of $S(t)$.

$\mathscr{P}_{it}(\cdot)$:   the probability measure employed by person i at time t.

$U_i(t)$: the real-valued continuous utility function of person i.

Notes

[1] Relating to completeness of sets of possible outcomes, see Bausor (1985).

[2] A similar reversibility arose in the symmetric characterization of motion in preentropic models in physics. See Mirowski (1984).

[3] For a survey of the important issues and results of this literature, see Grandmont (1977).

[4] Similar issues of reversibility of time have been significant in physics. Treating time as another dimension led to a sense of reversibility that seemed to work well in Newtonian mechanics, since positional displacement with respect to a background Cartesian grid could successfully be treated as symmetrically reversible. In the thermodynamics of closed systems, however, such intertemporal symmetries violate the Second Law, and the time-as-dimension characterization had to be supplemented with formal notions of entropy.

[5] Structurally, this model resembles Bausor (1982–1983, 1984), except that here the connection between expectations and perceptions of past history appears only implicitly, and is submerged within the function tethering current expectations to past experience. There it arose as an explicit component of the model's overall structure.

[6] This asserts nothing about "transaction costs." These accrue not in the *ex post* transfer, but in the marketing effort. Similarly, the accumulation of inventories, perhaps through production, is not reflected in $B(t)$, which refers only to contracted trades, not endowments. Both transactions costs and inventory fluctuations, as well as productive activities, enter this model as a separation of this period's endowment, net of trades, from next period's initial endowment. Transaction costs may, but need not, be incurred in terms of any commodity.

[7] Since the rank of $B(t)$ is bounded by $(n - 1)$ whenever condition 4.8 is satisfied, trades at no nontrivial solution price vector are possible only when $n > m$. In this example, $n - m = 2 > 0$.

[8] Conditions 4.8 and 4.12 together imply 4.10. Significantly, in historical time, market clearing alone is not sufficient for equilibrated coordination in the sense that people's intentions are satisfied.

[9] In cases of finance, the commodity (debt) exchanged for funds may be created in the act of trading, but there is a trade nonetheless. One acquires money and liabilities while one's trading partner acquires bonds.

[10] That $[\mathscr{E}(t), 2^{\mathscr{E}(t)}, \mathscr{P}_{it}(\cdot)]$ is a probability space should be clear once it is recognized that $2^{\mathscr{E}_i(t)}$ is a Borel Field: $2^{\mathscr{E}_i(t)}$ contains both the complement of each of its members, and every countable union of its members. Note also that probability spaces are defined over sample space of the form $\mathscr{E}(t)$ rather than, for example, $\hat{E}(t)$, the set of all possible future trade sequences, in order to explicity articulate in terms of the probabilities the conditional nature of anticipated outcomes on motivated decisions.

References

Arrow, Kenneth J., Block, H. D., and Hurwicz, Leonid. 1959. On the Stability of the Competitive Equilibrium, II. *Econometrica* 27(1):82–109.

Bausor, Randall. 1982–1983. Time and the Structure of Economic Analysis. *Journal of Post Keynesian Economics* 5(2):163–179.

Bausor, Randall. 1984. Toward a Historically Dynamic Economics: Examples and Illustrations. *Journal of Post Keynesian Economics* 6(3):360–376.

Bausor, Randall. 1985. The Limits of Rationality. *Social Concept* 2(2):67–83.

Cencini, Alvaro. 1984. *Time and the Macroeconomic Analysis of Income.* London: Frances Pinter.

Debreu, Gerard. 1959. *Theory of Value.* New Haven, CT: Yale University Press.

Georgescu-Roegen, Nicholas. 1971. *The Entropy Law and the Economic Process.* Cambridge, MA: Harvard University Press.

Grandmont, Jean-Michel. 1977. Temporary General Equilibrium Theory. *Econometrica* 45(3):535–572.

Hicks, J. R. 1939. *Value and Capital.* Oxford: Clarendon Press.

Hicks, J. R. 1979. *Causality in Economics.* New York: Basic Books.

Mirowski, Philip. 1984. Physics and the Marginalist Revolution. *Cambridge Journal of Economics* 8:361–379.

Muth, John F. 1961. Rational Expectations and the Theory of Price Movements. *Econometrica* 29(3):315–335.

Prigogine, Ilya. 1980. *From Being to Becoming.* San Francisco: Freeman.

Robinson, Joan. 1980. Time in Economic Theory. *Kyklos* 33(2):219–229.

Samuelson, Paul A. 1939. Interactions Between the Multiplier Analysis and the Principle of Acceleration. *Review of Economics and Statistics* 21:75–78.

Samuelson, Paul A. 1941. The Stability of Equilibrium: Comparative Statics and Dynamics. *Econometrica* 9:97–120.

Samuelson, Paul A. 1947. *Foundations of Economic Analysis.* New York: Athenaum.

Shackle, G. L. S. 1968. *Uncertainty in Economics, and Other Reflections.* Cambridge University Press.

Shackle, G. L. S. 1972. *Epistemics and Economics: A Critique of Economic Doctrines.* Cambridge University Press.

Shackle, G. L. S. 1974. *Keynesian Kaleidics: The Evolution of a General Political Economy.* Edinburgh: Edinburgh University Press.

Shackle, G. L. S. 1979. *Imagination and the Nature of Choice.* Edinburgh: Edinburgh University Press.

Shubik, Martin. 1975. The General Equilibrium Model Is Incomplete and Not Adequate for the Reconciliation of Micro and Macroeconomic Theory. *Kyklos* 28:545–573.

Vickers, Douglas. 1984. On Relational Structures and Non-equilibrium in Economic Theory. Mimeograph.

Winston, Gordon C. 1982. *The Timing of Economic Activities.* New York: Cambridge University Press.

5 THE ROLE OF FORMALISM IN ECONOMIC THOUGHT, WITH ILLUSTRATION DRAWN FROM THE ANALYSIS OF SOCIAL INTERACTION IN THE FIRM

Donald W. Katzner

Economists tend to use the word "analysis" rather glibly to describe the things that they do. The list of these things is long, including verbal description, numerical manipulation, model building in its many forms, and so on. In all usages, however, the underlying goal of analysis is the same: to make sense out of or to understand worldly phenomena. And in all cases, analysis proceeds by organizing and explaining the thoughts one has about the phenomena in question.

The most widespread approach to analysis in economics is called *formalism*. To economists, a formalist analysis consists of identifying (usually quantifiable) variables, assuming the existence of relations among them, assuming that the relations exhibit certain properties or characteristics, and working out at length the implications of all of these assumptions. Such analyses may also concern themselves with maximization, and with solutions and proofs of existence of solutions for some system of (simultaneous) relations.

This chapter explores the role of formalism in economic thought: where it came from, what it does, and what are its prerequisites and limitations, its power and potential. The argument of the chapter is illustrated with an analysis of the social interactions among employees in the economic firm.

The author would like to thank Robert W. Drago, Philip Mirowski, and Douglas Viskers for their help.

It should be made clear at the outset that what follows is neither an essay on methodology nor on epistemology. Most methodologies and epistemologies appearing in economics today make room for formalist constructions in analysis, although they use and interpret such structures in a variety of different ways (Katzner, forthcoming). And in all cases, whatever the methodological and epistemological foundation of an investigation, if formalism is to be employed, certain issues have to be faced. These latter issues are the focus of attention here.

History

A quick glance at the current issue of almost any modern economics journal reveals the pervasiveness of formalism in economic analysis. But the appearance of formalism in economics is only a late development in the long evolution of formalism as a mathematical school of thought. The emergence of formalism in the history of mathematics has been chronicled recently by Kline (1980). His story follows:

All ancient civilizations sought truths: truths about the properties of the physical world, truths about the nature of man and his behavior, etc. Most obtained these truths from theology. The Greeks, however, thought that the mind of man, aided by observation, is also capable of discovering truths. Moreover, since (the Greeks believed) the universe is designed according to mathematical principles, and since the relationships among numbers underlie and unify nature, truths may be learned through the application of mathematics. This reasoning was based on three precepts: First, mathematics is concerned with abstractions, and one abstract concept would encompass the essential features of every physical occurrence of that concept. Second, all discussion would begin with axioms or self-evident truths that no one could doubt. And third, each conclusion was to be derived deductively from the axioms. In their search for the mathematical laws governing the universe, the Greeks created, among other things, Euclidean geometry.

From the ancient Greeks up to the beginning of the nineteenth century A.D., Western thinkers (with a few exceptions) thought that all known truths about our physical world were described by Euclidean geometry. Furthermore, any unknown truths about physical reality were merely parts of Euclidean geometry that had not yet been detected. All of this was shattered in the nineteenth century with the discovery that non-Euclidean geometries could also be used to accurately represent the properties of physical actuality. Hence Euclidean geometry is not necessarily the true description of real physical space. Although the Greek program of employing mathematics to reveal truths about the world had been extraordinarily useful, it did not reveal truths in the sense originally intended. Axioms could no longer be regarded as unquestionable self-evident truths. They may be suggested by experience but they, along with the conclusions to which they deductively lead, still have only limited applicability.

About the same time that mathematicians began to understand that the mere usage of mathematics did not necessarily yield truths, they also realized that their discipline had evolved over the years in a sloppy haphazard fashion, leaving many poorly understood concepts and numerous logical errors. Consequently, the second half of the nineteenth century witnessed their attempt to correct these deficiencies by axiomatizing their arguments. Such efforts led to the recognition of at least three noteworthy principles: First, all deductive systems necessarily contain undefined terms. Second, every set of axioms should be shown to be consistent, that is, not permit the derivation of contradictory propositions from it. Finally, each individual axiom in any set of axioms should be independent of (not derivable from) the remaining axioms in that set.

By 1900 mathematicians believed that they had completed the reconstruction of their arguments in axiomatic terms. But almost immediately contradictions were uncovered in their new mathematics. In response to this state of affairs four schools of thought arose, each claiming to provide a contradiction-free approach to the nature of mathematics. According to the logistic school, all mathematics was secured from logic. Since the laws of logic constituted a body of consistent truths, so did mathematics. The set-theoretic school claimed that all mathematics was derived from a consistent theory of sets. The latter could be obtained by restricting the type of sets that were admitted for discussion. The intuitionist school asserted that mathematics was independent of the real world. Mathematical thinking consisted of mental construction of its own universe based on fundamental mathematical intuition. Intuition, not logic, also determined the soundness of argument. One did not deduce from axioms. Rather, to do valid mathematics was to construct entities in a finite number of steps. Defining sets by describing the characteristics of their elements and using nonconstructive proofs of the existence of things were not legitimate. Consistency was furnished by correct thought as judged by intuition.

The last of the schools of thought was the formalist school. Contrary to all of the other approaches, mathematics to the formalist was a collection of formal systems, each with its own concepts, axioms, and theorems. All axioms (both logical and mathematical) were expressed as formulas or collections of mathematical symbols. All deductions were manipulations of formulas according to the specified logical axioms. And every formal system had to be shown to be consistent within itself.

Each of these four schools vigorously attacked the others. Because interest here centers on formalism, it is worth noting at this juncture two criticisms leveled against the formalist school. On one hand, their mathematics was labeled as abstract and having little meaning in actuality. Infinite sets, for example, were a part of the mathematics of the formalist school, and were (and are) totally foreign to human experience. On the other hand, the consistency of a formal system did not guarantee the existence in the real world of things (such as equilibrium price vectors) proved by formalists to exist in nonconstructive existence theorems. Discussion will return to these points later on.

All of the four schools made claims of consistency. The intuitionists based consistency on intuition. The remaining three groups either asserted that their axioms led to consistency or believed that their axioms were sufficient to establish it, although they had no proof. But in 1931, Gödel showed that the consistency of any mathematical system sufficiently wide so as to include the arithmetic of whole numbers can never be established. He also demonstrated that in such a system there always is at least one proposition which, together with its negation, cannot be proved. Thus for the logicists, set-theorists, and formalists, who relied on axiomatic foundations, no system of axioms permitted proof of all theorems that fell within its structure. Moreover, there was no guarantee that contradictions could not arise in any of their systems. The principle that all systems should be consistent was impossible to enforce.

Gödel's results (combined with others that emerged at roughly the same time on the unprovability of specific propositions) fragmented mathematicians into an even greater number of competing factions. Many of these, including the formalist school, persist to this day.

The introduction of formalism in economics is relatively new. To be sure, functions have been maximized and systems of simultaneous equations have been solved as far back as Cournot (1960). And many later nineteenth-century economists such as Jevons (1965), Pareto (1966), and Walras (1954) subsequently applied mathematics to the study of economic phenomena. But all of this occurred before the emergence of the formalist school in the early years of the twentieth century. It is only very recently that the formalist approach, whereby axioms are explicitly postulated and their implications derived, appeared as a method of analysis in economics. The culmination of the transference of formalism from mathematics to economics appeared in 1959 in Debreu's *Theory of Value* which is still regarded by many as the apotheosis of the axiomatic method in economics. Debreu may also have been the first economist to expressly acknowledge and sanction formalism.

In the Preface to the *Theory of Value* he wrote:

> The theory of value is treated here with the standards of rigor of the contemporary formalist school of mathematics.... Allegiance to rigor dictates the axiomatic form of the analysis where the theory, in the strict sense, is logically entirely disconnected from its interpretations. (Debreu, 1959, p. viii)

Another aspect of the appearance of formalism in economics is the focus by economists almost exclusively on quantifiable aspects of the thing under investigation. Now quantification is neither a necessary nor a sufficient condition for formalism. Indeed, it is possible to do a formalist analysis without any sort of quantification at all (see Katzner, 1983). But by the time that Cournot started what eventually became a movement toward formalism, virtually all economists employing mathematics in their trade had accepted the equivalent of Lord Kelvin's dictum:

> ... when you can measure what you are speaking about and express it in numbers, you know something about it; but when you cannot measure it, when you cannot express it in numbers, your knowledge is of a meager and unsatisfactory kind: it may be the beginning of knowledge, but you have scarcely, in your thoughts, advanced to the stage of *science*, whatever the matter may be. (Thomson, 1891, pp. 80, 81)

Thus the introduction of mathematics and later of formalism in economics seems to have gone hand in hand with quantification.

The Prerequisites of Formalism

As described above, formalist analysis usually begins with the specification of variables and relations among them. But before even arriving at this starting gate, considerable abstraction and discipline of thought are required just to be able to accomplish the necessary specifications. The statement, "Let there be J variables and I relations among them," can and should be justified. And so discussion now focuses on what has to be done to set the stage for a formalist analysis. In anticipation of subsequent argument, a certain kind of intellectual tension is worthy of mention at the beginning.

Meyerson (1962, chs. 1, 2) has argued that when thinking about the world in terms of discrete objects and discrete laws (relations among objects), both the objects and the laws are not changed by displacing them in space. Nor are these laws modified by the passage of time, that is, they persist unaltered through time. Furthermore, to be able to understand the assertion, "An event happening to object A causes or determines another event happening to object B," it must also be supposed that A and B persist without transformation over time as well. But the nature of our world is such that changes in A and B are perceived as time moves on. These perceptions, then, can only reflect "apparent transformation" which, at a deeper level, does not actually occur. Hence there is always a tension that can never be completely overcome between what an analyst thinks and what he sees.

Similarly with change itself. To think about change in such a context requires that evolving reality be reduced to discrete laws that govern its metamorphosis. These laws are set against fixed objects and environments that are inviolate through time and which, on account of their constancy, permit change to be detected by comparison and contrast. This kind of change is called displacement or motion. But as before, apparent change is still perceived in the "fixed" objects and environments, and the tension between what one thinks and sees remains.

The Dialectical Nature of Thought

This tension (and others) reflects, in part, the dialectical characteristics embedded in the processes of thought. To see what is involved, notice first that in certain cases, the human mind is perfectly capable of sharply delineating the boundaries of an idea. The result is what Georgescu-Roegen (1971, pp. 43–45) has called an arithmomorphic concept. Such concepts have the property that they can be clearly distinguished and separated from all others. They are distinctly discrete and there is no overlap between them and their opposites. The velocity of a moving object is an arithmomorphic concept as is the weight of a pot of water and the length of a train.

On the other hand, there are concepts whose boundaries human powers seem unable to clearly and precisely define. Exact characterizations are either arbitrary in that they do not conform to standard notions or are extraordinarily difficult to employ. Where, for example, does one quality of experience leave off and another begin? Democracy and nondemocracy are two different ideas, each with a variety of shades of meaning and, what is more important, with certain shades of democracy overlapping certain shades of nondemocracy. Concepts such as these may be referred to as dialectical (Georgescu-Roegen, 1971, pp. 45–47). Dialectical notions are distinct, though not, as their arithmomorphic counterparts, discretely so. Each is surrounded by its own penumbra of meanings. Any dialectical concept is distinguishable from all others (including its opposite), since no two penumbras can be identical. But, although impossible with arithmomorphic concepts, a country can be both a democracy and a nondemocracy at the same time.

Now formalism, as it appears in economics, is clearly based on arithmomorphic concepts. But with dialectical contexts, since a thing can be both A and not A at the same time, the formalist rules for constructions and deductions do not apply. In particular, deductive logic can not be employed because it requires the discrete distinction of the objects on which it operates. One may still, however, make assumptions and reason with dialectical ideas, as the following passage due to Russell shows:

> Not only are we aware of particular yellows, but if we have seen a sufficient number of yellows and have sufficient intelligence, we are aware of the universal *yellow*; this universal is the subject in such judgements as "yellow differs from blue" or "yellow resembles blue less than green does." And the universal yellow is the predicate in such judgements as "this is yellow." ... (Russell, 1959, p. 212)

Dialectical reasoning can be checked in at least two ways (Georgescu-Roegen, 1971, p. 337). The first is by use of the ancient Socratic method: systematic questioning of all aspects of argument. The second is by working through arithmomorphic similes. Dialectical reasoning can often be likened to various arithmomorphic arguments, although none of these test arguments is ever capable of replacing the original in its entirety. Error uncovered by either the Socratic method or the employment of deductive logic in an arithmomorphic simile clearly casts doubt on the original dialectical reasoning. But even though it provides a certain comfort and satisfaction, a lack of detection of error does not imply correctness.

Most important concepts in economics are really dialectical in character. In actuality, for example, there is generally no such thing as the single, unique price of a good.[1] Rather, any commodity usually has an entire penumbra of prices at which it is sold. Moreover, because of the great variety of forms in which commodities normally can be produced, the line marking the "end" of one commodity and the "start" of another is often difficult to determine. Thus in saying that certain goods are sold in certain markets at certain prices, the underlying conceptual referents of "goods", "markets", and "prices" are purely dialectical. Other examples of dialectical concepts are the preferences of an individual, the technology of production, and the various forms of competition that may appear in markets, etc.

Formalist analysis in economics abstracts from such concepts to secure discretely distinct (arithmomorphic) notions which are then converted into variables. It is among these kinds of variables that formalist relations are defined and manipulated. As will be seen below, the relations themselves may be viewed as abstractions from underlying dialectical processes. In this sense, formalisms in economics may be described as arithmomorphic similes extracted from a dialectical base.

Arithmomorphic Abstraction

Consider a dialectical idea such as the price of good x, and suppose the arithmomorphic notion of the price of x is drawn from it. Suppose further that the arithmomorphic price of x is permitted to range over all nonnegative real numbers. Thus the arithmomorphic variable called "price of x" is obtained. An arithmomorphic variable, then, is defined by extracting an arithmomorphic concept from a dialectical one and specifying the collection of discretely distinct realizations or values that the concept may possess.

Although the variable "price of x" is quantitative, there is nothing in the construction of an arithmomorphic variable requiring that measurement be possible. To illustrate, from the dialectical notion of the form of competition in the market for x, extract an arithmomorphic counterpart. On 3-by-5 cards, say, write down descriptions of each of the various forms of competition that may appear in the market for x—one description on each card. Take these descriptions to be discretely distinct even though the prose on each card may appear to be imprecise and fuzzy. Assume that the relevant group of investigators agrees that this collection of descriptions is appropriate for the purpose at hand. Then the variable "form of competition in the market for x" may be defined as that which takes on as values the description on any 3-by-5 card in the collection. Another example of such a variable (and one employed in the sections on the firm below) is the (set of) activities in which an employee engages while at work. Each of its variable values, too, may be thought of as a description on a 3-by-5 card.

The question of whether the 3-by-5 cards in a given collection of variable values can be supplanted by numbers that meaningfully measure the descriptions on them in some way is a separate matter. To answer it requires formalisms that are entirely different from those employed in the analysis of the particular economic phenomena under scrutiny. Measuring the descriptions on the 3-by-5 cards implies that all of the important information on the cards is encapsulated in certain abstract properties, and that the specific form in which these properties arise in the description on any one card permits that card to be replaced by a single number conveying the same information as on the card.[2] For example, if each card described a person of a certain "oldness", and if oldness were all that mattered, then a number representing the age of the person described could possibly be substituted for the description on the card. The formal conditions under which such replacement is valid in general are complex. To be able to measure ordinally, say, requires the presence of a reflexive, transitive, and total ordering relation defined among the 3-by-5 cards such that the interval topology, based on the equivalence classes generated by this ordering, has a countable base. The details and the requisites for other forms of measurement are not considered here.[3] Suffice it to say that the more (relevant) information on the card that is not reflected by the number assigned to the card, and the more extraneous information entrapped by the number itself, the less meaningful the measure. Thus the price of x is not a good measure of the quality of the commodity x since the price of x contains information having nothing to do with the quality of x, and there are many aspects of the quality of x that need not be mirrored in its price. In any case, it has already been noted that measurement is not a prerequisite of formalism, and none is assumed in present discussion. Arithmomorphic variable values then, are generally viewed as descriptions on 3-by-5 cards that are discrete and unchanging over time.

Suppose now that the variables and relations for a formalist analysis have been distilled from their dialectical foundations. (The extraction of arithmomorphic relations from dialectical processes is the topic of the subsection "From Processes to Functions.") Several issues concerning the properties of the spaces of variable values, the meaning of the relations defined on them, and the apparatus for the manipulation of these relations still have to be discussed. In the next few paragraphs each is considered in turn.

Specification of spaces of variable values (the sets over which the variables range) and the properties these spaces are to possess is one of the important elements in proceeding to the start of any formal analysis. Indeed, Hofstadter (1979, pp. 611–613) has suggested that the proper choices in this regard may be crucial to the solution of many real problems. Economists, however, have tended to ignore the issue. When variables are quantifiable, the relevant spaces are almost always taken to be Euclidean. Other possibilities are seldom considered, in spite of the proven usefulness of non-Euclidean spaces for analyzing the physical world. As of now, nonquantifiable spaces have hardly been employed in formal analysis in economics, and there is still much to learn about them. One specification of such a space has been given by Katzner (1983, secs. 3.2, 3.3). In any case, the specification of the space over which a variable ranges contains implicit theoretical statements about the variable itself.

Also implicit in the specification of spaces and their properties are rules for manipulation of the variable values. The weakest rule that one can give is a scheme for classification. Somewhat stronger is the designation of order, that is, the imposition of an ordering relation among the elements of the space.[4] Thus in the section on social interaction below, values of the variable "activities in which a worker engages while on the job" are classified by certain "rule sets" and ordered according to their impact on output. With enough quantification present, the arithmetic operations of addition, subtraction, multiplication, and division provide still further manipulative tools.

It should also be noted that although an infinite number of descriptions on 3-by-5 cards can never be written down, infinite collections (both countable and uncountable) of such cards can certainly be imagined. Economists and other social scientists do so all the time (Katzner, 1983, sec. 7.2). Infinite sets of nonquantifiable elements may be accepted in the same sense that infinite sets of numbers are employed in quantitative contexts: Such sets exist only in the minds of investigators and have no basis in reality. In this way, the set of all values of the variable "activities in which a worker engages while on the job" is thought of as a possibly uncountable set in the section on social interaction. Recall that such conceptualizations are the source of one of the criticisms aimed at the formalist school many years ago.

Arithmomorphic relations among arithmomorphic variables are frequently expressed as mathematical functions. And, of course, the definition of function does not rely on measurement: Let y and x be two variables defined over sets called, respectively, the domain and range. (These may actually be vectors of variables such as $y = (y_1, \ldots, y_J)$ and $x = (x_1, \ldots, x_I)$.) Then the function f, often written as

$$x = f(y)$$

is a rule which assigns to each element of the domain a unique element in the range. When y and x are not quantifiable, f is defined by indicating which value of x is associated to each value of y. This is the meaning of the functions involving nonquantified variables used to analyze social interactions in the firm in the section on social interaction. In the numerical case, f may be characterized either by listing the associations between x and y or by summarizing them in a formula such as

$$x = f(y) = y + 2$$

Consider, for a moment, the latter. The formula $x = y + 2$ is generally taken to be a rule which indicates that values of x are obtained from values of y by adding the number 2. But according to Wittgenstein (see Wright, 1980, pp. 21–38), it can not be said that every time one sees $x = y + 2$, one is committed to interpret its meaning in this way. Individuals are always free to choose their interpretation at each encounter. There is no reason why a person could not invoke the above interpretation of $x = y + 2$ today and employ an entirely different one tomorrow.

Naturally, individuals can be trained to understand $x = y + 2$ in a certain way. Or they can negotiate over its meaning and possibly agree on an interpretation. But someone else with another kind of training or not a party to the negotiated agreement may well come along and comprehend the meaning of $x = y + 2$ differently. This is because each individual learns meanings by making inductive inferences from past experience. These understandings are one's own and can never be conveyed to another. For two persons to arrive at the same meaning, then, they must have the same experiences and must make the same inferences from them—an unlikely occurrence in the absence of negotiation or similar training.

The upshot is that the relations of any formalist analysis are always subject to new interpretations and changed meanings, and such is the case even if the dialectical foundation from which it springs were to remain constant. Thus the same formalist analysis of a given phenomenon at two separate times can not guarantee the same conclusions in advance. Formalism, then, can not be said to provide an absolute standard against which the conclusions of other types of analyses can be compared.

It remains, in this subsection, to consider the rules for manipulating the relations of a formalist analysis. As with the formalist school, these rules turn on the principles of deductive logic. Although deductive logic has no relevance in the underlying dialectical base of the analysis, its force upon application in arithmomorphic abstractions is well known.

The most fundamental operation that can be performed on functions is composition or elimination of variables by substitution. Thus, two functions f and g, say

$$x = f(y) \qquad \text{and} \qquad y = g(z)$$

may be combined into h by eliminating y:

$$x = h(z)$$

where

$$h(z) = f[g(z)]$$

and h is referred to as the composition of f and g. To be useful, function composition must exhibit two characteristics: It must be closed, that is, the composites it produces must always be functions, and it must be associative.[5] The simplest algebraic structure conforming to these properties is called a *semigroup*.[6] Hence the least that can be postulated about the functions of a formalist analysis is that they are elements of a semigroup under function composition.[7]

Additional techniques for manipulating functions may also be introduced. Inverting functions to obtain inverses and partial inverses is a possibility (Katzner, 1983, ch.4). In the quantifiable, case functions may also be added, subtracted, multiplied, divided, differentiated, integrated, and so on. Clearly, each insertion of a new manipulative rule complicates the algebraic structure required to support formalist analysis.

It should be emphasized that the postulation of a semigroup structure does not imply the presence of ordinal, cardinal, or ratio measures. First of all, the conditions for the existence of such measures are not all met by semigroup structures. And second, the functions of the semigroup may express the substantive relations of the analysis rather than the relations required for the construction of numerical scales. Thus the convenience of numerical representations, with their attendant arithmetic tools of manipulation, is not necessarily available. What is at hand are the discrete variable values and the functions or laws relating them, both of which persist as constants through time, the operation of composition for manipulating functions which is closed and associative, plus any other elements such as inverses that may be introduced for analytical purposes. All dialectical facets of thought have been exorcised.

Time and Change

As far as human capacity to sense nature is concerned, there is no such thing as an "instant of time". Rather, time is perceived as a series of imprecise and overlapping durations in which the future becomes the inexactly felt present and then slips into the past. It is a dialectical concept (Georgescu-Roegen, 1971, pp. 69–72). The idea of instants of time (or discretely distinct time periods) all lined up one after the other is an arithmomorphic abstraction. It permits identification of the linear continuum as the standard reference for keeping track of the movement of time. The use of dynamic equations (differential or otherwise) in formalist analysis depends on it.

Time and change are tightly interwoven; one can hardly be discerned without the other. Change, unobservable at an instant of time, is capable of detection only over durations. Although the distinction between sameness and change rests ultimately in the beholder, judgments as to whether a change has actually occurred turn on the relation of the thing in question to its "other". Change can only appear in contrast to the environment in which it is set. And because there are no clear-cut boundaries delineating where it begins and ends, change, like time, is dialectical in character (Georgescu-Roegen, 1971, pp. 63, 69).

One way of describing change is with the notion of process (Georgescu-Roegen, 1971, pp. 213–215). A process involves something happening, certain events or changes taking place over time. Each process is defined by the happenings that make it up. All remaining events constitute the process'

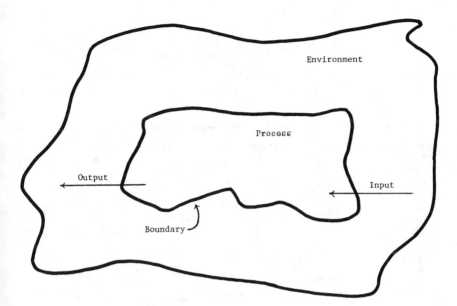

Figure 5–1

environment. The process itself can only be understood in terms of the relationship beween these two collections of occurrences which dialectically overlap each other.

   To extract an arithmomorphic analytical representation of a given process, that is, to reduce change to motion or displacement as described earlier, an arithmomorphic boundary partitioning reality is drawn between the process and its environment. (Figure 5–1 provides a schematic illustration.) Included in this boundary is a specification of the finite (arithmomorphic) period of time over which the process is considered. Neither occurrences entirely within the process nor entirely within its environment can be seen. Only arithmomorphic objects crossing the boundary that remain unchanged over time are capable of observation. (Recall that any change actually perceived in these arithmomorphic objects is regarded as merely apparent change having no significance.) Thus the analytical representation of the process consists of the record of boundary crossings over the interval of time in question. Elements crossing from the environment to the process are called *inputs*; those passing from the process to the environment are *outputs*. (In figure 5–1, only one input arrow and one output arrow are drawn. These are intended to represent schematically all inputs into and outputs from the process.)

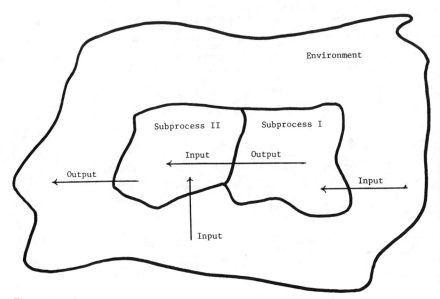

Figure 5–2

Observe that in taking the analytical representation of a process to be an arithmomorphic boundary, all intentions of analyzing what goes on within the process must be given up. Of course, it is always possible to peer "inside" the process by drawing a second arithmomorphic boundary and dividing the original process into two subprocesses, so that the output of one subprocess provides part or all of the input for the other (figure 5–2). But the two subprocesses are themselves independent processes, and the events occurring within each remain hidden from view. Note also that since a process is considered to have only a finite duration, whatever transpired before and whatever might happen after the relevant time period is ignored.

From Processes to Functions

Just as the variables of formalist analysis may be seen as emerging from dialectical concepts, so may the functions of formalist analysis be thought of as extractions from dialectical processes. Although the reduction of dialectical processes to arithmomorphic analytical representations of them has been described in the previous section, additional steps are needed to convert the latter into functions. These steps are now considered with special reference to the case of neoclassical production for illustrative purposes. The production function appearing in the following section as equation 5.2 is of the same sort as that derived here.

Let an analytical representation of a dialectical process be given and suppose the interval of duration is $\{t: \ 0 \leq t \leq t^0\}$, where t is a real (arithmomorphic) variable representing time. (It is convenient, henceforth, to use the term "process" synonymously with its analytical representation.) Thus the process (that is, its analytical representation) starts at $t = 0$ and ends at $t = t^0$. The first step is to thin all boundary crossings to not-necessarily-quantifiable arithmomorphic entities. If there are J distinct arithmomorphic input-boundary-crossing variables indexed by $j = 1, \ldots, J$, and if $y_j(t)$ denotes the value of input variable j at time t (that is, an input boundary crossing at t), then the vector of input boundary crossings at t is $y(t) = [y_1(t), \ldots, y_J(t)]$, and the collection of all input boundary crossings for the duration of the process is

$$Y = \{y(t): \ 0 \leq t \leq t^0\}$$

Similarly, with $x_i(t)$ representing the value of output variable i at time t, where $i = 1, \ldots, I$, and with $x(t) = [x_1(t), \ldots, x_I(t)]$ the complete set of output boundary crossings for the process appears as

$$X = \{x(t): \ 0 \leq t \leq t^0\}$$

The pair (Y, X) is one (arithmomorphic) description of the process.

The representation of a process as the culmination of all input and output boundary crossings encompasses several special instances which are worthy of brief mention (see Georgescu-Roegen, 1971, pp. 215–217). To begin with, some inputs might enter the process and, like catalysts in a chemical reaction, subsequently exit without noticeable change. This can be captured by the statement that

$$x_i(t + k) = y_j(t)$$

for appropriate i and j, and some positive real number k. In another instance, some entering inputs could be completely "used up" by the process and never exit as outputs, while certain exiting outputs produced by the process may have no counterpart as entering inputs. Lastly, inputs might be modified or only partially used up by the process, and hence exit in a somewhat different form from that in which they entered. Here the entering inputs may be regarded as different variables from the exiting outputs. These special cases find illustration in the production process of growing corn, in which land is often described as an input that is unchanged by the process; rain an input that is completely used up; ears of corn an output that does not appear as an input; and an entering spade that exits with increased wear, an input that is modified by the process.

It is also possible in a production process to divide inputs into two categories: those that are flows per unit of time (such as seed and fertilizer in the corn example) and those that are "agents" that use or act on the flows (like labor and spades). But such a distinction is not worth pursuing in the present discussion (Georgescu-Roegen, 1971, pp. 219–234).

Of course, a process need not always be depicted by the same pair (Y, X), although only one pair can be observed for every process. Conceptually, for any given process, different input values of the same variables at the same times—that is, different sequences of input boundary crossings—would generally give rise to different sequences of output boundary crossings or output variable values. Let $\mathcal{Y}$ be the set of all conceivable sequences, Y, of input variable values and $\mathcal{X}$ be the collection of all possible sequences, X, of output variable values. Then the complete arithmomorphic analytical representation of the process is the set of ordered pairs, $f(Y, X)$, where X is in $\mathcal{X}$, Y is in $\mathcal{Y}$, and the ordered pair (Y, X) is in $f(Y, X)$ provided that X is the output sequence when Y is the input sequence. (To speak about neoclassical production, one would have to add a condition of efficiency or maximization in the specification of f.) If correspondences such as f are to be the functions employed in a formalist analysis, then the distillation from the original dialectical process stops here.

Otherwise, the next step in reducing a process to a function is to focus attention on one of the output variables and ignore all others. Dropping the subscript on x, let $x(t)$ now represent the value of the selected output variable at time t. Keep $y(t)$ as before. Assuming that the ordered pairs in $f(Y, X)$ associate exactly one X in $\mathcal{X}$ to each input sequence Y in $\mathcal{Y}$, the relation f becomes a function and may be written as

$$X = f(Y)$$

However, f is not a function in the usual sense. To see why, observe that Y and X actually describe, respectively, a vector of functions of t and a (scalar) function of t. These functions are frequently denoted by the previously introduced symbols $y(t)$ and $x(t)$. Thus f is really a functional, mapping functions y into a single function x, or

$$x = f(y)$$

where the functional argument t, though present, has been excluded to simplify notation (Georgescu-Roegen, 1971, p. 236).

Occasionally, functionals are taken as the functions in a formalist analysis by economists. More often, however, ordinary functions are employed. The final step is securing such functions is to make assumptions about the nature of the $y(t)$ and $x(t)$. Indeed, appropriate specification of $\mathcal{Y}$ and $\mathcal{X}$ is capable of turning f into either a static or dynamic function. If, for example, one were to suppose that

$$y(t) = y(t') \quad \text{and} \quad x(t) = x(t'),$$

for all t and t', and for all $y(t)$ in $\mathcal{Y}$ and $x(t)$ in $\mathcal{X}$, then all functions $x(t)$ and $y(t)$ are constant functions, and the functional f becomes an ordinary function of (not-necessarily-quantifiable) arithmomorphic variables that are independent of time. This may also be written as

$$x = f(y)$$

where y and x are now interpreted as ordinary time-independent vector and scalar variables.

It is clear, then, that the arithmomorphic functions employed by economists in formalist analyses may be viewed as extractions from dynamic, dialectical processes. Following the above path in the case of neoclassical production, the initial process is diluted to a static, technical structure that merely indicates possible (efficient) ways to combine inputs into outputs. Naturally, the deletion of time precludes serious discussion of change.

Social Interaction in the Economic Firm:
An Example of Formalism

The next task is to provide an example of a formalist analysis. This will not only illustrate what formalism can do, but will also serve as the basis for subsequent discussion of its power and limitations. To fully display the depth of formalist argument, it is necessary that the example be both detailed and complete. Furthermore, to be able to distinguish the power of formalism as distinct from that of quantification (remember that arithmomorphic extraction does not imply measurement), the example focuses almost exclusively on nonquantifiable entities. In presenting the example, the preceding section's derivations of concepts, variables, and functions from their corresponding dialectical thought-forms are not repeated for each concept, variable, and function employed. Rather, all such derivations are taken as having already been accomplished, and discussion begins with these concepts, variables, and functions in their arithmomorphic state ready for use.

The Problem

The idea of *production function* is one of the cornerstones on which the neoclassical theory of the perfectly competitive firm rests. Given technology, a production function describes the maximum output obtainable from every possible combination of inputs. In one common version, the theory postulates certain nonnegativity, smoothness, increasingness, and convexity traits of technology which are represented as properties of the production function. It then supposes that the firm, being faced with "fixed" market prices, bases input and output decisions on profit maximization. Thus the firm's input demand and output supply are derived as functions of input and output prices. The characteristics of these latter functions, i.e., the so-called comparative-statics propositions, are deduced from the initial restrictions placed on the production function.

As pointed out earlier, this theory has no choice but to treat the production process as a "black box". And the theory clearly draws the boundary of the process in such a way that inputs go in, output comes out, and no questions are asked in between. But unfortunately, it is equally clear that, in addition to inputs and technology, production also depends on the specific people involved in the production process and on what they do and do not do while employed. Individuals, after all, are hired to perform particular tasks within the limits of certain rules. A salesman has to decide how to approach and deal with prospective buyers; a carpenter may have to choose the order in which wood is cut and nailed together. Hence with the same technology and numerical input quantities, output can vary significantly according to whether the rules are reasonable, the extent to which the relevant individuals are willing to follow them, and the extent to which they foster cooperation within the firm. Cases in which output has lagged at certain times due to nontechnological "internal" problems even in the most well-supplied and technologically "advanced" firms are observed often.[8] At the opposite extreme, productivity has been known to soar during periods in which other social arrangements obtained.[9] These issues can only be considered by drawing the boundary of the production process somewhat differently.

The formalist analysis presented here attempts to begin such a program by developing an economic model of the "perfectly competitive" firm which attempts to account for a small part of the social interaction naturally occurring among employees. Nonlabor inputs are treated in the traditional fashion. But rule structures, influence, cooperation of workers, and incentive schemes are introduced[10] and the potential for still further generalization is suggested. Both individuals and the firm itself are taken to be maximizers. Input demand and output supply functions are derived and their (comparative statics) properties relating to modifications in workers' skills and preferences are studied. The meaning and importance of Pareto optimality (efficiency) within production also is considered. The argument follows in the tradition of Coase (1937), Dunlop (1958), Leibenstein (1976), and Simon (1956b), formalizing and pursuing many of their ideas. It draws heavily on Gintis and Katzner (1979).

The Firm

Let there be K workers in the firm and index them by k, where $k = 0, \ldots, K$. Designate the director by $k = 0$. Assume lines of authority are pyramidal (with the director at the top) so that every worker $k \neq 0$ has exactly one supervisor. All workers except those at the bottom end of a line of authority have at least one subordinate. Any worker who supervises k, or the supervisor of k, or the supervisor of the supervisor of k, etc., is said to be *above k* in authority. Of course, the director is above all $k \neq 0$, and k is *below* all those above him. The *co-workers* of k are those workers who have the same supervisor as k. The set of all workers can be partitioned into nonoverlapping and exhaustive subsets, each of which is a class of all mutual co-workers. Suppose there are J such classes enumerated by $j = 1, \ldots, J$.

As an illustration, consider the pyramid drawn in figure 5–3. There are 19 workers, each denoted by a dot and assigned a number. The dot associated with 0 represents the director. Lines indicate the flow of authority from the director on down. Thus worker 3 supervises 7 and 8 and, in turn, is supervised by the director. Persons 5, 1, and 0 are all above worker 11, while 17, 18, and 19 are below him. There are 9 co-worker classes: $\{1, 2, 3\}$, $\{4, 5\}$, $\{6\}$, $\{7, 8\}$, $\{9, 10\}$, $\{11\}$, $\{12, 13, 14, 15\}$, $\{16\}$, and $\{17, 18, 19\}$. Observe that worker 5 is neither above nor below persons 2, 6, and 10. Nor is he a co-worker of these individuals.

Each worker k supplies labor time e_k to the firm. All units of labor time coming from the same person are homogeneous and can not exceed some maximum. During time supplied, the employee performs activities or acts a_k which fall within the terms of the work contract.[11] These activities involve social interactions among employees and are limited by the technological imperatives of production. It is not necessary that the a_k be quantifiable: As described earlier; the only restriction is that each "value" of a_k be capable of distinct, discrete verbal description. The collection of values over which a_k may range is called k's *activity* set and is denoted by A_k. Write $a = (a_1, \ldots, a_K)$ and $A = A_1 \times \cdots \times A_K$. In addition to activities, each worker also

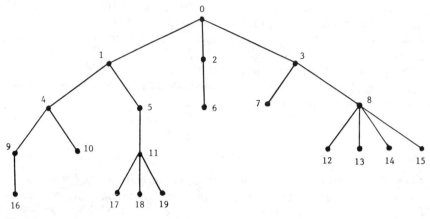

Figure 5–3

provides rules that constrain the activities of all workers below him. The furnishing of rules may be thought of as an "administrative" activity separate from all other activities and singled out for special attention. Recalling the example of figure 5–3, worker 5 say, receives rules from 1 and 0, and issues rules for 11, 17, 18, and 19. Such rules are defined by the subsets of the activity sets they determine. Rules may be so restrictive as to dictate exactly what must be done (i.e., select a single element from the relevant activity set) or they may allow for considerable flexibility and choice. Moreover, the nature of the rules so promulgated may be legally limited.[12]

It is worth remembering at this point how far these notions of activities and rules really are from their underlying dialectical counterparts. All of the subtle variations in activities in which one activity overlaps another have disappeared in the discretization of the values that the variable "activity" may take on. Either a worker does a particular job or he does not—there is no in-between. The designation of rules as a subset of these activity variable values, then, imposes greater rigidity and less flexibility in communication among persons than one would, as a practical matter, expect. That is, the nuances of the rules themselves, as well as those of the way in which they are transmitted, are necessarily lost in the formalization of this kind of human interaction.

Consider the rules received by person k' from above. If k is above $k' \neq 0$, let $R_{kk'}$ vary over possible rules prescribed by k for k'. Then $R_{kk'} \subseteq A_{k'}$. The collection of rules imposed on k' by all persons above him (including the director) is

$$\rho_{k'} = \cap_k R_{kk'} \qquad (5.1)$$

where the intersection is taken over all k above k'. Note $\rho_{k'} \subseteq A_{k'}$. It is not necessary that the sets $R_{kk'}$ be nested, that is, become smaller, as k moves from 0 to k'—although in practice, actual rule sets may wind up having this property. If, for example, the director wants to have certain things done in certain ways, then he promulgates rules for all workers ensuring that his wishes are met. Rules issued by persons between the director and k' may permit more freedom than the director's rules. But k' is constrained by the director's more restrictive rules anyway and can not take advantage of larger rule sets even if issued by intermediate persons above him. Of course, for a sequence of rules imposed on k' to be viable (consistent), $\rho_{k'}$ can not be empty. Assume that workers obey all rules handed down from above and that there are no monetary costs associated with the implementation of any rule.

Persons not at the bottom of the pyramid of authority post rules for all individuals below them. Let r_k be the vector of rules issued by worker k. The components of r_k are the $R_{kk'}$ for appropriate k'. Take r_k to vary over some admissible set, $\mathscr{R}_k$, of vectors of rules. For notational simplicity write $r = (r_1, \ldots, r_K)$ and $\mathscr{R} = (\mathscr{R}_1, \ldots, \mathscr{R}_K)$, where it is understood that if, say, k' has no workers below him then $\mathscr{R}_{k'}$ is empty and $r_{k'}$ has no meaning. Both $\mathscr{R}$ and the director's rule vector, r_0, are presumed given.

Output, in the present context, depends on quantities of labor time and nonlabor inputs employed by the firm as well as on activities (consistent with rules received from above) and rules for subordinates chosen by workers. Suppose, insofar as their contribution to output is concerned, the firm regards all individuals from the same co-worker class as more-or-less identical. The labor hours contributed by co-worker class j may be viewed as homogeneous and combined in

$$z_j = \sum_k e_k$$

where the sum is taken over all persons in class j. Let y_i represent quantities of nonlabor input i, where $i = 1, \ldots, I$, and let x denote output. Write $y = (y_1, \ldots, y_I)$ and $z = (z_1, \ldots, z_J)$. Then the firm's production function is given by

$$x = f(y, z, a, r) \qquad (5.2)$$

defined for all $y > 0$, $z > 0$, a in A and r in $\mathscr{R}$. Actually since it only serves to limit the values that a can take on and does not affect output directly, r need not be listed as an argument of f. But retaining r in the production function introduces no difficulties and at the same time provides convenience and suggestiveness that is useful below. In the currently fashionable theory of the firm, y and z are picked by the firm and the presence of a and r are ignored. The following retains selection of y and z within the province of the firm but views the choice of a and r (except r_0) as coming from the worker. Determination of y and z are considered first for fixed (but not-necessarily-quantifiable) values of a and r.

Let the firm pay each employee k a wage w_k per unit of time according to the incentive function w^k where

$$w_k = W^k(a_k, r_k) \qquad k = 1, \ldots, K \tag{5.3}$$

and W^k is defined on $A_k \times \mathscr{R}_k$. Nonmonetary incentives such as the possibility of promotion and guaranteed long-term employment are not considered. Because rules dictated from above restrict person k to a subset ρ_k of A_k (recall equation 5.1), some wages w_k might not actually be available to him. Moreover, since the firm makes no distinctions between co-workers, it is reasonable to require that for any pair of workers k' and k'' in the same co-worker class, incentive functions reward equal work with equal pay. Let "equal work" be defined for k' and k'' in terms of some equivalence relation $\ominus_{k'k''}$ on $(A_{k'} \times \mathscr{R}_{k'}) \cup (A_{k''} \times \mathscr{R}_{k''})$. Then the firm provides equal pay for equal work when for all $(a_{k'}, r_{k'})$ in $A_{k'} \times \mathscr{R}_{k'}$ and all $(a_{k''}, r_{k''})$ in $A_{k''} \times \mathscr{R}_{k''}$,

$$(a_{k'}, r_{k'}) \ominus_{k'k''} (a_{k''}, r_{k''})$$

if and only if

$$w_{k'} = w_{k''}$$

Supposing, moreover, that all workers in each co-worker class execute equal work, there are only J distinct wage rates paid by the firm namely, $w_1, \ldots,$ w_J. Note the aforementioned fixity of (a, r) in the production function 5.2 now implies that the w_j play the role of given parameters. Under these conditions the profit, π, of the firm is expressed as

$$\pi = qf(y, z, a, r) - p \cdot y - w \cdot z$$

where p is an I-vector of nonlabor input prices, $w = (w_1, \ldots, w_J)$, q denotes the price of the output, and the dot indicates "inner product." To keep matters simple, the director is paid out of profits rather than provided a wage.

The selection of incentive functions W^k by the firm (or its director) deserves comment. On one hand, the W^k may be constant functions assigning the same wage to every (a_k, r_k). Alternatively, those values of $(a, r) = (a_1,$

$\ldots, a_K, r_1, \ldots, r_J)$ which enhance the productivity or profitability of the firm may be rewarded with a higher wage by the W^k. In the latter case, however, suppose that for fixed values of $q, p_1, \ldots, p_I, y$, and z, output is higher at (a', r') than at (a'', r''). If profit is also to be larger at (a', r'), then it is necessary for the firm to set the W^k so that the additional wages paid employees at (a', r') over those paid at (a'', r'') are less than the additional revenue received at (a', r'). Were this not always the case, then the most productive (a, r) need not be the most profitable, and hence moving to increase productivity might reduce profitability. Formally, the collection of incentive functions $\{W^k\}$, one for each employee $k = 1, \ldots, K$, is said to be *profit-efficient*[13] whenever

$$f(y, z, a', r') \geq f(y, z, a'', r'')$$

implies

$$qf(y, z, a', r') - p \cdot y - \sum_{j=1}^{J} z_j W^j(a', r') \geq$$

$$qf(y, z, a'', r'') - p \cdot y - \sum_{j=1}^{J} z_j W^j(a'', r'')$$

for all (a', r') and (a'', r'') in $A \times \mathcal{R}$, and all $y > 0$ and $z > 0$, where W^j is a representative incentive function for co-worker class j. Profit-efficient incentives, then, have the property that productivity increases due to changes in (a, r) always are translated into greater profit. Note that in addition to incentives which provide wage raises that are smaller then resulting revenue increases, all collections of constant incentive functions are also profit-efficient.

As usual, p and q are determined in perfectly competitive input and output markets. Continuing with the restriction that a, r, and hence w are fixed, assume further that f, as a function of y and z, has sufficient nonnegativity, smoothness, increasingness, and convexity properties to validate the propositions stated below. Now let x, y, and z be chosen so as to maximize π. Then in the traditional way, values of marginal products at the maximum are equated to input prices:

$$qf_i(y, z, a, r) = p_i \qquad i = 1, \ldots, I$$
$$qf_{I+j}(y, z, a, r) = w_j \qquad j = 1, \ldots, J$$

where p_i is the price of input i and f_i (or f_{I+j}) is the partial derivative of f with respect to its ith (or $I+j$th) argument. Solving and substituting the solution into 5.2 yields the ordinary input demand and output supply functions,

$$y_i = h^i(q, p, a, r) \qquad\qquad i = 1, \ldots, I$$
$$z_j = h^{I+j}(q, p, a, r) \qquad\quad j = 1, \ldots, J \qquad\qquad (5.4)$$
$$x = h^{I+J+1}(q, p, a, r)$$

except that here x, y, and z also depend on a and r. As long as the latter remain fixed, the well-known comparative statics properties of such functions apply. To the extent that the given vector (a, r) does not reflect equal work by all pairs of workers in the same co-worker class, these results must be modified accordingly.

Thus even in this more general setting, the time-honored theory of the economic firm remains essentially intact. But it now is embedded in a world which recognizes that individuals are responsible for carrying out the activities of production, and that the way these responsibilities are met is a significant element in determining the firm's output and profitability. The coordination and accomplishment of the activities of production alone, without direct reliance on a price mechanism for guidance is, according to Coase (1937, pp. 388, 389), the distinguishing feature in the economist's notion of a firm. The next section looks at the individual's decision making and at some of the coordinating instruments that bring the activities of production to fruition.

Workers

Two coordinating instruments, of course, have already been built into the model. First, rules are issued from the director down through the pyramid of authority and these serve to define the activity limits within which each worker may operate. Second, an incentive function (equation 5.3) is furnished for each worker in an attempt to induce him to choose, within boundaries set by the rules imposed upon him, those activities and rules for others that are best from the point of view of the firm. A third coordinating instrument, introduced here, is the leadership and influence exercised by supervisors in their provision of information, training, encouragement, and advice to subordinates. Such leadership is needed to support supervisors' authority since the latter often is insufficient to guarantee "correct" choices of activities and rules by subordinates (see Simon, 1957a, pp. 14, 15). This last coordinating instrument is accounted for by supposing that each worker $k \neq 0$ perceives a goals and premises $(g\text{-}p)$ function

$$g_k = G^k(a_k, r_k) \qquad\qquad (5.5)$$

on $A_k \times \mathscr{R}_k$, in which g_k varies over ordinal numbers expressing what he thinks to be the preferences of his supervisor for points in $A_k \times \mathscr{R}_k$. The G^k

are taken to be given and the characteristics they might be expected to possess are not discussed. g-p functions are independent of incentive functions. They rely on social rather than economic pressures for their effect.

It should be noted in passing that, among other things, workers may also be influenced by the values of their co-workers, and by the information (relevant for their job or otherwise, true or false) circulating around the firm. These kinds of social interactions are not difficult to include; but since, in light of present purposes, there is little to be gained by doing so, the necessary effort is not worth expending.[14] Instead, attention now focuses briefly on workers' decisions.

To complete the above description of the economic firm, workers are required to choose the activities they perform and the rules they issue. Generally these are picked simultaneously along with labor time supplied and consumption. It will simplify matters considerably, however, if decisions regarding activities and rules are kept both separate from and prior to those concerning labor supply and consumption. In each case the worker is assumed to be a constrained utility maximizer. Observe that once activities and rules are obtained (as described below) the worker can treat his wage per unit of time as a fixed parameter according to equation 5.3. Hence the calculation of labor time e_k, for every worker $k \neq 0$, proceeds in the usual manner by maximizing a utility function over consumption-leisure space subject to an appropriate budget constraint.

Turning to the selection of activities and rules, worker k's (k $\neq$0) utility function is written to make the role of incentives and influences explicit: Let

$$\mu_k = u^k(a_k, r_k, w_k, g_k) \tag{5.6}$$

be defined for all appropriate values of (a_k, r_k, w_k, g_k). Substitution of 5.3 and 5.5 into 5.6 yields

$$\mu_k = U^k(a_k, r_k) \tag{5.7}$$

where

$$U^k(a_k, r_k) = u^k[a_k, r_k, W^k(a_k, r_k), G^k(a_k, r_k)]$$

and $k = 1, \ldots, K$. Suppose (a, r) emerges uniquely from the simultaneous maximization[15] of $U^k(a_k, r_k)$ for all $k \neq 0$, subject to the constraints that a_k is consistent with all rules imposed from above, i.e., a_k is in ρ_k, for $k = 1, \ldots, K$. Recall that the ρ_k consist of intersections (equation 5.1) of certain components of r. Obviously, the latter constraints ensure that every ρ_k coming out of these K maximizations is nonempty. Thus workers choose internally consistent values for (a, r), the firm hires a vector (y, z) as indicated at the end of the last subsection, and the firm's output and profit are determined.

The assumption of prior determination of (a, r) also permits a simple explanation of the functioning of labor markets. In labor market j (there is one for each wage) the supply of labor is generated by aggregating over workers participating in that market. The behavior of each is based on a utility-maximizing, consumption-leisure choice as indicated above. Labor demand is secured as the sum across firms of the relevant functions derived from profit maximization, as in 5.4. (It is necessary to suppose here, as it is within the single firm, that all workers in the market, regardless of where they work, do "similar" jobs and are rewarded with the same pay.) The market wage w_j is obtained from appropriate components of the predetermined vectors (a, r) for all participating firms in conjunction with incentive functions like 5.3. If this wage is too low so that demand is greater than supply, then firms adjust incentive functions so that the "same work" receives a higher wage. If the market wage is too high, competition among workers alters incentive functions obversely. Thus, although relative incentive scales are maintained to encourage the worker to behave (while on the job) in the interest of the firm, their absolute levels are varied to equilibrate demand and supply.

At this point, three implicit assumptions ought to be brought out into the open. First, only social interaction among workers connected along lines of authority is considered here. Such interaction appears in the issuance and acceptance of rules and incentives, in the attempt by supervisors to influence subordinates through goals and premise functions, and in the response of workers to these elements as reflected by their choices of activities and rules for others. Social interaction among co-workers, such as the interplay of personal values and the sharing of information mentioned earlier, has been ruled out. Were this not done, individual utility maximization could be more complex since decisions made by one person might then depend on those made by others. Second, upon selection of activities from utility maximization, each worker k is presumed to carry out his chosen activity a_k according to expected standards. In other words, performance is not determined separately after the selection of all (a_k, r_k). If performance were permitted to vary, then output could not yet be found from the production function 5.2 as described above since the vector (a, r) actually performed would still not be known. Third, it is supposed that each subordinate and his supervisor has identical perceptions of the former's activity set, of the rules prescribed by the latter for the former, and of the preferences of the supervisor for points in the subordinate's set $A_k \times \mathcal{R}_k$ (as appearing in the g-p function facing the subordinate). Thus confusion resulting from differing perceptions is precluded. The Wittgensteinian possibility that a subordinate conceives of his job in different qualitative terms from his supervisor (e.g., applies paint to a wall less thickly than the supervisor expected), and hence induces an unexpected quality to the firm's output, does not arise.

Skill and Preference Modification

It is now time to examine some of the comparative statics properties of input demand and output supply functions (equations 5.4) with respect to (a, r) and the functions W^k, G^k, and u^k lying implicitly in the background. To do so, however, first requires the development of analytical structure. In the traditional theory of the firm, such structure—upon which derivations of comparative-statics propositions with respect to q and p rest—is found in conventional economic concepts like "isoquant," in the nonnegativity, smoothness, increasingness, and convexity characteristics of production as a function of input magnitudes, and also in the commonly used traits of quantitative spaces and functions that permit such things as differentiation and the definition of numerical order. Clearly none of this is available here and it is therefore necessary to start from scratch.

Discussion begins with three notions of order. Fix $k \neq 0$. For any a'_k and a''_k in A_k, write $a'_k \geq a''_k$ whenever replacement of a''_k by a'_k in the firm's production function does not lower output no matter what the values of the remaining components a_{k° in (a, r), where $k^\circ \neq k$. Next, for any pair of nonempty, admissible rules R'_{kk° and R''_{kk° imposed by k on k°, define $R'_{kk^\circ} \geq R''_{kk^\circ}$ provided that $R'_{kk^\circ} \subseteq R''_{kk^\circ}$ and if a'_{k° is in R'_{kk° and a''_{k° is in $R''_{kk^\circ} - R'_{kk^\circ}$, then $a'_{k^\circ} \geq a''_{k^\circ}$. In other words, R'_{kk° restricts k° to a subset of R''_{kk° on which output is at least as high as that at any point of $R''_{kk^\circ} - R'_{kk^\circ}$. Take $r'_k \geq r''_k$ to mean $R'_{kk^\circ} \geq R''_{kk^\circ}$ for all k° below k. Finally, for all (a'_k, r'_k) and (a''_k, r''_k), put $(a'_k, r'_k) \geq (a''_k, r''_k)$ if and only if both $a'_k \geq a''_k$ and $r'_k \geq r''_k$. All three relations are reflexive, transitive and antisymmetric; and all generate the usual derivative relations $>$ and $=$ appropriately defined (see Gintis and Katzner, 1979, pp. 283, 284). Confusion will not arise by employing the same symbol of order, namely $\geq$, for all three meanings. (Note that $\geq$ also refers to "greater than or equal to" when numbers are involved.) Context determines the appropriate interpretation.

The following concepts provide a vocabulary in terms of which subsequent comparative statics propositions emerge. The incentive function W^k is called *nondecreasing on* A_k whenever $a'_k \geq a''_k$ ensures $W^k(a'_k, r_k) \geq W^k(a''_k, r_k)$ numerically, for any a'_k, a''_k, and r_k. It is said to be *nondecreasing on* $A_k \times \mathcal{R}_k$ as long as $W^k(a'_k, r'_k) \geq W^k(a''_k, r''_k)$ arises from $(a'_k, r'_k) \geq (a''_k, r''_k)$, for every a'_k, a''_k, r'_k, and r''_k. Similarly, G^k can be non-decreasing on A_k or $A_k \times \mathcal{R}_k$. Now worker $k \neq 0$ is *incentive motivated* if for all a'_k, a''_k, r'_k, and r_k'', the numerical inequality

$$W^k(a_k', r_k') \geq W^k(a_k'', r_k'')$$

implies (recall equation 5.7):

$$U^k(a_k', r_k') \geq U^k(a_k'', r_k'')$$

He is *vertically influenced* when

$$G^k(a_k', r_k') \geq G^k(a_k'', r_k'')$$

(also a numerical relation) forces

$$U^k(a_k', r_k') \geq U^k(a_k'', r_k'')$$

again for all a_k', a_k'', r_k', and r_k''. And he *internalizes the values of the firm* provided that for all a_k', a_k'', r_k', and r_k'', if $(a_k', r_k') \geq (a_k'', r_k'')$, then

$$U^k(a_k', r_k') \geq U^k(a_k'', r_k'')$$

The last three definitions respectively depict worker k's preferences as receptive to incentives, influence, and the expansion of output. With W^k and G^k nondecreasing on $A_k \times \mathcal{R}_k$, any person k exhibiting one or more of these characteristics cooperates "naturally" in the carrying out of production within the firm.

Suppose that the preferences of worker k are permitted to vary. Let $\mathcal{U}^k$ be a class of utility functions each of which represents a unique preference-order possibility for k. Thus $\mathcal{U}^k$ contains no increasing transformations of any of its elements. Likewise, take $\mathcal{W}$ to be a collection of admissible incentive functions. Consider any $\bar{U}^k$ and $\hat{U}^k$ in $\mathcal{U}^k$ and use the symbolism $(\bar{a}_k, \bar{r}_k)$ and $(\hat{a}_k, \hat{r}_k)$ to denote the (unique) vectors chosen by constrained utility maximization from, respectively, $\bar{U}^k$ and $\hat{U}^k$. If

$$(\bar{a}_k, \bar{r}_k) \geq (\hat{a}_k, \hat{r}_k)$$

then $\bar{U}^k$ is said to *dominate* $\hat{U}^k$. Alternatively, k is referred to as being *more highly motivated by incentives* under $\bar{U}^k$ than under $\hat{U}^k$ provided

$$W^k(\bar{a}_k, \bar{r}_k) \geq W^k(\hat{a}_k, \hat{r}_k)$$

for all W^k in $\mathcal{W}$. In the former instance, preferences dominate when they generate more productive choices; in the latter, k is more highly motivated by incentives under certain preferences if choices based on these preferences lead to larger wages regardless of the incentive function. The idea that k can be *more highly motivated by influence* under $\bar{U}^k$ than under $\hat{U}^k$ is described analogously.

The last definitions introduced here have to do with the skills of the worker. Let $A_k \subset A_k^*$, where $A_k \neq A_k^*$, for some k. Person k is said to have become *more skilled* if the following two conditions are met: (i) A_k^* is substituted for A_k in making his decisions, and (ii) for all (a_k^*, r_k^*) and (a_k, r_k) such that $r_k^* \geq r_k$, if a_k is in A_k and a_k^* is in $A_k^* - A_k$, then $(a_k^*, r_k^*) \geq (a_k, r_k)$. Skills are thus improved when act sets expand to include activities leading to increased output. But this definition by itself guarantees neither that k will use his new skills (i.e., actually choose an act from $A_k^* - A_k$) nor that co-workers will not attempt to subvert them. As will be seen momentarily, the first possibility can be prevented by invoking one of the notions of cooperation discussed above. To handle the second requires a final concept: The firm is *receptive to new skills* of k whenever, upon substitution of A_k^* for A_k in the simultaneous constrained maximization of all U^k, the ρ_k (defined in equation 5.1) generated by that maximization contain at least one element of $A_k^* - A_k$.

Several properties of the firm's output supply function $h^{I + J + 1}$ (from 5.4) with respect to a, r, W^k, G^k, and u^k can now be described. Each assumes that workers are in a utility-maximizing stance and asks what happens to output when certain things change and appropriate maximizations are repeated. Labor time and nonlabor inputs, that is (y, z), are assumed fixed. The properties are listed below in a series of six propositions. Proofs are available elsewhere.[16]

Theorem 1. Let the firm be receptive to new skills of k and suppose k internalizes the values of the firm. If k becomes more skilled and no other worker alters his chosen acts and rules, then output either rises or remains unchanged.

Theorem 2. Let the firm be receptive to new skills of k and let W^k be nondecreasing on A_k. Suppose k is incentive motivated. If k becomes more skilled and no other worker alters his chosen acts and rules, then output either rises or remains unchanged.

Theorem 3. Let the firm be receptive to new skills of k and let G^k be nondecreasing on A_k. Suppose k is vertically influenced. If k becomes more skilled and no other worker alters his chosen acts and rules, then output either rises or remains unchanged.

Theorem 4. Let k change preferences. If the new utility function dominates the old and if no other worker alters his chosen acts and rules, then output either rises or remains unchanged.

Theorem 5.   Let k change preferences and W^k be nondecreasing on A_k. If k is more highly motivated by incentives under the new utility function and if no other worker alters his chosen acts and rules, then output either rises or remains unchanged.

Theorem 6.   Let k change preferences and G^k be nondecreasing on A_k. If k is more highly motivated by influence under the new utility function and if no other worker alters his chosen acts and rules, then output either rises or remains unchanged.

To the extent that the weak inequalities ($\geq$) in the previous list of definitions are replaced, in theorems 1–6, by their associated strong inequalities ($>$), the conclusions of these theorems can be strengthened to assert that output must rise. If, in addition, incentives are profit-efficient, then profit must rise or remain constant with output.

Thus, in the narrow context of this arithmomorphic model and with the deletion of all dialectical possibilities, new skills and new preferences will, under certain conditions, increase output and profit. Alternatively put, in choosing among individuals to fill its positions, the firm should be interested not only in skills but in other attributes, like incentive motivation, as well. Further comparative statics questions—such as (i) if output is fixed and labor time and nonlabor inputs vary, what is the impact of alterations in skills and preferences? and (ii) in what ways are theorems 1–6 and the answer to (i) affected by permitting x, y, and z to all change simultaneously?—require still additional structure and are not pursued here. The problem of how to select the incentive functions W^k so as to maximize profit given individual utility functions also is ignored. Instead, attention now turns to the issue of efficiency within the firm.

Internal Pareto Optimality

It is well known that under certain conditions in a perfectly competitive economy, equilibrium is Pareto optimal. Thus, with initial endowments given, with consumers buying output quantities and supplying factor quantities so as to maximize utility subject to their budget constraints, with firms selling output quantities and buying input quantities so as to maximize profit, and with supply equal to demand in all markets, quantities of outputs and inputs can not be redistributed among consumers and firms without lowering some output or making at least one person worse off. This proposition is fundamental to the Walrasian vision of microeconomic reality. Its significance lies in the efficiency property it imparts to equilibrium distributions of inputs, outputs, and consumption. For to say such a distribution is Pareto optimal means that the utility (or output) level of any one consumer (or, respectively, firm) achieved in the distribution is the largest possible given the remaining allocations of the distribution. In other words, perfect competition "wastes" nothing at equilibrium. Thus, as suggested by Smith (1937, p. 423), the "invisible hand," which coordinates market behavior based on maximization, leads individuals to an end which they do not intend and which benefits society.

Previous discussion has attempted to analyze more completely the production process within the perfectly competitive firm by drawing its arithmomorphic boundary so as to more fully describe how production takes place. A model accounting for part of the social interaction of employees in their jobs has been proposed. Each worker picks rules for those beneath him and likewise is constrained in the selection of this own activities by rules imposed from above. In making these choices workers also are subjected to various influences and incentives. As indicated, everything takes place in the context of rationality and perfect competition. And so, with individuals still making decisions on the basis of maximization, the traditional question once again arises concerning the end toward which workers and the firm are lead by the nonmarket invisible hands that, under varying circumstances, coordinate behavior internally within the firm: Is it wasteful or efficient?[17]

The first thing to notice is that efficiency in the economy is entirely independent of efficiency within the firm. Pareto optimality may arise in the distribution of consumption, output, and input quantities with considerable waste in production itself. Obversely, decisions concerning activities and rules could result in efficient production even when the optimality of economy-wide equilibrium fails—perhaps due to the presence of monopoly or other market imperfections. (Previous argument may be modified in the traditional manner to accommodate whatever form of imperfect competition one might wish to impose on the firm.) In what follows, then, interest centers on efficiency in production only. As before, the vector (y, z) is taken to be fixed. Notation is simplified by abbreviating the production function (equation 5.2) to

$$x = f(a, r)$$

The same analytical structure introduced to develop the comparative statics of input demand and output supply functions (see the previous subsection) is employed.

Let $g\text{-}p$ (goals and premise) functions G^k and incentive functions W^k be given for every $k \neq 0$. Write $a^\circ = (a_1^\circ, \ldots, a_K^\circ)$ and $r^\circ = (r_1^\circ, \ldots, r_K^\circ)$. A vector (a°, r°) in $A \times \mathcal{R}$ is called *internally Pareto optimal in production*, or just *Pareto optimal*, provided that there is no other (a, r) in $A \times \mathcal{R}$ such that

$$U^k(a_k, r_k) \geq U^k(a_k^\circ, r_k^\circ)$$

for all $k = 1, \ldots, K$,

$$U^k(a_k, r_k) > U^k(a_k^\circ, r_k^\circ)$$

for at least one $k = 1, \ldots, K$, and

$$f(a, r) \geq f(a^\circ, r^\circ)$$

where all $\geq$ refer to numerical relations. Thus at a Pareto optimum, no reorganization of production in terms of activities and rules can make one worker better off, and no other worker worse off, without lowering output. Note that the director is not included in this concept of Pareto optimality.

On the basis of notions of incentive motivation, internalization of the values of the firm, and vertical influence defined earlier, different sets of conditions sufficient for Pareto optimality obtain. These are stated as three propositions. The parallel between them and theorems 1–3 above is worth noting. Once again, proofs are ignored.[18] It is convenient to prescribe one assumption beforehand, namely, that both the $\geq$ on A_k and the $\geq$ on $\mathcal{R}_k$ be total for every $k \neq 0$. (Note this implies that $\geq$ is total on $A_k \times \mathcal{R}_k$ for all $k = 1, \ldots, K$.) In consequence, the characterizing implication in each of the definitions of nondecreasingness of W^k and G^k on $A_k \times \mathcal{R}_k$, incentive motivation, internalization of the values of the firm, and vertical influence points in both directions. Thus, for example, W^k is now nondecreasing on $A_k \times \mathcal{R}_k$ whenever

$$(a_k', r_k') \geq (a_k'', r_k'')$$

if and only if

$$W^k(a_k', r_k') \geq W^k(a_k'', r_k'')$$

for all a_k', a_k'', r_k' and r_k''. With the totality of $\geq$ on the A_k and $\mathcal{R}_k$ in force, the propositions are as follows:

Theorem 7. Let incentives be profit-efficient and suppose all workers internalize the values of the firm. If (a°, r°) maximizes profit over $A \times \mathcal{R}$, then (a°, r°) is Pareto optimal.

Theorem 8. Let incentives be profit-efficient, let all workers be vertically influenced, and suppose G^k is nondecreasing on $A_k \times \mathcal{R}_k$ for each

$k = 1, \ldots, K$. If (a^o, r^o) maximizes profit over $A \times \mathcal{R}$, then (a^o, r^o) is Pareto optimal.

Theorem 9. Let incentives be profit-efficient, let all workers be incentive motivated, and suppose W^k is nondecreasing on $A_k \times \mathcal{R}_k$ for each $k = 1, \ldots, K$. If (a^o, r^o) maximizes profit over $A \times \mathcal{R}$, then (a^o, r^o) is Pareto optimal.

Each of the above theorems assumes as one of its hypotheses that (a^o, r^o) maximizes profit over $A \times \mathcal{R}$. This supposition by itself is not enough to guarantee Pareto optimality. Although it implies that $(a_k^o, r_k^o) \geq (a_k, r_k)$ for every (a_k, r_k) in $A_k \times \mathcal{R}_k$ and all $k \neq 0$, to establish the propositions still requires that (a_k^o, r_k^o) also maximize each worker's utility. This is ensured by the remaining assumptions.

An answer to the big question, namely, under what conditions does internal equilibrium within the firm result in Pareto optimality? is now within easy reach. Recall g-p functions, incentive functions, and production functions are given along with the pyramid of authority, the director's rules, and individual activity and admissible rule sets. Workers alone choose their acts and the rules they issue. In conformity with earlier argument, then, *internal equilibrium* is defined as a vector $(\bar{a}, \bar{r})$ such that $(\bar{a}_k, \bar{r}_k)$ maximizes the utility of worker k subject to (a_k, r_k) being within the collection of all rules, ρ_k, imposed upon him from above, where $k = 1, \ldots, K$. According to earlier assumptions alluded to but not spelled out, such an equilibrium always exists. Let $\bar{\rho}_k$ be the constraint set determined by $(\bar{a}, \bar{r})$ for $k \neq 0$. Now if, in addition to the hypotheses of theorems 7, 8, or 9, the profit-maximizing vector (a_k^o, r_k^o) also lies in $\bar{\rho}$ for all $k \neq 0$, then in every case, $(a_k^o, r_k^o) = (\bar{a}_k, \bar{r}_k)$. Hence internal equilibrium is Pareto optimal. Evidently, internalization of the values of the firm, vertical influence, and incentive motivation, each in its own way, makes some contribution towards preventing wastefulness in the carrying out of production.

The Limits of Formalism

The study of social interaction in the economic firm just considered displays all of the characteristics of a formalist analysis. It has concepts such as profit efficiency and incentive motivation, and variables like firm profit and workers' activities. Its axioms include assertions about the existence of production and utility functions, each having enough properties to permit appropriate maximization, along with statements about certain ordering relations among activities and rules, also with specific properties. Functions are manipulated by composition or substitution of variables (for example, in passage from equation 5.6 to equation 5.7), addition, and multiplication (recall the definition of profit efficiency). Variable and function values[19] are manipulated by classifications (the designation of rule sets), by the aforementioned ordering relations (as in the definitions of nondecreasing incentives), and by ordinary arithmetic operations (see the definition of firm profit). And deductive reasoning is employed throughout.

The main implications obtained by applying manipulative procedures and deductive reasoning to the concepts, variables, and axioms, are the assertions about the impact on output (and profit) of skill and preference modification among employees, and about the relationship between profit and utility maximization and internal equilibrium on one hand, and internal Pareto optimality on the other. The first group of implications are summarized in theorems 1–6; the second in theorems 7–9 and the subsequent conclusion linking internal equilibrium within the firm to internal Pareto optimality. Still further implications also could have been explored. For example, a version of the proposition that becoming more skilled increases a worker's wage could be established (Becker, 1975), and by lifting the previously imposed requirement that rules are costless to implement, the optimum firm size could be calculated (Calvo and Wellisz, 1978; Williamson, 1967).

As argued in the section on prerequisites, all of the concepts, variables, and functions employed in this analysis are distinctly discrete arithmomorphic extractions from nondiscrete dialectical entities. In addition, none of the manipulative rules of classification, order, composition, arithmetic operations, and even deductive reasoning has any basis at all in the underlying dialectical scheme. Each is an abstract notion introduced solely for the purpose of generating implications. Different arithmomorphic extractions, different manipulative rules, and hence different implications can not be ruled out. There can be little doubt, then, that the old criticism of the formalist school, which arises because of the abstractness of the formalist approach and which, as a consequence, questions its relevance in studying reality, has not been escaped in the application of formalism in economics. The results that one obtains by using formalism in economics are necessarily somewhat removed from ordinary life.

The complaint that formalism is too abstract clearly derives from the loss of dialectical content required for the construction of formalist models. A small portion of this loss has been described specifically for the model concerned with social interaction as the loss resulting from the fact that only certain very special kinds of activities and rules are permitted. All other variables in the model involve similar losses. Moreover, additional losses of dialectical content emerge from the functions employed. Still further losses come from the abstraction that maximization is the driving force behind firm and worker behavior. Since every one of these abstractions is arbitrary, and since none of them can be justified as the "correct" representation of reality, the criticism that the model is some distance away from describing the actual social interactions in the economic firm can not be dismissed out of hand. It is not that the specific assumptions of some formalist models are better than others. Rather it is that all such sets of assumptions (each of which serves as the basis for a separate formalist model) are constrained by the arbitrary limits imposed so as to be able to use formalism in the first place.

Note that measurement is not at issue here. The same problem of the relationship of the real world to the constructs, axioms, and implications of formalist analysis turns up regardless of whether the variables employed may legitimately be represented by numbers. Attacking the meaningfulness and appropriateness of certain numerical quantifications is certainly not the same thing as an assault on the use of formalism. But since, as has already been pointed out, measurement requires its own (independent) formalisms, any difficulties relating to formalism in general necessarily pertain to the use of formalism to derive measures in particular. Thus, as is the case with all formalist argument, one may also ask about the real-world relevance of introducing abstract measures into the investigation of actuality.

The second criticism of formalism invoked by the opponents of the formalist school, namely that nonconstructive proofs of existence may establish the abstract existence of entities in models but can never establish the existence of such entities in reality, is also germane to the application of formalism in economics. Hence, to show—the proof is nonconstructive—that internal equilibrium always exists as the outcome of utility maximization on the part of each worker (a proposition asserted but not proved in an earlier section) is not to demonstrate the existence of internal equilibrium in a real firm. Economists often fill such a gap between what is shown to exist in a model and what is seen to exist in reality by interpreting the latter as the former. In other words, what one would observe by looking at an actual firm at any moment would be identified as an internal equilibrium. This then permits the assertion that the model explains what is seen. As a further illustration, observations of price and quantity sold in a particular market during a period of time are frequently understood as equilibria in a model of the market containing demand and supply functions.[20] That is, the observations are explained as the outcome of the interaction of demand and supply.

Thus, to the extent that formalist analysis in economics employs nonconstructive entities, interpretation of these entities is essential if the links between the analysis and actuality are to be comprehended. The formalist approach itself gives no clues or standards for determining what these interpretations should be. And of course, different interpretations yield different explanations of the same thing.

In addition to the above limitations, formalism also faces the Wittgenstein problem that the meanings of the relations of a formalist analysis are not absolute and unchanging over time: One is not committed to the same understandings of them each moment they come up.

It should be emphasized that all of these limitations emerge solely from the particular discipline that formalism imposes on our mental forms. Thus the issue of relevance of formalist analysis in understanding reality derives from the things that have to be thrown out, the concessions that have to be made, in order to proceed from dialectical foundations and arrive at the abstract starting gate where formalist analysis can begin. The reason for caution over the meaning of formalist relations may be attributed to the abstraction procedure, which results in functions that are deceptively well defined. Lastly, the necessity for interpretation of nonconstructive entities emerges from the abstract manipulative rules that are employed in leaving the starting gate and developing formalist analyses.

The Power of Formalism

And what, then, can be said for the use of formalism in economics? To be sure, formalist analysis may always be employed in arithmomorphic simile to look for error in dialectical reasoning. But it also has a broader application in the building of arithmomorphic metaphors of dialectical experience. Metaphors in economics serve as both an instrument of thought and as a device for communicating meaning (McCloskey, 1983). Their force lies in that they transfer the sense of one person's vision to another. They are figures of communication in which one thing, say thing A, is likened to a different thing, call it thing B, by speaking of A "as if" it were B. A market operates as if to equate demand and supply. Economic analysis is heavily metaphorical and formalism provides one way of developing metaphors.

And these metaphors are powerful! They permit an analyst to focus his or her thoughts in a concrete and precise fashion on variables and relations that seem important by current professional standards.[21] In the example of formalism given earlier, the production function incorporates the idea that inputs are related to output. But production is more than just a technological process: Social interactions among employees are entangled in its structure and influence both output and firm profit. Confining attention in this manner permits the drawing of specific conclusions about the effects of improved worker skills on the output and profit of the firm, and about the efficiency of the production process itself. The model and these conclusions constitute an "ideal type" or mental construction which isolates what are thought to be "fundamental" forces of reality for study by themselves in the absence of the "secondary" and still less important forces also thought to be present. Hence the investigator can gain an understanding of the ideal system functioning alone as a "first step" in his exploration of reality. At a later stage (and this is rarely attempted by those employing formalism) dialectical reality may be introduced and the initial formalism abandoned.

These metaphors also provide standards for judging real-world behaviors; that is, in our earlier example, standards for deciding whether actual firm and worker behavior is, in fact, maximizing. Lastly, the metaphors are relatively easy for those who wish to pursue similar analyses within the formalist framework to modify and extend as new techniques, new concepts, and new assumptions are introduced. Again referring to the earlier example, novelty appears in the use of nonquantifiable variables and in the formalization of the idea that social interaction among employees is, in certain specific ways, significant in production.

But formalist metaphors are still extractions from dialectical perceptions of reality. They are abstract. They often contain nonconstructive entities requiring interpretation. And so on. Hence such metaphors can only be regarded as very crude "approximations" of the real world. With this in mind, an epilogue to our discussion of the optimality of internal equilibrium might run as follows:

According to theorems 7–9, internalization of the values of the firm, vertical influence, and incentive motivation each helps to prevent wastefulness in production. But none, by itself, is enough. And the very real possibility exists that actual economic behavior may not reasonably fit any of them. Moreover, the assumptions of totality of $\geq$ on each A_k, and on each $\mathscr{R}_k$, and of output-maximizing (a_k^o, r_k^o) lying in $\bar{\rho}_k$, are equally tenuous. The first insists on a kind of independence among the activities of workers. The second throws out all rule sets from each $\mathscr{R}_k$ except those that form a certain kind of nested sequence under set inclusion. And the third requires that rules issued by different persons also line up in a very special way. The Lordstown case[22] is an example in which the hypotheses of these theorems generally do not seem to apply. In reality, the forces allocating activities and rules within actual firms may be insufficient to secure the nonwastefulness of internal equilibrium.

Marshall was similarly circumspect in his view of the demand-supply analysis of an isolated market:

The theory of ... equilibrium ... of demand and supply helps indeed to give definiteness to our ideas; and in its elementary stages it does not diverge from the actual facts of life, so far as to prevent its giving a fairly trustworthy picture of the chief methods of action of the strongest and most persistent group of economic forces. But when pushed to its more remote and intricate logical consequences, it slips away from the conditions of real life. (Marshall, 1948, p. 461)

Why is formalism as a general approach so compelling and appealing to economists? One reason is the power (described above) of the metaphors it is able to produce. Moreover, in the arithmomorphic contexts in which it is set, formalism has rendered errors in deductive reasoning easier to detect; it has deepened understanding; and it has increased the simplicity, elegance, and generality of argument. It has provided a clear and precise way of organizing thoughts and it has made available the efficient language of mathematics for use in developing and reporting research (Debreu, 1959, p. viii; 1984, p. 275). And, most important, it has led to what are considered to be significant arithmomorphic results.

Citing the fact that the subject does not have a "unique, rigorous, logical structure," Kline characterizes mathematics as "... a series of great intuitions carefully sifted, refined, and organized by the logic men are willing and able to apply at any time" (Kline, 1980, p. 312). These intuitions have had an enormous impact on economics, largely entering our discipline through formalist analyses. Even though mathematics may be inconsistent, even though the correct foundation for it may never be determined, and even though it is incomplete, mathematics has still been effective in various fields—and no one knows why (Kline, 1980, p. 7). Mathematics, after all, has been instrumental in sending man to the moon. In the guise of formalism, it has been employed throughout economics. Also as formalism, it appears in the study of social interaction in the firm. Perhaps the most important accomplishment of mathematical formalism in economics is the demonstration of the possibility of coherence in a world of individuals motivated solely by their own self-interest. While not as spectacular as placing a man on the moon, this may still be regarded as progress.

Notes

1 See the papers by Bausor and Mirowski in this volume (chs. 4 and 6).
2 An expanded discussion may be found in Katzner (1983, sec. 2.2).
3 See, for example, Pfanzagl (1971).
4 Specification of order alone does not, in general, imply (ordinal) measurement as the term

is commonly used (Pfanzagl, 1971, pp. 75, 79).

[5] For example, if $w = e(x)$, $x = f(y)$, and $y = g(z)$ are three functions, then associativity of function composition means that eliminating first x and then y gives the same result as eliminating y first and then x.

[6] A semigroup is a nonempty set on which a closed and associative operation has been defined.

[7] See Mirowski, this volume, ch. 6.

[8] One of the more notorious examples centers around the famous strike at General Motors' Lordstown plant. At the time, this plant was supposed to be the technological showcase for the American automobile industry. But in 1972 things went awry. (See Rothschild 1973, ch. 4; and O'Toole 1977, pp. 89–93.)

[9] The Eagle Project at the Data General Corporation would appear to illustrate the point. (See Kidder 1981.)

[10] The role of individual personality traits, though potentially significant (Filer 1981), is ignored.

[11] A similar variable is introduced and described by Whyte (1955, p. 192).

[12] It is interesting that at least one observer has identified rule changes dictated from above as one of the chief causes of the 1972 Lordstown plant strike (O'Toole 1977, p. 91). See note 8.

[13] This definition of profit efficiency is slightly different from that given by Gintis and Katzner (1979) in that here the weak instead of the strong inequality is employed.

[14] The interested reader is referred to Gintis and Katzner (1979).

[15] Conditions that ensure that functions of nonquantifiable variables can be maximized uniquely are discussed in Katzner (1983, sec. 5.4).

[16] Except for the last, these propositions roughly correspond to theorems 7–11 (or, in the reprinted version, 11.3–1 to 11.3–5), respectively, in Gintis and Katzner (1979). Because they are concerned with profit instead of output, in each case Gintis and Katzner require the extra hypothesis of profit efficiency. The proofs of theorems 1–5 here essentially carry over from those in Gintis and Katzner, with the last step involving profit efficiency omitted. The proof of theorem 6 is analogous to that of theorem 5.

[17] Leibenstein has coined the term "X-inefficiency" to refer to whatever wastefulness might be present (Leibenstein, 1976, p. 95).

[18] Theorems 7 and 8 are more or less identical to, respectively, theorems 5 and 6 (or, 11.2–5 and 11.2–6 in the reprinted version) in Gintis and Katzner (1979). As previously indicated in note 16, proofs of the former are essentially the same as those of the latter. The proof of theorem 9 is similar to that of theorem 8.

The deduction that $d'_w \ominus d^o_w$ in the proof of theorem 5 given by Gintis and Katzner requires $\ominus$ to be total on D_w (their notation). Totality of $\ominus$, however, follows from totality of $\geq$ on A_k and of $\geq$ on $\mathcal{R}_w$—assumptions that were left out of the original. This omission is remedied here in the remainder of the present paragraph. It also has been corrected in the reprinted version of the paper.

[19] Actually, function values are special instances of variable values.

[20] In this case, there are other well-known interpretations. For example, the observations may be thought of as lying on a "dynamic" time path which is converging to equilibrium.

[21] Current professional standards are determined by a complex social and historical interaction among present and the work of past economists involving, in part, the techniques of analysis themselves.

[22] See notes 8 and 12.

References

Becker, G. S. 1975. *Human Capital.* New York: National Bureau of Economic Research.

Calvo, G. A., and Wellisz, S. 1978. Supervision, Loss of Control, and the Optimum Size of the Firm. *Journal of Political Economy* 86:943–952.

Coase, R. H. 1937. The Nature of the Firm. *Economica* 4:386–405.

Cournot, A. 1960. *Researches into the Mathematical Principles of the Theory of Wealth,* N. T. Bacon trans. New York: Kelley.

Debreu, G. 1959. *Theory of Value.* New York: Wiley.

Debreu, G. 1984. Economic Theory in the Mathematical Mode. *American Economic Review* 74:267–278.

Dunlop, J. T. 1958. *Industrial Relations Systems.* New York: Holt, ch. 1.

Filer, R. K. 1981. The Influence of Affective Human Capital on the Wage Equation. *Research in Labor Economics* Vol. 4. R. G. Ehrenberg (ed.). Greenwich, CT: JAI Press, pp. 367–416.

Georgescu-Roegen, N. 1971. *The Entropy Law and the Economic Process.* Cambridge, MA: Harvard University Press.

Gintis, H., and Katzner, D. W. 1979. Profits, Optimality and the Social Division of Labor in the Firm. *Sociological Economics,* L. Lévy-Garboua, ed. London: Sage, pp. 269–297. Reprinted as ch. 11 in D. W. Katzner, 1983.

Hofstadter, D. R. 1979. *Gödel, Escher, Bach: An Eternal Golden Braid.* New York: Basic Books.

Jevons, W. S. 1965. *The Theory of Political Economy,* 5th ed. New York: Kelley.

Katzner, D. W. 1983. *Analysis without Measurement.* Cambridge, UK: Cambridge University Press.

Katzner, D. W. (Forthcoming.) Alternatives to Equilibrium Analysis, *Eastern Economic Journal.*

Kidder, T. 1981. *The Soul of a New Machine.* Boston: Little, Brown.

Kline, M. 1980. *Mathematics: The Loss of Certainty.* New York: Oxford University Press.

Leibenstein, H. 1976. *Beyond Economic Man.* Cambridge, MA: Harvard University Press.

Marshall, A. 1948. *Principles of Economics,* 8th ed. New York: Macmillan.

McCloskey, D. N. 1983. The Rhetoric of Economics. *Journal of Economic Literature* 21:481–517.

Meyerson, E. 1962. *Identity and Reality.* K. Loewenberg trans. New York: Dover.

O'Toole, J. 1977. *Work, Learning and the American Future.* San Francisco: Jossey-Bass.

Pareto, V. 1966. *Manuel d' economie politique.* Trans. into French by A. Bonnet. Geneva: Droz.

Pfanzagl, J. 1971. *Theory of Measurement,* 2nd ed. Würzburg—Vienna: Physica-Verlag.

Rothschild, E. 1973. *Paradise Lost: The Decline of the Auto-Industrial Age.* New York: Random House.

Russell, B. 1959. Knowledge by Acquaintance and Knowledge by Description. *Mysticism and Logic and Other Essays*. London: Allen & Unwin, pp. 209–232.

Simon, H. A. 1957a. *Administrative Behavior*, 2nd ed. New York: Macmillan.

Simon, H. A. 1957b. *Models of Man*. New York: Wiley.

Smith, A. 1937. *An Inquiry into the Nature and Causes of the Wealth of Nations*. New York: Random House.

Thomson, Sir W. (Baron Kelvin). 1891. Electrical Units of Measurement. Lecture delivered on May 3, 1883. In *Popular Lectures and Addresses*, Vol. 1. London: Macmillan, pp. 80–143.

Walras, L. 1954. *Elements of Pure Economics*. W. Jaffé trans. Homewood, IL: Irwin.

Whyte, W. F. 1955. *Money and Motivation*. New York: Harper & Row.

Williamson, O. E. 1967. Hierarchical Control and Optimum Firm Size. *Journal of Political Economy* 75:123–138.

Wright, C. 1980. *Wittgenstein on the Foundations of Mathematics*. Cambridge, MA: Harvard University Press.

6 MATHEMATICAL FORMALISM AND ECONOMIC EXPLANATION

Philip Mirowski

It seems to us nowadays a very simple thing to assign dimensions to magnitudes, so simple that we are apt to forget the extremely important implication of the assertions. When we assert that a certain derived magnitude always has certain dimensions, we are in fact asserting the complete accuracy of the law which determines that derived magnitude under all possible conditions. If there is any doubt whatever about the universality of the law, then there is a corresponding doubt about the dimension of the derived magnitude. . . .

—Campbell, 1957, p. 416

Investigate whether mathematical propositions are not rules of expression, paradigms—propositions dependent on experience but made independent of

*I would like to thank Don Katzner, Robert Paul Wolff, David Ellerman, and Michael McPherson for their helpful and critical comments on an earlier draft. Although (or perhaps because) I did not end up writing the paper that any of them had suggested, they should bear no liability for my errors and extravagances.

Because I found in the course of researching this paper that there was a large literature on the role of mathematics in economics, but most authors seemed unaware of any but their own contributions, I have appended an extensive bibliography which touches upon the issues raised in this paper.

*it. Ask whether mathematical propositions are not made paradigms or ob-
jects of comparison in this way. Paradigms and objects of comparison can
only be called useful or useless, like the choice of the unit of measurement.*

—Wittgenstein, 1976, p. 55

*It is difficult to contemplate the evolution of economic science over the last
hundred years without reaching the conclusion that its mathematization was
rather a hurried job.*

—Georgescu-Roegen, 1976, p. 271

§1. Is there really nothing useful or novel to be said about the relationship between the study of economic phenomena and the casting of economic
inquiry in quantitative and mathematical format? Everyone is fully aware
that the trend over the last century has been toward ever greater mathematical sophistication as part and parcel of the professionalization of the discipline of economics. Everyone is equally aware that this trend has provoked
periodic controversies over the meaning and significance of this conjuncture. Where awareness, or perhaps self-consciousness, is deficient is in the
areas of the historical determinants of mathematical conceptualization, and
of recent developments in the history and philosophy of mathematics.

Economists seem singularly oblivious to the forces that have shaped
their present mathematical practice. While this undoubtedly serves as a
bulwark against seizures of metaphysical loss of nerve, it also invites out-
siders to indulge in sarcasm. Suppose a working economist were confronted
by a well-known physicist, addressing a respected body of philosophers of
science, who proceeded to state:

> ... the traditional view in this country from the time of Newton has been that
> science is the study of the nature of reality and different branches of science
> merely study different aspects of the same reality: Mathematics being the branch
> which is concerned with the quantitative aspects of reality exemplified in its
> simplest form by various kinds of measurements. Towards the end of the last
> century as a result of the interaction between logic and mathematics changes
> began to take place and pure mathematics moved along a path which seemed to
> diverge from the path taken by the other sciences. While physicists and engineers
> seemed to show a distinct preference for the mathematics of the older kind,
> practitioners of social and economic science, which have come into their own
> fairly recently, found that the new mathematics was quite useful in making both

their qualitative and quantitative arguments more obscure for laymen. (Sharma, 1982, p. 276)

Surely this aperçu is ill-tempered, and a bit of a low blow, but it is actually to be found in the pages of a very reputable philosophy journal, which has been known to print serious discussions of economic method on occasion. In this respect, 1982 seemed a year particularly notable for the airing of dirty laundry, with a Nobel laureate making essentially the same accusation in the pages of the most respected generalist periodical in the natural sciences (Leontief, 1982). Now, one could always write these little incidents off as a bad run of luck; but as a matter of form, economists would probably rather tend to think that a commitment to rational discussion would require a measured rebuttal; or at the very least, a little effort to sort out the issues. Suppose we decide to look for an answer. What lines of defense are deployed in the existing literature of economics?

§2. There are two generic responses. The first (which we shall dub Defense$_1$) is most readily accessible in Paul Samuelson's Nobel Prize lecture (Samuelson, 1972, p. 2). Tracing the pedigree of the idea to Joseph Schumpeter, he states that the "subject matter presents itself in quantitative form": that is, economics is held to be "naturally quantitative". In this view, while discussions of economic phenomena do not require any particular mode of discourse, the mathematical mode is the most convenient, because it is concise and well suited to the subject matter (Samuelson, 1952, p. 63). Further, although this extension is rarely stated explicitly, the quantitative character of the subject matter not only justifies mathematical formalism in general, but also justifies any subset of that formalism, since mathematics is presumed to be a unified and consistent body of technique *par excellence*.

Far from being original with Schumpeter, Defense$_1$ dates back to the earliest progenitors of a particular style of political economy, that associated with neoclassical economic theory. It can be found in the programmatic statements of the founders of that school; for example, in William Stanley Jevons' *Theory of Political Economy*:

> It is clear that economics, if it is to be a science at all, must be a mathematical science ... simply because it deals in quantities.... The symbols in mathematical books are not different in nature from language.... They do not constitute the mode of reasoning they embody; they merely facilitate its exhibition and comprehension. (Jevons, 1970, p. 78)

§3. The second defense of the mathematical method is somewhat more modern. (Let us call it Defense$_2$.) In this view, mathematical formalism is merely the imposition of logical rigor upon the loose and imprecise common discussion of economic phenomena. The efficacy of this regimen derives from the discipline of axiomatization. A major statement of this position can be found in another Nobel Prize lecture (Debreu, 1984). The most influential expositor of this defense was Tjalling Koopmans; his advocacy is worth quoting in the original:

> The appropriateness of mathematical reasoning in economics is not dependent upon how firmly or shakily the premises are established. Let us assume for the sake of argument that the attempt to establish premises or at least to explore their implications is worthwhile, that is, economics itself is worthwhile. In that case the justification for mathematical economics depends merely on whether the logical link between the basic premises economists have been led to make and many of their observable and otherwise interesting implications are more efficiently established by mathematical or by verbal reasoning. (Koopmans, 1954, p. 378)

Since it is deemed impractical for those who have invested the time and energy in mastering the special techniques of axiomatization to also offer a verbal restatement of their activities, in contrast to the first defense, no claim is made that mathematics is "just another language," or even that it is incumbent upon mathematical economists to communicate with the uninitiated (Koopmans, 1954).[1] No intrinsic link between the essence of economic phenomena and the character of mathematical and analysis need be postulated, because, in this view, mathematical formalism *is* logic (Koopmans, 1957, p. 143).

In Defense$_2$ economics is portrayed as a workaday card file of axiomatized formal models: prudent practitioners are encouraged to be agnostic concerning the principles of the draw of cards from an otherwise orderly deck. Here one detects a certain distaste about enthusiasms over correspondence to reality.

§4. These two defenses (like so very much else) did not originate in economics, but rather replicate earlier controversies in mathematics and physics. Defense$_1$, the claim that the ontology of phenomena is in its very quiddity patterned along mathematical lines, is found in Greek antiquity; in the eighteenth century, the success of celestial mechanics fostered the more widespread belief that, "The true system of the world has been recognized, developed, and perfected." This ontological manifesto, cut free from its previous moorings in theology, is echoed by many in our own time. For example, Eugene Wigner, the 1960 Nobel prize recipient in physics, has asserted, "The statement that the laws of nature are written in the language of mathematics was properly made 300 years ago; it is now more true than ever before" (Wigner, 1967, p. 288).

Defense$_2$ developed out of some controversies among mathematicians around the turn of the century (Kline, 1980, ch. XI). Concern over the logical foundations of mathematics led David Hilbert to found the formalist school, the purpose of which was to establish once and for all the certitude and dependability of mathematical proof techniques and practices. Hilbert believed that mathematics should not be comprehended as factual knowledge of the book of nature, but rather as a formal symbolic structure: abstract, austere, and without explicit reference to meaning. He specifically limited proof techniques to the rigidly confined manipulation of symbols according to previously validated formulas or logical axioms. The consistency of arithmetic itself, and hence of all of the other branches of mathematics, was to be settled for all time. "To the formalist, then, mathematics proper is a collection of formal systems, each building its own logic along with its mathematics, each having its own concepts, its own axioms, its own rules for deducing theorems, and its own theorems" (Kline, 1980, p. 249). Closely allied with the formalists was the set-theoretic school of Zermelo and Fraenkel. This school developed and extended the basic axioms of sets, from which it was hoped that all other mathematics could be derived. Some modern exponents of this school, a group of mathematicians writing under the collective pseudonym of Nicholas Bourbaki, have been particularly influential in this respect; many of their techniques and their attitudes are present in the mathematical economics of the Arrow-Debreu variant (Debreu, 1959, p. x; Samuelson, 1983).

Both of these justifications of the employment and efficacy of mathematics are inadequate and have been vulnerable to rational criticism. For our purposes, their deficiencies can be explored upon two levels: that of recent developments in the history and philosophy of mathematics, and that of the history of economic theory. Because it is more recent and, among economists, more commonplace, let us examine Defense$_2$ first.

§5. The formalist program in mathematics has been subject to paroxysms of doubt and dissension since the 1930s, although the tremors have yet to trouble any economists. The first crisis of self-confidence, which has now even been popularized in certain best-sellers (Hofstadter, 1979), is a set of propositions derived from the work of Kurt Gödel. The full import of Gödel's theorem is still a wellspring of philosophical controversy; thus prudence dictates that we rely only upon its least contentious interpretation (Nagel and Newman, 1958).

Gödel showed that a consistency proof of a system meeting Hilbert's requirements and simultaneously strong enough to formalize arithmetic could not be given within that same system, assuming, in fact, that the system was consistent. This followed from Gödel's Incompleteness Theorem, which stated that, given any set of axioms for a system strong enough to express arithmetic, there exist sentences true in arithmetic which are formally underivable within that system. If any of these sentences are incorporated into the system as axioms, they then become trivially derivable, but then there exist other unprovable but true sentences. Thus, "mathematical proof" does not inevitably coincide with the use of a formalized axiomatic method. The demonstration that, "there are limitations on what can be achieved by axiomatization contrasts sharply with the late 19th century view that mathematics is coextensive with the collection of axiomatized branches.... As Paul Bernays has said, it is less wise today to recommend axiomatics than to warn against an overvaluation of it" (Kline, 1980, p. 263). The existence of such "formally undecidable propositions" to a certain extent undermines the "law of the excluded middle", and with it, much of the faith that mathematics is less fuzzy than the conventional vernacular.

A second attack on the formalist program came, not from within mathematics, but from philosophers associated with the ideas of the later Wittgenstein (especially, Wittgenstein, 1978). Although Wittgenstein's aphoristic writings prevent even the enthusiast from claiming his philosophy prosecutes a unified thesis, the aspect of it relevant to the formalist program is his critical exploration of the belief that mathematical practices could be unambiguously codified in axiomatic systems. One aspect of mathematical practice that he subjected to scrutiny was the role of ostensive definition and the rational persistence of unintended interpretations in an axiomatic system.[2] A second aspect, taken loosely, is that any collection of rules, such as a system of axioms, is incapable of definitively enforcing itself. To imagine otherwise is to descend into an infinite regress of the sequential postulation of rules whose purpose is to enforce certain interpretations of higher-level rules, and so on, *ad nauseam* (Levinson, 1978; Mirowski, this volume, ch. 7). Again, it is not the internal research project of mathematics that is deflated by these events, but rather the widespread confidence that mathematics embodies obvious superiority in the areas of consistency, clarity, and limpid communication.

§6. It would seem a worthwhile project to try to bring the recent history of metamathematics to the attention of economists, if only because one so frequently hears that mathematical methods constitute a neutral language, which only conveys what is consciously put into it. This belief is then further confounded with some auxiliary notions of the inherently value-free character of a class of theories. Again quoting Koopmans:

... that the mathematical method when correctly applied forces the investigator to give a complete statement of assuredly noncontradictory assumptions has generally been conceded as far as the relations of the assumptions to the reasoning is concerned. To this may be added that the absence of any natural meaning of mathematical symbols, other than the meaning given to them by postulate or by definition, prevents the associations clinging to words from intruding upon the reasoning process. (Koopmans, 1957, pp. 172–173)

Gödel's theorem alerts us to the fact that completeness and consistency are by no means as straightforward and effortless as here supposed. Again, let us try to be as clear as possible about what Gödel's theorem does and does not mean in this instance. It does not mean that there is anything illegitimate about the use of any particular branch of mathematics in order to make or illustrate a thesis in economics. It does mean, however, that the simple fact of the employment of mathematics in economic arguments cannot guarantee that the exhibition of assumptions is somehow more complete or less disingenuous than in the conventional vernacular. It does mean there is no certainty that the list of assumptions will not need augmentation in the future. It does mean that the Leibnizian dream of a universal algorithm has been severely tarnished in the twentieth century. These facts directly contradict Koopmans' assertions quoted above.

Further, the philosophical work of Wittgenstein cautions us to pause and wonder if those mathematical symbols really are so very free of clinging associations. The austere and asocial nature of mathematics sounds a little odd, coming out of the mouth of a social scientist. Koopmans' advocacy of the mathematical method makes it sound too much like snake oil, a universal panacea for all fuzzy thought. In therapeutic contrast, the metamathematical tradition sounds the tocsin that the axiomatic formalist method can be *potentially* strewn with pitfalls. These rather abstract arguments can be brought down to earth by means of a detour through the history of economic thought; it can provide the concrete counterexamples to Koopmans' assertions.

Interestingly enough, we can pick up the scent of the trail in Koopmans' own work. Almost in passing, he comments that, "A utility function of a consumer looks quite similar to a potential function in the theory of gravitation ...". (Koopmans, 1957, p. 176). Although he opts not to elaborate on that statement, let us explore it further. Suppose we are describing a mass-point moving in a three-dimensional Euclidean space from point A to point B, as in figure 6–1. The conventional method of describing this motion, developed in the early- to mid-nineteenth century, would postulate a 'force' decomposed into its orthogonal components, multiplied through by the spatial displacement of the mass-point, also suitably decomposed. In order

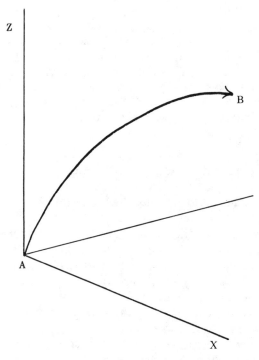

Figure 6–1

to incorporate cases of nonlinear displacement and acceleration, the "work" done in the course of the motion from A to B was defined as the summation of the infinitesimal forces multiplied times their displacements:

$$T = \int_A^B (F_x\,dx + F_y\,dy + F_z\,dz) = (\tfrac{1}{2})mv^2 \Big|_A^B$$

The writings of Lagrange, and more importantly of Hamilton, argued that the total energy of this system also depended in a critical way upon the *position* of the mass-point. This was subsequently clarified in the following manner: suppose that the expression $(F_x\,dx + F_y\,dy + F_z\,dz)$ was an exact differential, which implies that there exists a function $U(x,y,z)$ such that

$$F_x = (\delta U/\delta x); \qquad F_y = (\delta U/\delta y); \qquad F_z = (\delta U/\delta z)$$

The function $U(x,y,z)$ defines a gravitational field, which later was identified as "potential energy". The sum of potential and kinetic energies, $T + U$, was then understood as being conserved within the confines of a closed system. This conservation law, in turn, clarified and encouraged the employment of constrained maximization techniques (such as the Principle of Least Action, Lagrangean multipliers, and the Hamiltonian calculus of variations) in the description of the path of the mass-point under the influence of the impressed forces.

As Koopmans indicates, the similarity between this model and conventional neoclassical price theory is quite striking. In fact, if one merely redefines the "forces" to be prices, the displacements to be infinitesimal changes in the quantities of individual goods x, y, z "kinetic energy" to be expenditure; and relabels the gravitational potential field to be "utility", then one arrives at the standard model of neoclassical price theory.[3] Constrained maximization (or minimization) of an imponderable quantity leads directly to a conservative field, which in turn fixes the permissible configurations of forces/prices.

Is this remarkable similarity merely an accident? Koopmans is silent on this issue, but examination of the origins of neoclassical theory reveals that its progenitors consciously and willfully appropriated the physical metaphor and imported it into discussion of economic theory in order to make economics a mathematical science (Mirowski, 1984b). The most curious aspect of this program to make economics more rigorous and more scientific is that *not one* neoclassical economist in over one hundred years has seen fit to discuss the appropriateness or inappropriateness of the adoption of the mathematical metaphor of energy in a prerelativistic gravitational field in order to discuss the preferences and price formation of transactors in the marketplace. This lacuna raises two immediate questions: do neoclassical economists have any inkling whence their favored mathematical techniques are taken? And, if one accepts the account of the matter that says they were directly appropriated from physics, has this really made any significant difference either for the subsequent evolution of research or for the communication of the results? Meticulous exploration of these questions should serve to reveal the lack of foundations of the allegation that the mathematical method encourages "a complete statement of assuredly noncontradictory assumptions" and "prevents associations clinging to words from intruding."

§7. In answer to the first question, neoclassical economists generally have no coherent conception of the genesis of their mathematical techniques, nor, indeed, of the extent of the similarities of their practices to those in physics. This is evident from the singular deterioration of the level of discourse whenever the role of mathematics in the development of economics is broached: on these occasions the preacher buried within the economist's husk comes bursting forth with homilies about elegance and progress and science and truth and efficiency. The actual context of use and meaning is the first casualty in the rush to testify the faith; the second casualty is any curiosity about what contemporary mathematicians and physicists are saying about how they use mathematics. Examples of these shortcomings can be found in assertions that the definition of economy as the maximization of an objective function under constraint was an "obvious" inference after the invention of the calculus (conveniently ignoring the two-century lag), and in assertions by some eminent neoclassical economists that economics has no analogue to the conservation of energy, nor, indeed, to any aspects of physics at all (see Mirowski, 1984c).

There is an irony at the heart of this stubborn oblivion on the part of the partisans of Defense$_2$. Their method of axiomatic formalism, which they tout as being utterly transparent and logical, seems to elude all of their attempts to discuss it transparently and logically. The method which reveals the clinging associations of words is incapable of revealing its own clinging associations: its own employment cannot be justified on its chosen grounds. Those familiar with the philosophy of mathematics will recognize this as another example of a general phenomenon of the twentieth century, examples of which include the Russellian paradoxes of set theory, as well as Gödel's theorem: indirectly self-referential systems are the bane of the formalist program.

§8. And now, to the second question: the fact of the appropriation of mathematical techniques from the physics of the nineteenth century has clearly influenced both the content and the mode of research in economics. These clinging associations are the residue of the projection of a metaphor from physics onto the sphere of the economy, where aspects of economic experience were then subject to reinterpretation. An enumeration of the myriad ways in which the mathematical model smuggled a hidden agenda into political economy would be a very substantial undertaking in the intellectual history of the discipline. (See Mirowski, forthcoming.) Our pretensions are more modest in the present context, and therefore, we shall have to rest content with approaching this problem in stages, weaving it together with a parallel evaluation of the defenses of mathematics in economics. To this end, in this section we shall provide a preliminary assay of the physical residue in economic theory, only to delve more deeply into issues of mathematical structure in sections §10 and §18–20 below. The following is a list of suggestions as to the multifarious influences of the physical metaphor:

A.   There is nothing obvious about the definition of human rationality as the maximization of an objective function over a stationary field (Mirowski, this volume, ch. 7). This elevation of the significance of extrema did not arise first in social theory, but rather in physics, as the principle of least action. The physics of constrained extrema was interpreted as evidence supporting the existence of a God who had constructed the world in the most efficacious and coherent manner. This minimization or maximization was global in the most comprehensive sense, and encouraged the attitude that "efficiency" could be defined within some absolute framework. In its evolution from Maupertuis to Euler to Hamilton, the principle of least (or varying) action shed its theological skin, but the notion of the efficiency of extrema persisted, and it was this connotation which was recruited to tame the multiform and unruly phenomenon of rationality. The predisposition of the modern economist to "optimize" over someone's "objective function" is neither an empty tautology nor a harmless metaphor: it presumes an inordinately large amount of structure about the nature of desires and objectives, the role of time, the understanding of causality, the unimportance of process, the conservation of the domain of the objectives, the relative constructs of the world of the actor and its reconstruction by the social analyst, the separation of the phenomenon and the act of choice, and much, much more (see Bausor, this volume, ch. 4; and Mirowski, 1984c).

B.   The metaphor of energy/utility which neoclassical economics appropriated was derived from the physics of a specific historical period: the years of the mid-nineteenth century just prior to the elaboration of the second law of thermodynamics. The mathematics of pre-entropic physics was the pinnacle of the development of static mechanism (Prigogine, 1980), where all physical phenomena are portrayed as being perfectly reversible in time, and no system exhibits hysteresis. Nineteenth-century physical laws were thought, by definition, to possess no history. The stubbornly ahistorical bias of neoclassical economics has been excoriated by critics such as Joan Robinson, and bemoaned by such partisans as Hicks (1979) and Shackle (1967). What the latter do not realize is that one cannot superimpose a history onto neoclassical processes without undermining the physical metaphor and the mathematical techniques that were the cause of its success.

C.   In pre-entropic physics, all physical phenomena are variegated manifestations of a protean energy which is fully and reversibly transformed from one state to another. When this idea was transported into the context of economic theory, it dictated that all economic goods were fully and reversibly transformable into utility, and thus into all other goods through the intermediary of the act of trade. The introduction of money into neoclassical economic theory has always been tenuous and tentative, at best (see below, section §18; and Clower, 1967). The problem has been, strangely enough, metaphorical. In the mathematics, the analogue to money has not been the lubricant that reduces the friction in a mechanical system; it has been rather a superfluous intermediate crypto-energy which all other energies have been constrained to become in transit to their final state. The mathematics says one thing; the accompanying commentary another.

D.   As a prerequisite for the application of constrained extrema techniques in physics, it has long been recognized that energy must be conserved as a mathematical rather than an empirical imperative (Theobald, 1966). A major theme in Western economic theory has been persistent controversy over what should be conceptualized as being conserved in the economy. Neoclassicals, in opting for the mathematics of energetics, have implicitly chosen the utility field to be conserved. Lack of self-consciousness concerning this choice has resulted in no end of muddle in neoclassical discussion of such issues as knowledge and uncertainty (Bausor, this volume ch. 4).

E.   There was a flurry of activity in the 1940s and 1950s which portended the liberation of neoclassical value theory from any dependence upon the utility concept. The motivations behind this self-denying ordinance were never seriously aired, although a rationally reconstructed history (Wong, 1978) can easily be clarified by making a list of the various ways our understanding of the folk-psychology of utility renders it dissimilar to energy. (Parenthetically, it also can explain why economists cannot be bothered to take twentieth-century psychology seriously.) The failure of this abortive research program can be gauged by the extent to which the axioms of revealed preference are isomorphic to those of a gravitational field.[4]

F.   Problems with the energetics metaphor sometimes assumed a very prosaic cast. For example, the components of forces can take on negative values without disrupting the physical intuition; but negative prices seemed to be pushing the analogy a bit too far. We shall return to this issue in section §10 below.

The more one is willing to become embroiled in the history of physics and mathematics, the more one could expand this list. For our present purposes, I presume it offers sufficient evidence to counter the claim that it makes no appreciable difference where mathematical analogies and techniques come from, because once appropriated, they are freely amended to express only what is transparently intended. At least in this respect, mathematics is not a colorless and secure coat into which the analyst can slip in order to shield himself from the vagaries of human discourse.

§9. There is another respect in which mathematics cannot be a neutral vehicle for abstract thought. Mathematics not only influences what is to be said; it also influences to whom you can speak. In retrospect, it seems clear that the physico-mathematical origins of neoclassical economics substantially shaped the structure of the nascent economics profession, thus determining what sort of person would be sanctioned to think about the economy. The defenders of mathematical neoclassical economics have always treated this fact with disarming ingenuousness. Alfred Marshall, the force behind the propagation of economic studies at Cambridge, wrote in the preface to the eighth edition of his *Principles*:

The new analysis is endeavoring gradually and tentatively to bring over into economics, as far as the widely different nature of the material will allow, those methods of the science of small increments (commonly called the differential calculus) to which man owes directly or indirectly the greater part of the control that he has obtained in recent times over physical nature. It is still in its infancy; it has no dogmas, no standard of orthodoxy ... there is a remarkable harmony and agreement on essentials among those who are working constructively by the new method; and especially among such of them as have served an apprenticeship in the simpler and more definite, and therefore more advanced, problems of physics. (Marshall, 1920, pp. xvi–xvii)

But of course there was a dogma and a standard of orthodoxy: that was why agreement had been achieved so rapidly and so painlessly by the early neoclassicals: the standards, the metaphors, and the very gestalt of a specific mode of theorizing had been imbibed during an apprenticeship in physics or engineering (Mirowski, 1984b). While those on the wrong end of the bayonet in the marginalist revolution regarded that cadre as if they had dropped from another planet with their symbolic quantification of qualities, their abstract optimization, and their haughty wielding of the saber of science, the revolutionaries themselves immediately recognized each other as comrades in arms. Some, with Marshall as the premier example, tried to justify the revolution to the larger populace; but by then it was already entering its first phase of consolidation.

Perhaps the most important aspect of the mathematization of any intellectual project is its sociological impact upon the membership of the discipline. It is only fairly recently that the issue could be seriously discussed (Bloor, 1973, 1978, 1983; Colvin, 1977). One can only speculate as to the sublimations and fears that acted to place mathematics beyond the pale in any discussion of the social influences on science (Restivo, 1983), since evidence of the social functions of mathematics may be found as far back as the birth of modern physics. Few who revere Isaac Newton as the towering genius of Western science are aware that he originally composed his *Principia* in the popular vernacular so as to encourage its wide dissemination; but subsequent disputes with other natural philosophers prompted him to recast it into its now familiar mathematical format. Newton himself tells us in the *Principia*:

... considering that such as had not sufficiently entered into the principles could not easily discern the strength of the consequences, nor lay aside the prejudices to which they had been many years accustomed, therefore, to prevent the disputes which might be raised on such accounts, I chose to reduce the substance of this Book into the form of Propositions (in the mathematical way), which could be read by those only who had first made themselves masters of the principles established by the preceding Books." (quoted in Westfall, 1980, p. 459)

Years later, Newton recited a similar story to his friend William Derham. He abhorred contentions, he said. "And for this reason, namely to avoid being bated by little Smatterers in Mathematicks, he told me, he designedly made his Principia abstruse." (Westfall, 1980, p. 459)

Such revealing admissions concerning the sociological role and function of mathematics are common enough in the historiographic record, once one ventures beyond the hagiography of science.

Mathematics is a primary tool in the creation of a well-behaved audience for a particular discourse, the establishment of an orthodoxy which automatically serves to exclude dissension. It is a prosaic but nonetheless accurate observation that the time spent in mastering the mathematics and the translation of those symbols into the orthodox statements of a discipline is a regimen sufficient to discourage the skeptical and reinforce the self-esteem of the willing recruit.

How can a system of obscure symbols be responsible for the maintenance of orthodoxy? First, it is a restricted language, and like any such language (say, the Latin at a Roman Catholic Mass, or the jargon of Freudian analysis), it possesses a certain ritual efficacy over and above its content. Such a language expresses social relations by its very use, and independent of any conscious intent.

Secondly, mathematics is a singular sphere of human discourse where the assertion of the discreteness of intellectual constructs is pushed to its extreme, resulting in the most rigidly inflexible claims that the manipulation of concepts is either unambiguously correct or unambiguously incorrect. This construction of knowledge is particularly serviceable in the context of the classroom, where discipline and the hierarchical status of teacher and student are projected into the realm of knowledge itself. Once internalized, mathematics seems to police itself, sanctioning the correct application of its own rules. This undoubtedly accounts for the fact that most mathematicians would rather adopt Platonism than be confronted with the idea that they themselves participate in the construction of mathematics (Penrose, 1982). (Unfortunately, most mathematics classes are not conducted along the lines of Socratic dialogue as in the ideal world of Lakatos (1976).)

Third, the illusion of self-policing rules are reproduced in the social theories which depend heavily upon mathematical formalization. Many of the "constraints" binding the actors in mathematical social theories partake of the character of "natural" limitations because mathematics is incapable of encompassing the process of interpretation and the freedom and exhilaration of the redefinition of a problem context which is the prerogative of human rationality (Mirowski, this volume, ch. 7). This hemmed-in conception of the human dilemma would appear as more plausible to a mathematician than, say, a rhetorician, because it is precisely that freedom of interpretation which they were taught to curb in their schooling. To put this bluntly, mathematics fosters the impression that the actors who are the subject of analysis are determined by alien extraneous forces.

Fourth, the discrete character of mathematics encourages what Colvin and Bhaskar call "the norm of closure," which, briefly, signifies the creation of a system restricted in time and in space, in which a constant conjunction of events is maintained in the isolated ideal, and upon which is imposed a tendency to atomism and a prohibition of novelty by combination.[5] Colvin (1977) suggests that the norm of closure comes to transform the social structure of the discipline that embraces it. For example, research itself in such a discipline becomes more fragmented, and the issues themselves come to be seen as more and more discrete and isolated. The conviction gains currency that rigor is identical with the most extreme ontological individuation. The industrialization of research becomes more feasible and desirable, and the responsibility for the success or failure of the research program becomes diffused over large numbers of workers oblivious to the "big picture". A certain anomie sets in, with mathematical workers appealing ultimately to epistemologically vague "elegance" or "simplicity" as the prime justification for their endeavors. Legitimation in the field comes to be confused with the norm of closure, so there arises a very low threshold of toleration for debate which does not seem to be headed toward closure. Pronounced changes in the field also seem ominous.

Fifth, the penetration of mathematics induces a particular form of hierarchy within a discipline, where mathematical theorists become separated from a lower class of researchers whose task it is to connect the theoretical terms to empirical data and to reprocess the "highbrow" theory into "lowbrow" expositions and contexts. As Colvin (1977, p. 116) writes, "In this type of work differentiation, it is the theorist, rather than the experimentalist, who projects the capacities of arithmomorphism to the hilt, in that he is able to slide fairly casually over the domain of the grounds of reality, where the experimentalist might ordinarily hold sway, in order to reinforce the theoretical position of the arithmomorphic norm." Thus mathematics frees the theorist from having to create a context of justification. Hence it is notable that in the history of physics it has not been the literary natural philosophers but rather the mathematicians who have proposed some of the most outrageous analogies in the course of their endeavors: heat flows like a liquid; electricity and light undulate like waves on a pond; electrical inductance behaves like a gravitational mass; and so on (Olson, 1958). While these analogies often ride roughshod over the multiform particularities of the actual phenomena, their acceptance and adoption is encouraged by the separation of the discipline into mathematical theorists and applied practitioners. The mathematical theorists can disregard mundane phenomenological problems and choose descriptions they find agreeable because they resemble other existing mathematical constructs, however farfetched. The applied practitioners and experimentalists, aware of their second-class status (perhaps due to an earlier failure in pursuing the mathematical frontiers of their discipline), acquiesce in the analogies of the theorists and work to find some common ground between the phenomenon and the formalism. The relevance of this dynamic to the explanation of the appropriation of the physical metaphor of energy by neoclassical economists should be obvious.

§10. There is no more stark illustration of the difficulties of Defense$_2$ than the evolution of what is today widely considered the pinnacle of neoclassical economic theory, the Arrow-Debreu (AD) general equilibrium model. While it is the case that the AD model deploys some of the most sophisticated mathematics to be found in any branch of social theory, there has never been serious defense of the tenets that its axiomatic structure has improved the tenor and clarity of theoretical discussion or revealed exhaustively all of the necessary assumptions underlying the neoclassical world view, or even that the model adequately represents the issues that have vexed economists prior to its inception.

The history of the AD model is admirably summarized by Weintraub (1983). The progenitor of the model, Léon Walras, did innovate the inscription of utility functions and production functions, as well as invent the artifice of the market-clearing auctioneer, but his work contained many anachronistic features from classical economics, and his only attempt at providing a solution for the model consisted of counting the number of equations and unknowns. After an interval of neglect, a few mathematicians observed that the counting method did not guarantee the existence of an equilibrium solution consisting of a strictly positive set of prices and outputs (Baumol and Goldfeld, 1968, pp. 267–280). Abraham Wald in 1934 succeeded in providing the first proof of existence and uniqueness of a positive equilibrium price vector. The rather primitive techniques used in these papers—for example, the bald assumption of price as a monotone decreasing function of output, or the unjustified postulation of convergent sequences of Δ's (see Wald in Baumol and Goldfeld, 1968, pp. 281–287)—next attracted the attention of other mathematicians. John Von Neumann in 1944 shifted the premises of the inquiry by postulating global characterizations of objective functions and constraint sets, which in turn required solution concepts based upon the convexity of sets. In the early 1950s, there was a rush to apply further topological techniques, such as the Brouwer and Kakutani fixed-point theorems (see Takayama, 1974, pp. 260–265), in order to provide more "elegant" formalization of existence and uniqueness of competitive equilibrium. By the time of the contributions of Arrow and Debreu, there was no longer any pretense that the object was to find the solution to a set of equations or inequalities; there was, instead, the more modest goal of "proving that a number of maximizations of individual goals under independent restraints can be simultaneously carried out" (Koopmans, 1957, p. 60).

Even a cursory examination of this history reveals that "the box of tools", the language purportedly free of "clinging associations", took on a life of its own. Walras imported his model from physics without understanding a critical flaw in the analogy: negative solutions for forces and displacements are quite common in physical problems, and cause no problems of interpretation, because they are seen as representing the relative orientation of the phenomenon in space; negative solutions for outputs, and more significantly, prices, posed a much more sticky problem of interpretation in economics. Instead of seeing this as a seriously damaging drawback of the physical metaphor, or deciding that the algebraic structure of nineteenth-century physics was inappropriate in the context of the economic sphere, twentieth-century *mathematicians* sought to augment the model with more assumptions in order to banish the anomaly. Initial auxiliary hypotheses concerning inequalities and the free disposal of superfluous goods gave way to changes in the mathematical solution technique. These changes in technique, and the movement toward global and topological considerations, in turn altered the content and the goals of the research program. Physicists do not generally hold proof of existence and uniqueness of a solution to a model high on the roster of their research accomplishments, because they aim for constructive proofs. The movement toward nonconstructive proof techniques in economics was a portent of a larger-scale tectonic shift in the conceptualization of what an economic system did, and what an economist could hope to say about it.

One of the fault lines of this tectonic drift has been charted by Garegnani (1983), albeit in another context. He argues that the transition from classical to neoclassical economics was accompanied by a lagged transition from the notion of equilibrium as the "center of gravity" of a limited set of forces to the notion of equilibrium as a sequence of temporary market-clearing prices. Garegnani sees this shift as motivated by internal failures in the neoclassical theory of capital, but we would instead suggest that it is symptomatic of the wholesale reinterpretation of the economic system caused by the adoption of advanced mathematical techniques. The classical theory of competition and equilibrium sought to ground the phenomenon of market price in prior and independent physical determinants, which would fully characterize a long-run equilibrium price of production independent of transitory variations in demand (Levine, 1980; and this volume, ch. 2). The importation from physics of the metaphor of constrained extrema implied that physical surroundings be reinterpreted as a domain of free choice, rather than a self-contained determinate environment. The invariant point of departure for analysis was shifted from the world to preferences/energy. Walras and the other early neoclassicals attempted to retain the classical conception of competition as a center of gravity, but subsequent generations of economists realized that the very conception of *order* in neoclassical theory must diverge from that characteristic of classical economics (Mirowski, forthcoming).

The Western tradition of economic theory is united in its search for order amidst the seeming anarchy of the market; but throughout the parade of individual theories, harmony has been a very plastic notion. The order of the classical economists was a social arrangement sanctioned by natural law (i.e., the laws of physics and the presumed constancy of a given class structure) which was used to explain the reproduction and growth of a national economy. The neoclassical conception of order as represented in the AD model is the potential consistency of individual mental constructions sanctioned by personal constrained optimization over noneconomic initial conditions (i.e., stylized preferences and rules for the transformation of commodity identities, as well as endowments). The stark contrast between the two conceptions of equilibrium is marked by the fact that Arrow-Debreu systems must impose ad hoc auxiliary conditions that ensure individuals can subsist on initially given endowments without engaging in exchange, and that minimum consumption requirements are covered in equilibrium (Takayama, 1974, p. 264). Classical economics spoke the language of *persistence*, whereas the mathematics of energetics and constrained extrema dealt in terms of *invariance*. It is flatly not the case that neoclassical economists first decided that it was better to think of the economy as an aggregate of invariant preferences rather than a system of persistent social relations; instead, economists baldly mimicked physics and its attendant mathematical formalism, and then only discovered gradually that their world picture had to be strategically stretched and shrunk to conform to the metaphor of the transformation and the conservation of energy (Mirowski, 1984b, 1984c).

The transformations in the ideas of order, competition and equilibrium are thus the direct result of the adoption by neoclassicism of its characteristic mathematical techniques. Classical economics postulated a preordained equilibrium of nature which the market generally, but not invariably, acted to ratify. There was no requirement that all generic commodities had to trade at the identical price; nor, indeed, was there any imperative that markets continuously clear. Arrow-Debreu economics, on the other hand, can only implement its mathematico-physical metaphor by imposing the law of one price for any generic commodity and by defining equilibrium prices as those that clear the market.[6] A moment's reflection should reveal that heightened mathematical concern with constrained optimization implies the law of one price as a lemma; whereas preoccupation with proofs of existence and uniqueness in the presence of exogenous stable preferences ordains that the function of price is to clear the market.[7] The fact that it was the mathematics that came first and the economics second is demonstrated by the curiousum that in neoclassical textbooks the motivation for the law of one price is disposed of in a paragraph or less, while any discussion of the identification of equilibrium with the clearing of the market is relegated to the literature of industrial organization or the endless quest for the "Keynesian synthesis". However incongruous, these two pillars of neoclassical theory are introduced *en passant* by the inscription of p_i or $\Sigma_i p_i(D_i - S_i) = 0$. This happens just as unselfconsciously as a literary economist inadvertently introduces an unintended or ill-considered idea in a rhetorical flourish.

Not only has the mathematical development of the AD model altered the content of the theory; it has also continued to allow the sort of errors of economic reasoning that have been deplored in premathematical economic theory. A single example, albeit a somewhat important one, should suffice to demonstrate this thesis. The attraction of mathematical formalism resides largely in its promise of consistency. In the preface to one of the canonical sources of the AD model (Arrow and Hahn, 1971), the authors state their purpose is not the description of an actual economy. However, on page 346 they write: "... we must conclude that the failure of the market mechanism to establish equilibrium—if such failures are in fact observable—must be due to the elements of the actual economy that the economy of section 13.4 neglects." Now, the statements in the preface and on page 346 are patently inconsistent. One nonconstructive proof in one particular model that contains one ideosyncratic conception of the preferences of its agents—one of many possible descriptions of a technology—one incompletely specified definition of private property (Ellerman, this volume, ch. 3), in conjunction with one algorithm governing the adjustment of prices can in no stretch of the imagination absolve those rather large classes of phenomena from any responsibility for failure of actual market coordination. This is not an insignificant or minor non sequitur, however much it is mitigated by the coy reference to observation, because it brings us back full circle to the question:

what is the significance of the formalist program in economics? If it is asserted to have no necessary significance outside of some semiotic practices of a closed fraternity, then that is one thing. Alternatively, if it is asserted that it is a superior method of illuminating questions about the nature of order and coordination in economic life which date back to John Maynard Keynes, or Adam Smith, then that is quite another thing. It makes one wonder if formalists take their own methodological pronouncements seriously.

§11. Defense$_2$ is untenable, which probably explains why its partisans prosecute it with such modest vigor and enthusiasm. As frequently as not, when persistently pressed about the merits of the axiomatic method, those same proponents retreat to the following position: "Let us live and let live. Just give us our teaching posts and our graduate students and our journals, and let us cease this tiresome discussion of method. Let history judge." On the face of it this is an admirable sentiment, the request of every scholar to be left in peace. Nevertheless, in this context it is the subtle extension of the formalist program: it redirects attention away from the ends and purposes of research and back toward more vague impressions of scientific method and means. It denies the possibility of any rational discussion of the impact of formalist practices upon the remainder of the economics profession, either through the alteration of analytical content, or through transformations in the sociological structure of the profession. It ignores the fact that formalists are at present in the ascendancy in the profession. And, finally, it is not even good neoclassical economics: if resources are scarce, then presumably it is desirable to foster competition among various research programs.

It is in this sense that the formalist program serves to hinder rational communication in economics.

§12. Now let us turn to Defense$_1$, which, in contrast to Defense$_2$, will provide us with much more substantial material upon which to ponder. To reiterate, Defense$_1$ insists that the subject matter of economics is "naturally quantitative"; and it is this fact which dictates that mathematical expression is more convenient, more concise, and admirably suited to its subject matter. Defense$_1$ is frequently yoked to another thesis to the effect that mathematics is just another language, so that comparisons of convenience and conciseness are thought to be carried out among languages freely translatable and of the same epistemic efficacy, at least beyond the sphere of the naturally quantitative.

Various considerations broached in previous sections (especially §8 and §9) provide us with the initial means to evaluate this defense. The whole question of "convenience" seems to dovetail with the neoclassical appeal to "efficiency", as if this referred to some unique and unambiguous criteria, independent of context or of the vantage point. We have already observed that the importation of mathematical techniques brought with it subtle and telling metamorphoses in the subject matter, as well as having profound impact upon the sociology of the discipline. If the convenience of mathematics were to be portrayed as some sort of global optimum, then that optimization would necessarily involve the comparison of the status quo with worlds embracing different economic theories, different conceptions of science, different social structures of research, etc. Since such comparisons are not even remotely possible, assertions of convenience reduce to Panglossian notions that what is, is right.

It might be objected that this misconstrues the meaning that partisans of Defense$_1$ intend in their use of the term "concise". Perhaps they wish to bracket the whole question of the evaluation of theories by presuming we are already in possession of the "correct" theory, and only then confronted with the prospect of choice between a mathematical formulation and one in English, perhaps also assuming our audience is fluent in both modes of discourse. Given that the economy as we know it operates within a regime of numbers, would it not be more concise to choose mathematical expression? This sentiment has been criticized by Ken Dennis in two articles on problems of translation in mathematical economics.

Dennis (1982) argues that for purposes of exposition, there is no hard and fast dichotomy between mathematical language and the vernacular; mathematical models constitute a subsystem of notations which, by necessity, remain embedded within a framework of conventional language. Samuelson (1952, p. 59) saw the fact that mathematics is taught using the vernacular as support for his thesis that mathematics is just another language; but it could equally well be interpreted as showing that mathematics and the vernacular are not completely separable and self-sufficient communication systems. If this point is granted, then the predisposition to view logic and systematic exposition as an intrinsic property of mathematical symbols becomes the source of much confusion. Rigor and concision derive as much from the precision with which the analyst is capable of performing the translation between the subsystem of the mathematical model and the English commentary, as it does from the appropriate handling of the rules of mathematical manipulation. Errors in transit from a differential to a "marginal cost" will render an analysis void of sense as readily as errors in differentiation or integration. To illustrate the importance of this fact, Dennis provides numerous examples of what he calls the "double standard of high mathematical rigor and low semantic comedy." The formalist may feel this vindicates his or her disdain for the vernacular, but this overlooks the fact that there will never be an escape from the conundrum of translation in economic theory, and thus the notion of an absolute ranking of convenience of either mathematics or the vernacular is an empty one. The proportion of symbols from the respective systems will differ, along with style and semantical conventions, but these are merely the reflections of the personality of the author, and not the imperative of some spectral Platonic mandate. Since no axiom system can be fully and finally specified, there will always be room for originality. In fact, since economists are so rarely first-class mathematicians, most of the contributions economists can reasonably aspire to make to their chosen discipline must come in that twilight zone of semantical interpretations of previously developed mathematical structures.

§13. There remains the issue of what it means for a phenomenon to be "naturally quantitative".

To an economist, the broaching of this question may seem to be the worst form of hair-splitting. "Prices are numbers. Everyone can see that." It is true that prices are quoted as numbers, but that does not settle their relationship to mathematical techniques, nor does it begin to explain why prices are quoted as numbers. The remainder of this paper will consider these two questions in some detail.

Those who insist that the naturally quantitative character of prices, commodities, etc., suffices to justify the employment of mathematics in economics run up against the problem that they would not like to extend a blanket justification to any deployment of mathematical symbols in economic theory. Clearly, any old math will not do. Consider Schumpeter's comment:

> But the use of figures—Ricardo made ample use of numerical illustrations—or of formulae—such as we find in Marx—or even the restatement in algebraic form of some result of nonmathematical reasoning does not constitute mathematical economics: a distinctive element enters only when the reasoning itself produces the result that is explicitly mathematical. (Schumpter, 1954, pp. 954–955)

The distinction between legitimate and illegitimate mathematical economics is somewhat vague. Is Marx quarantined because he employed algebra instead of the calculus? Did Ricardo fail because he did not cast his discourse in the format of theorem-proof lemma? Why is it that Jevons and Walras disparaged the mathematical models of William Whewell as illegitimate? And why is it that Cournot is widely considered to be the first mathematical economist, even though there were many who preceded him (Theocharis, 1961)?

There is a tangle of issues here to be sorted through. Initially, one might suggest that the illegitimate use of mathematical symbols in economics might be defined as ineptitude or errors in the manipulation of mathematical symbols. Whewell got his sums of infinite sequences of fractions wrong; Marx botched the transformation problem; Ricardo was embarrassed by his 93-percent labor theory of value. The problem with this interpretation is that the "legitimate" mathematical economists are equally as guilty of these errors. Prudently restricting ourselves to the long deceased, we discover: Cournot (Cournot, 1897, pp. vi–vii); Walras (Walras, 1965, letter 1679, n. 3; letter 211, n. 4; letter 331; letter 1009); Pareto (Volterra in Chipman, et al., 1971, p. 368); (Wicksell, 1958, pp. 141–158); and Marshall (Marshall, 1975, pp. 4–5).[8] The curious predicament that besets those who maintain that mathematical exposition banishes error from discourse is the fact that historically, everyone makes errors of manipulation. Candid observers such as David Hume understood this long ago:

> There is no Algebraist nor Mathematician so expert in his science, as to place entire confidence in any truth immediately on his discovery of it, or regard it as anything more than a mere probability. Every time he runs over his proofs, his confidence encreases; but still more by the approbation of his friends; and is rais'd to its utmost perfection by the universal assent and applauses of the learned world. (Quoted in Kitcher, 1983, p. 41)

It cannot be simply errors of manipulation of mathematical rules which deem that a particular application of mathematical formalism to economic theory is inappropriate.

Perhaps, alternatively, the reason particular theorists are disqualified as mathematical economists is that they did not avail themselves of formalist proof techniques. But surely this criterion would be much too restrictive, since formalist proof techniques were only propagated in the late nineteenth and early twentieth century; and even today, many who would consider themselves mathematical economists only use the format intermittently, and often in a desultory manner. Further, formalist proof techniques are not coextensive with the entire project of mathematics, as we have indicated above in section §5 in our discussion of Gödel's theorem. Moreover, the structure of mathematical proof is neither independent of historical context, nor has it always conformed to a certain rigid format. This is due to the fact that every mathematical proof skips an indeterminate number of steps, as well as the fact that the standards of mathematical proof have changed drastically over time (Kitcher, 1983, pp. 42, 191; Kline, 1980). Thus, conformity to a particular proof format is not a valid passport to the pantheon of the mathematical economists.

Given that we have already claimed in section §12 that mathematical argumentation can never be entirely divorced from linguistic expression, the statement that there exists a particularly appropriate mathematical economics must mean that a specific subset of mathematical technique is ideally suited to prosecute discussions of the operation of the economy. It does not appear that any other coherent interpretation can be given to dicta represented by the above Schumpeter quote; and yet, I have not found a single economist willing to make this argument.[9] Instead, all partisans of Defense$_1$ treat all of mathematics as if it were a single unified body of knowledge, indiscriminately and equally fit for economic discussions. The conflict between credo and practice has not been reconciled within the bounds of Defense$_1$.

§14. It is possible, with the aid of section §6 above, to offer a very brief explanation of the observed fact that *neoclassical* economists do not lavish equal praise upon all competent examples of the employment of mathematical formalism in economic theory, however much their methodological statements suggest this should be the case. As previously observed, mathematics was integrated into economic theory simultaneously with the marginalist revolution, which appropriated a specific model from nineteenth-century physics and merely changed the names of the variables. An unintended consequence of this event was that a very narrow subset of mathematics came to be identified with neoclassical theory: that is, the mathematics developed specifically within the context of the physical theory of the late eighteenth and nineteenth centuries, the calculus of constrained extrema.

When a Schumpeter says that Ricardo and Marx were not really mathematical economists, the only consistent interpretation of this statement is that they did not employ techniques of constrained maximization. When Cournot is cited as the first legitimate mathematical economist, it is not because he theorized in terms of utility (he did not), nor because he provided proofs to accompany his mathematical symbols (ditto), but because he applied optimization techniques to fixed revenue and demand functions. When Whewell is denied the status of a mathematical economist, it is because he simply found the solution to a set of algebraic equations. When an Edgeworth or a Pareto is remembered while a Bortkiewicz or a Palomba or a Mandelbrot is forgotten, it is preponderantly due to their respective attitudes toward and incorporation of constrained extrema in their work.

One of the greatest misperceptions in the history of the discipline of economics is that which credits neoclassical theory with the wideranging appreciation and appropriation of mathematical tools. On the contrary, the neoclassical "box of tools" is very small: a purse, or a pouch. Neoclassicism has become little more than constrained optimization in ever-more baroque guises.

§15. Disregard of the twentieth-century doctrine that there is no single unified body of techniques called "mathematics" (Kline, 1980, pp. 275–277) and the conventional belief that the economy is naturally quantitative are really two aspects of the same idea. One of the most profound intensifica tions of the abstract character of mathematical speculation occurred in the late nineteenth century, when geometry was divorced from the study of physical space; shortly thereafter, algebra came to be distinguished from the study of number (Wussing, 1984; O'Malley, 1971). Hilbert once said that although he spoke in terms of points, lines, and planes, the terms he employed could just as well have been mug, chair, and spoon. The rise of abstract algebra suggested that most existing mathematical theorems were merely different realizations of more general principles governing the relationships between abstract objects possessing a very few basic properties. Poincaré flippantly summarized this trend by defining mathematics as the art of giving the same name to different things. For Poincaré and others, there was a kernel of Platonism buried in this epigram, since mathematical formalism does tend to encourage the imposition of the aura of persistence and essence upon unruly and disparate phenomena (Meyerson, 1962). This imperative to uncover the one in the many would only make sense if, at some fundamental level, everything really partook of some abstract unity (Giedymin, 1982, p. 31).

It was the further elaboration of the implications of abstraction by Kurt Gödel, through the assignment of statements to their "Gödel numbers", where any string could simultaneously be interpreted as a metamathematical statement as well as some assertion in arithmetic, that ultimately undermined the confidence in this approach. This escalation of abstraction finally led to the realization that there is no single unique meta-structure embedded either in the elaboration of all mathematics, or in the symbolic expression of events. The history of abstraction surprizes us with proliferation as well as with unification (see Lakatos, 1976).

Understanding the historical timing of this realization is a prerequisite for the explanation of economists' impressions of the significance of mathematics. The physics model appropriated by the progenitors of neoclassicism was generated around the middle of the nineteenth century, just before the spread of the furore over the significance of the non-Euclidean geometries. The first generation of neoclassicals were contemporaries of Klein's Erlanger Program (Kline, 1972, p. 917), which became the group theoretic man-

ifesto, but the economists remained unacquainted with it. The next major
wave of neoclassical economists in the 1930s–1950s was also unaware of
foundational issues in mathematics and their attendant controversies. These
economists came either from physical science backgrounds (Harcourt, 1984,
p. 500), which eschewed these ideas in the interests of pragmatism; or else
they were heirs of the Bourbaki tradition, the major school of formalists who
have shrugged off foundational challenges, and pursued the dream of a
unified mathematics. (The backgrounds of economists in the post-Vietnam
era are even more narrow.) Thus, perhaps it is not at all unusual that neoclassical economists are predisposed to believe that there is a unified corpus
of mathematical technique, which then must be isomorphic to the patently
obvious quantitative character of prices, outputs, money, and so forth.

§16. On a few rare occasions, prominent mainstream mathematical economists have seen fit to elaborate upon the idea that the economy is naturally quantitative, although inevitably these episodes take the form of remarks
in passing or asides. After an intensive search, the few instances I could find
in the entire postwar period are best represented by:

> The logical justification of the use of diagrams (in economic theory) lies in the *fact*
> [my italics–P.M.] that the postulates underlying the analytical description of
> space are identical with those used to represent the joining and separating of
> commodity bundles and the multiplication of such bundles by numbers. (Koop-
> mans, 1957, p. 174)

> Having chosen a unit of measurement for each one of them (the commodities),
> and a sign convention to distinguish inputs from outputs, one can describe the
> action of an economic agent by a vector in the commodity space R^l. The *fact* [my
> italics–P.M.] that the commodity space has the structure of a real vector space is
> a basic reason for the success of the mathematicization of economic theory.
> (Debreu, 1984, pp. 267–268)

The agreement over the interval of nearly thirty years is impressive. The
testimony that the economy is naturally quantitative does not consist of the
observation that prices are expressed as numbers. More fundamentally, the
proffered explanation of the efficacy of mathematical economics is that commodities naturally come in real or Euclidean sets. Curiously enough, this is
not expressly included in the list of axioms, but couched in the language of
fact, which presumably is intended to indicate that this is self-evident. To
rephrase this in the somewhat arcane terminology of classical economics,
exchange values are quantitative because they are merely a reflection of the
"fact" that use values are physically quantitative.

This argument is yet another corollary of the neoclassical predilection to appeal to physics-style arguments. The apparently extrasocial aspect of the sequence one apple, two apples, three apples,... is to provide the natural starting point for price and value. Unfortunately, it is precisely this dichotomy between the "natural" sphere of use and the "social" sphere of value that we wish to isolate as the untenable bulwark of Defense$_1$. If we are forced to judge by the criteria of use, then it is not at all clear that apples and oranges span a Euclidean vector space. Before we appeal to mathematical and philosophical arguments, it may prove instructive to note that various neoclassical economists have already voiced this caveat, albeit in contexts other than an evaluation of mathematical methods in economics.

The first manifestation that something was amiss can be associated with the work of Lancaster (1966) on his revision of the theory of neoclassical consumer demand. Lancaster sensibly suggested that commodities are not generally desired because of their phenomenological identity, but rather for some bundle of characteristics they presumably embody. In effect, Lancaster proposed an intermediate mathematical device which would translate "apples" into appropriate indices of sweetness, crunchiness, redness, "fostering the image of promoting our own health"-ness, and so on. Then, after a *particular* apple is encoded into the terms of the variables with which we express our desire and longing, these variables are entered into the new model utility function.

In the intervening years, sporadic reference has been made to Lancaster's work in bibliographies of consumer theory (Green, 1971), but it has not attracted further research; possibly because it had touched an exposed nerve. On a superficial level, it would seem that sweetness, crunchiness, etc., are rather more difficult to quantify than the apples themselves; therefore, to interpose these less-mathematically accessible variables between unobservable utility and the apples as discrete units seemed to weaken rather than strengthen the existing theory. Nevertheless, this attempted revision was significant, because it gave voice to a hesitation that had occurred to many who had given serious consideration to the utility function: from a strict utilitarian point of view, there is no such thing as a generic commodity. To every individual *qua* individual, each apple is different: some bigger, some stunted, some mottled, some worm-ridden, some coated with stuff that will kill me slowly, some McIntosh, some engineered to look and taste like tomatoes.... Although the thrust of the insight remained latent in Lancaster's article, reconsideration of these issues raised the possibility that the self-identity of the commodity, which is the necessary prerequisite of its basis as a cardinal number, is not at all psychologically present. The Lancaster model remained in the background as an irritant precisely because the natural ground of cardinality, the very quiddity of the definition of the commodity, melted into air; and all that survived was the faintest suggestion that the rigid standardization requisite for cardinality was *imposed* by the development of the market with its arbitrary bundling of characteristics.[10] Perhaps number is not a natural attribute.

Another version of this reticence appeared in Oskar Morgenstern's popular book on the accuracy of economic observations. As is rather frequently the case among neoclassical economists, Morgenstern took the opportunity to excoriate the accounting profession for producing what he considered to be meaningless numbers. He complained:

> Both balance sheets and . . . profit and loss accounts represent a mixture of figures that belong in widely separate categories. Yet these figures are treated conceptually and arithmetically as if they were completely homogeneous.... There simply cannot be a financial statement which is not ultimately the report of some physical event: money passing from one hand to another . . . or a record made of some physical entities allegedly in the possession of the business. The record, however, may contain an additional element, namely that of *evaluation* of the physical activity. (Morgenstern, 1963a, p. 72)

As the reader may realize, this is the same problem in a different setting. Business accounts impose a type of homogeneity upon their assets and liabilities, and thus a certain algebra (see Ellerman, this volume, ch. 3), which is hardly obvious, and in certain circles, is quite an object of contention. Oddly enough, Morgenstern seemed to feel that this was the fault of the businessmen, who deviously and wrong-headedly resisted dividing the world up into "figures [which] can be viewed as direct statements about fairly easily ascertained *physical* things such as cash, currency and bank deposits" (Morgenstern, 1963a, p. 75) and valuations dependent upon some theory. Here once again is the physicalist bias, but in a distorted mirror-image: now it is *money* that is the physical touchstone, and it is physical commodities that require some dubious theory of imputation in order for them to be subject to the same format of algebraic accounts. And once again, the irony is close at hand: is it not incongruous to refer to *money* as if it provided the physical foundation for the quantification of business records? The "natural" basis of quantification slips further from our grasp.

The level of subtlety of discussions surrounding this issue was raised incalculably by the appearance of Nicholas Georgescu-Roegen's *Entropy Law and the Economic Process*. In place of the excessive deference conventionally displayed when an economist invokes the name of physics, Georgescu-Roegen's familiarity with the subject prompted him to start from the premise that, "Physics, therefore, is not as free from metaphysics as current critical philosophy proclaims" (Georgescu-Roegen, 1971, p. 97). In practice, he agrees with the quote from Norman Campbell at the beginning of this chapter. He insists that the use of cardinal measure reflect a particular physical property of a category of objects. To quote his argument in detail:

> ... this simple pattern (of proportional laws in physics) is not a mere accident: on the contrary, in all these cases the proportional variation of the variables is an inevitable consequence of the fact that every one of these variables is free from any qualitative variation. In other words, they are all cardinal variables. The reason is simple: if two such variables are connected by a law, the connection being immediate in the sense that the law is not a relation obtained by telescoping a chain of other laws, then what is true for one pair of values must be true for all succeeding pairs. Otherwise, there would be some difference between the first and, say, the hundreth pair, which could only mean a qualitative difference. This characteristic property of cardinal laws ... constitutes the very basis on which Cantor established his famous distinction between ordinal and cardinal number. We arrive, Cantor says, at the notion of cardinal number by abstracting from the varying quality of the elements involved and from the order in which we have "counted" them. (Georgescu-Roegen, 1971, p. 102)

The elaboration of this conception of law-like structure can be seen, in retrospect, as the prime motivation behind most of Georgescu-Roegen's impressive *ouvre*. In the 1950s he argued that if commodities were cardinally measurable, then there would always be an uncaptured qualitative residual associated with any individual's esteem for them, and that this fact in itself, even in the absence of other psychological assumptions, would guarantee that indifference curves would always be convex. He later realized that it could only guarantee that indifference maps would be nonlinear; a much less interesting proposition (Georgescu-Roegen, 1971, p. 113). Nevertheless, this insight can serve to explain the failure of Lancaster's research program: the qualitative residual cannot be banished by appending any set of quantitative variables to existing neoclassical theory (Georgescu-Roegen, 1971, p. 76). To put it in a somewhat different manner: If utility really were measurable, then all units of one generic commodity could be made psychologically identical with any other commodity; all commodities could be reduced to other commodities; and we would be back to a classical theory of value which discovered value as embodied within the commodity. The question of the "natural" or "unnatural" quantification of economic phenomena is, properly interpreted, a metaphysical problem of identity. Hence Poincaré's remark that mathematicians give the same name to different things.

Although Georgescu-Roegen neglected to press the inquiry into the cardinal measurability of commodities in consumer theory, he did choose to do so in the theory of production (Georgescu-Roegen, 1976, pp. 72–73). His contributions in this area are decisive. First, he has observed that physics is not uniformly "quantified". There are many areas of study which have not been able to construct or discover proportional laws, presumably because they are more directly concerned with variations in qualities. Secondly, he points out that the technical role of an input in a production process *may* be specified in a physically quantitative relationship, but that quantification rarely has any direct relationship to the "cardinality" of the input in its incarnation as a commodity (Georgescu-Roegen, 1971, p. 218). In a simplistic example, oil is sold by the barrel, but its efficacy in one production process is measured by foot-pounds per BTU, and in another by sulfur content in milligrams per litre, and in a third process a measure of resistance relative to roughness (in terms of the diameter of sand particles that give the same effect at a high Reynolds number). One might retort that the fully appropriate measure of the commodity should be some such vector as (liquid volume, BTU rating, Reynolds number, ...); but this ignores the fact that if we extend the metric to encompass every possible aspect of every conceivable production process, we absurdly balloon the length of the list of generic "commodities" until cardinality is defined away, because there is no remaining identity of "oil". Third, he explains that algebraic operations upon the input units cannot be confused with algebraic operations intended to represent production processes. Production processes may be cojoined, or they be assigned membership to a set in the mind or on paper; however, they cannot strictly be added or multiplied (Georgescu-Roegen, 1971, chap. 9).

Georgescu-Roegen brings to bear all of these considerations to demonstrate that the neoclassical production function is a thoroughly slipshod construct which is incapable of any appeal to physicalist notions as justification of its mathematical structure. In fact, since a production process does not satisfy the first requirement of lawlike behavior—that is, inputs and outputs are not directly connected, in the sense outlined above in the lengthy quote from Georgescu-Roegen—it does not even qualify as an appropriately cardinal formalism. The devastating moral of this line of inquiry is that, "If we maintain that any scale is as good as any other, then such fundamental notions as decreasing marginal rate of substitution, constant returns, efficiency, etc., lose any meaning whatsoever" (Georgescu-Roegen, 1976, p. 274).

It would thus seem that by the 1970s most of the components of a powerful critique of the received doctrine that the economy is "naturally quantitative" could be harvested from the neoclassical theory literature; nonetheless, this critique never materialized. Although he hesitated to do so himself, Georgescu-Roegen's critique of production theory could easily have been extended to the theory of the neoclassical consumer. After all, consumption is also a process, and is treated in other respects by neoclassicals in a manner symmetrically to production.

It could have been pointed out that the common thrust of these varied writings is the overarching thesis that *there is no reason to believe that the algebras of economic quantities are isomorphic to the algebras used to characterize their physical manifestations.* An alternative interpretation would see metrics as constructed entities conditional upon the intended use, based upon the imposition of identity upon phenomenological diversity. Alas, this line of inquiry has lain dormant. We now return unerringly to that non-quantitative question, the motor of metaphysics: Why?

§17. There are at least two distinct answers to that question. The first derives from a certain tradition in anthropology and sociology, which claims that all cultures, preliterate and literate, are predisposed to base their explanations of their own social interactions upon their theories of the natural world and natural order (Barnes & Shapin, 1979; Douglas, 1966, 1970). As much as we might wish to feel superior to the Tiv or the Nuer or the Bushmen, the continuous invocation of and appropriation of physics by neoclassical economists documented in this essay reveals that we really all are brothers under the skin. One reason why the critique of "natural order" in the quantitative sphere has not been followed to its conclusions is that, as we have observed, this inquiry would reveal the social and conventional bases of quantification, and it would therefore undermine the direct lineage of economic magnitudes' descent from physical magnitude. Many unexplored programs of research remain that way because the abyss seems to yawn just inside of their perimeters.

The second answer to the question may be more palatable to those who find such functionalist explanations distasteful. Another major reason that the critique of a direct isomorphism between physical and economic algebras has languished in an undeveloped state is that the most perceptive and insightful critics have not marshalled one of the major mathematical devices of the twentieth century to their cause. That body of technique is a subset of the discipline of abstract algebra called group theory.

Group theory evolved out of work done on the theory of equations in the early nineteenth century (Wussing, 1984). It began as the documentation of certain patterns in the solutions of equations when various key parameters underwent permutation. After 1870 a more abstract view of groups gained ascendancy. Around the turn of the century it was recognized that the structure of groups could be employed to describe any arbitrary operation, not necessarily those restricted to the theory of equations or geometry, which conformed to a few simple rules. Groups provided the language for a discussion of very abstract patterns which, when interpreted, promised to uncover connections between many disparate areas of mathematics.

An abstract group is defined as:

I. A set of elements (a, b, c, d, . . .) which can be of finite or infinite order. The number of elements in the set is called the order of the group.

II. Any operation between any two elements, which we shall read from left to right. For example: a × b

This operation must obey the following rules:

i) *Closure*. If a and b are elements of the set, so is the result of a × b.

ii) *Associativity*. a × (b × c) = (a × b) × c

iii) *Identity Element*. The set must contain an element e such that:

$$e \times a = a \times e = a, \text{ for each element in the set.}$$

iv) *Inverse Element*. For every element a in the set there exists an element b such that:

$$a \times b = b \times a = e$$

We will follow standard notation and denote this inverse $b = a^{-1}$.

The central concept in abstract algebra is the group; the taxonomies of other abstract algebras generally involve the augmentation or diminution of the above set of rules. Some of these variants that we shall shortly find useful are the concepts of an Abelian group and a semigroup. In the former case, if we were to append a fifth rule to the above four to the effect that the operation must be *commutative*, that is, for every pair of elements:

$$a \times c = c \times a$$

then the group would be called an Abelian group. In the latter case, a set of elements and an operation which only conforms to the first two rules of closure and associativity is called a semigroup. As is to be expected, the less restrictive specification of a semigroup results in much diminished inference concerning its properties. Finally, any subset of the elements of a given group which, by themselves, conform to the rules i–iv is known as a *subgroup*.

One advantage of group theory is that knowledge of a small number of key characteristics of a group will serve to summarize all of the important information about the structure of an algebra. Poincaré observed that the theory of groups is ". . . the whole of mathematics divested of its matter and reduced to pure form" (quoted in Kline, 1972, p. 1146). Some of this power-ful capacity can be illustrated by the examination of the "table" of a group of small order; in this case, a group of order four. The group table displays all of the possible outcomes of application of the × operation between any two elements of the set.

GROUP TABLE

e	a	b	c
a	b	c	e
b	c	e	a
c	e	a	b

In this example, the group consists of the set of elements (a, b, c, e), and obeys the following rules:

$$a \times a = b; e \times a = a; e \times b = b;$$
$$a \times b = c = a \times a \times a;$$
$$b \times b = e = a \times a \times a \times a.$$

Inspection of the table is sufficient to reveal that this is indeed a group, since rules i–iv imply that no element of the set can appear more than once in any column or row of the table. The table is symmetric, in that the pattern of entries is identical above and below the diagonal running from the upper left to the lower right hand corner: this is indicative of the fact that the operation is commutative, and thus this group is Abelian. Knowledge of the fact that the group is of order four imposes sufficient restrictions upon the operation such that we know that there exist only two distinct structures for groups of order four, and that they both must be Abelian. Similarly, we know there is only one group structure of order three, and only one structure of order two, and that they also must be Abelian (Durbin, 1985, p. 103). Other theorems of group theory which we shall employ in this paper are: each group can only possess one unique identity element; each element of a group possesses a unique inverse; groups of prime order possess no subgroups except themselves and the isolated identity element (ie., the improper subsets). The reader might confirm these theorems from inspection of the group table.

Groups are more abstract than the more familiar ordinary algebra because they subsume its patterns under more general principles. For instance, suppose we restrict ourselves to the set of integers:

$$(\ldots, -3, -2, -1, 0, 1, 2, 3, \ldots)$$

and consider the group operation of ordinary addition. Inspection will reveal that this operation conforms to all of the rules governing a group: the sum of any two integers is an integer, the element "0" is the identity, the inverse of "n" is "−n", and closure is preserved by specifying that the group is of infinite order. Since addition is commutative, the group is Abelian.

Now instead suppose that we restricted ourselves to the set:

$$(\ldots, 2^{-3}, 2^{-2}, 2^{-1}, 2^0, 2^1, 2^2, 2^3, \ldots)$$

If we then specify the group operation to be ordinary multiplication, we find that we again have a group. An important step in coming to understand the abstract power of group theory is to observe that all of the formal patterns produced within this multiplicative group are exactly the same as the patterns displayed by the additive group of integers, so that for all practical purposes, they are the same group. (Here recall Poincaré's quip.) If two groups have the same pattern of entries in their group tables, then they are said to be *isomorphic* to one another.

However brief and inadequate this survey of group theory, it should sufficiently equip us with the means to explain how the critics of quantification and arithmomorphism in economic theory were hampered by their neglect of abstract algebra.

§18. For purposes of illustration, we shall initially focus our attention upon two neoclassical economists who have been concerned with problems of formalization and quantification: Robert Clower and Nicholas Georgescu-Roegen. Clower perceives his work as the tilling of the narrower field of monetary theory, whereas Georgescu-Roegen cultivates the broader field of production theory. Both would have profited immensely from detection of the isomorphisms between their respective programs of research.

The aim of (Clower, 1967) was an inquiry into the determinants of the trivial role played by money in syntheses of Keynesian and neoclassical theories. He decided that the major culprit was the mathematics of then-popular models, which effectively described barter economies in which every commodity indiscriminately performed the functions of money; hence, an independent money commodity was redundant. Of particular interest from our present point of view was his method of demonstrating his point. He presented the following tables as paradigms of different kinds of economies:

barter			pure money				non-pure money				
	C_1	C_2		C_1	C_2	C_3		C_1	C_2	C_3	C_4	
C_1	X	X	C_1	X	X	X	C_1	X	X	X	X	
C_2	X	X	C_2	X	X	0	C_2	X	X	0	0	
			C_3	X	0	X	C_3	X	0	X	X	
							C_4	X	0	X	X	

The C_i are indices for different generic commodities, $i = 1, 2, \ldots, n$. The X's are to be interpreted as indicating that the trade of commodities represented by the intersecting row and column is allowed to take place; the 0's indicate that a particular trade is not permitted. Although Clower's overriding concern is with money, the artifice of the tabular format leads him to briefly consider the more fundamental question: what qualifies as a legitimate trade? He takes it as a self-evident axiom that possession of a commodity qualifies as a virtual trade of that commodity for itself; that is, C_i can always be traded for C_i (and therefore, diagonal entries in the tables will always be X). Secondly, he posits that the exchange relation must always be symmetric; that is, if C_i is allowed to exchange for C_j, then it must also be the case that C_j is also allowed to exchange for C_i (thus Clower's tables will always be symmetric around the diagonal). Finally, he defines a money commodity as one which can be traded for any other commodity. From these axioms he deduces the theorem that the simplest economy where money performs a non-trivial function of the coordination of exchange must have at least three distinct commodities. Similarly, the smallest money economy which is capable of containing a subset which functions as a pure barter system must comprise at least four separate commodities. Since many of the models under consideration did not meet these criteria, Clower felt satisfied that he had identified the flaw in their arguments.

The reader will quickly recognize that Clower was groping his way towards an abstract algebric representation of trade.[11] The most critical artifact which prevented him from exploiting the group concept was his insistence upon binary trade/no trade entries in the bodies of his tables. If we temporarily overlook the fact that his table entries are not group elements because the operation is not closed, we can observe that much of what Clower wished to say (and much more) could be expressed using the theorems of group theory.

The imposition of diagonal symmetry upon the tables is a very strong restriction; we know that if we interpreted the operation of exchange as conforming to an algebraic group, then Clower must be insisting that all trades are commutative, and thus the group of exchange must be Abelian. (Possible definitions of the operation and the set of elements are discussed below.) In his own examples, however, this is not a matter subject to choice, since *all* groups of order five or lower must be Abelian. In other words, in order to consider exchange as a group process which is not commutative, we must build models of the economy which possess at least *six* distinct commodities. Moreover, by Lagrange's theorem (Hamermesh, 1962, p. 20), we know that the order of all proper subgroups of any arbitrary group are integer factors of the order of the original group. Therefore, any model of an economy where the number of distinct commodities is prime will possess no barter subeconomies similar to the one exhibited in Clower's table (c). Thus we witness an advantage of the group theoretic perspective: it helps us discern what the previous employment of other mathematical techniques has served to obscure. In the present instance, it indicates that any economic model that treats less than four functionally distinct commodities cannot seriously discuss the separate and distinct functions of money in the economy; and a model which would not surreptitiously impose the condition that all trades are commutative must possess at least six distinct commodities.

While these theorems instantiate how group theory might have helped to generalize Clower's results, they are simply extrapolations of his basic themes. A more important application of group theory could reveal that even at this most abstract level of the binary entries of trade/no trade, Clower could not succeed in illuminating the very core of the problem of money. The question that he posed was: under what conditions would the functions of money be non-trivial? Clower correctly noted that money would always be trivial in two-good models. What he did not notice was that as long as trade conforms to a group, and each good trades for at least one other good, and the group is Abelian, any particular commodity can be obtained through a finite sequence of trades, starting from any arbitrary endowment. Unless further structure is imposed upon the model (such as independent transactions costs or other external constraints on the trading sequence), money still has a trivial function in such an economic model. Clower could not observe that the axiomatic imposition of symmetry on his economy acted to neutralize the very role of money which he wished to highlight, because it was isomorphic to a world of barter where any commodity may be directly or indirectly traded for any other commodity. Once one becomes sensitized to the group formalism, one can immediately deduce these results from inspection of the abstract patterns displayed in a group table.

The seemingly harmless assumption that the activity of trade is commutative is freighted with profound and substantial theoretical content, much of which has never been explored in any detail in economics. The elaboration of this content will take up much of the remainder of this essay. In this section it may suffice to simply indicate some of the aspects of the submerged theoretical content. First, commutivity places some implicit restrictions upon the actors, who have up until now remained hidden in the wings. Commutivity means there must exist some set of traders willing to exchange X for Y, and another set willing to trade Y for X in the exact same circumstances (which includes the law of one price). Hence, people must differ in whatever it is that motivates their trading activities, and those activities *must have been coordinated prior to the realization of the trades*. In other words, there must exist diversity, but simultaneously, that diversity is neutralized through the restriction that it can in no way materially affect the outcome. Clower did not see that commutivity neutralized the role of an independent trade coordinator. Without the specification of different trader personalities, commutivity would condone a shoe salesman entering his own shoe shop to purchase shoes, and in fact, this would provide the major vehicle for taking up any slack in effective demand. Secondly, commutivity implies effective reversibility of any trade in time, rendering any attempts to model errors or historical change incoherent. Third, commutivity posits a symmetry which is frequently absent in actual economies. I can take money to the Safeway to buy food; but I can't take food into the Safeway to buy money. Fourth, commutivity imposes some very rigid conditions upon the concept of value, which we shall elaborate below in section §20.

Now let us relinquish the binary entries in Clower's tables, and in the process discover that monetary theory is merely a special case of a more general economic problem. We have noted that the structure of a group requires closure; this would mean that the entries in the tables whose purpose it is to describe trade must themselves be members of the set of commodities. Thus (as should be obvious) Clower's tables are useless in discussing prices, since the elements of his set are merely the names of generic commodities, such as: (Gucci shoes, hot dogs, beer mugs, iron ingots,...). In other words, *Clower's conception of trade is not quantitative.* Let us inquire into how we might rectify this serious omission.

Clower treats trades as if they were thoroughly abstracted away from the activities of the people "behind the scenes"; in this section, we shall do likewise. Suppose that there happened to be six discrete "endowments" sitting in a "market". There are also three permissible barter trades, sanctioned by some unspecified mechanism: one particular hat trades for a particular dozen eggs, a second dozen eggs trades for a pen, and three hats trade for ten dozen eggs. Employing the symbol T in order to signify the operation of trade, our rules are therefore:

$$1 \text{ hat } \text{T} \quad 12 \text{ eggs} = \quad 12 \text{ eggs}$$
$$12 \text{ eggs } \text{T} \quad 1 \text{ pen} = \quad 1 \text{ pen}$$
$$3 \text{ hats } \text{T} \; 120 \text{ eggs} = 120 \text{ eggs}$$

If we adopt Clower's axioms that a commodity always trades "virtually" for itself, and that all sanctioned trades are symmetric, then we deduce the further sanctioned trades:

$$1 \text{ hat } \quad \text{T} \quad 1 \text{ hat } = \quad 1 \text{ hat}$$
$$2 \text{ hats } \quad \text{T} \quad 2 \text{ hats } = \quad 2 \text{ hats}$$

$$\vdots \qquad \vdots \qquad \vdots$$
$$\vdots \qquad \vdots \qquad \vdots$$

$$12 \text{ eggs } \textcircled{T} \quad 1 \text{ hat} \quad = \quad 1 \text{ hat}$$
$$1 \text{ pen } \textcircled{T} \quad 12 \text{ eggs} = \quad 12 \text{ eggs}$$
$$120 \text{ eggs } \textcircled{T} \quad 3 \text{ hats} = 120 \text{ eggs}$$

Further, let us provisionally adopt one of the most fundamental assumptions of all of mathematical economics (which has never been discussed, much less evaluated). Let us suppose that the operation of trade is associative, so for instance:

$$(1 \text{ hat } \textcircled{T} \ 12 \text{ eggs}) \ \textcircled{T} \ 1 \text{ pen} = 1 \text{ hat } \textcircled{T} \ (12 \text{ eggs } \textcircled{T} \ 1 \text{ pen}) = 1 \text{ pen}$$

Consolidating all of the permissible trades into a single table, we arrive at:

$\textcircled{T}$	1 hat	2 hats	3 hats	12 eggs	120 eggs	1 pen
1 hat	1 hat	?	?	12 eggs	?	1 pen
2 hats	?	2 hats	?	?	?	?
3 hats	?	?	3 hats	?	120 eggs	?
12 eggs	1 hat	?	?	12 eggs	?	1 pen
120 eggs	?	?	3 hats	?	120 eggs	?
1 pen	1 hat	?	?	12 eggs	?	1 pen

Perusal of this table begins to reveal problems in the specification of Clower's tables, as well as problems in the specification of a group to characterize trade. The nature and significance of an "impermissible" trade is left tantalizingly vague in Clower's writings, and it is precisely upon the choice of conceptualization of these prohibited activities that much of the structure of the algebra founders. The question marks in the table signify trades other than those sanctioned by the unspecified "mechanism". If all of these entries were left empty, then we would be violating the first requirement of any abstract group, that any operation defined over a set should be closed. However, if a proscribed trade is not consummated, but instead remains virtual, how should the result be characterized? Taking a cue from Clower's contention that a commodity should always virtually trade for itself, we could posit that every blocked or prohibited trade is equivalent to a virtual trade of the initial commodity for itself, because the initiator of the blocked trade always retains the commodity offered. Thus, as an example:

$$1 \text{ hat } \textcircled{T} \ 2 \text{ hats} = 1 \text{ hat}$$

In this eventuality, the above table would find all of the question marks replaced with the entry heading the corresponding row. Unfortunately, this emendation would contradict Clower's original axiom of the symmetry of trades, undermining their purported commutative character.

Further attempts to rescue this representation of the algebra of exchange are rendered hopeless by the realization that Clower's axioms are self-contradictory. This is because *this conception of barter exchange in a finite order economy does not conform to the structure of an algebraic group*. Even were we to induce closure in the table by said replacement of the question marks by the row headings, any given row or column contains elements of the set which appear more than once. This violates group rules iii and iv in the sense that the row and column headings do not behave like distinct elements of a group. Taken in isolation, each commodity bundle acts as its own identity and inverse; but this does not extend to the system as a whole, the aggregate of commodity bundles.

Parenthetically, there exists the possibility that our criticism of Clower misses the mark because we have misspecified the group elements as commodity bundles. An alternative would be to specify each group element as consisting of an entire trade, say:

$$
\begin{array}{lll}
\text{A:} & 1\,\text{hat} & \to \; 12\,\text{eggs} \\
\text{B:} & 12\,\text{eggs} & \to \; 1\,\text{pen} \\
\text{C:} & 3\,\text{hats} & \to 120\,\text{eggs} \\
\text{D:} & 1\,\text{hat} & \to \; 1\,\text{pen} \qquad \text{and so on.}
\end{array}
$$

The group operation would in this case be the composition of these transformations: in this example, $A \times B = D$. The economic interpretation of the group operation would be that it identified compositions of trades that would end up "at the same place," in the way that both $A \times B$ and D end up at "one pen".

While there has been some very interesting work based upon this algebraic portrayal of exchange (Ellerman, 1984), it does not come to grips with the problems that concern Clower, (and us, we hasten to add), because it assumes them away at a very primitive level of analysis. First, this version is incapable of confronting the problem of impermissible or blocked trades, because, by definition, only "sanctioned" trades qualify as group elements. Secondly, it cannot explicitly confront the thorny issues of quantification, since it buries the notion of commodity equivalence in the primitive definition of the group operation: "one pen" counts as the "same result" in B and D. The seeming plausibility of this conceptualization ultimately rests upon the purported isomorphism of physical algebras to the algebra of trade discussed above in §16. Third, by focusing attention on the transformation rather than the commodity bundle, it assumes that trades are comparable along some axis in the absence of money, and therefore cannot distinguish situations in which the presence of money is either superfluous or necessary. Fourth, our critique of the incoherence of virtual self-trade also applies to this framework. For all of these reasons, the conceptualization of trade as a composition of transformations will not help us explain why prices are quantitative.

In this extended reconsideration of Clower's research agenda, we are forcibly struck by the persistent frustration of broaching the issue of the role of money in the context of an operation that lacks an identity element. Given the surfeit of trades that map any given commodity back onto itself, money is truly a superfluous concept. Hence Clower's critique dies aborning, because the problem is not restricted to the fundamental misrepresentation of money in mathematical economics; it extends to the fundamental misrepresentation of the operation of exchange.

Turning to the paper by Georgescu-Roegen (1976, pp. 271–296) on measure, quality, and optimum scale, we seem (at first blush) to be very far removed from any of the questions that motivated Clower's writings. Georgescu-Roegen avows his purpose is to demonstrate "that the ordinary concept of efficiency (as well as other equally important concepts of production theory) has no meaning if factors and products are not cardinally measurable." Nonetheless, there are two major similarities. The first, which we have already had occasion to mention, is the thesis that the laws of the prosecution of production processes are not necessarily isomorphic to the manipulation of their physical constituents. Clower suggests that the process of exchange is not adequately represented by the addition of physical units; Georgescu-Roegen holds the parallel brief for economic production processes. The second similarity resides in the fact that Georgescu-Roegen conceptualizes the analytical prerequisites for a plausible model of production by postulating an abstract operation, and then asking what axioms would guarantee that this operation was susceptible to cardinal measurement. It is fascinating that, just as in the case of Clower, he invokes some aspects of the basic structure of group theory without acknowledging it, and therefore misses using the analytical shortcuts provided by group structures. In fact, his axioms of cardinality (Georgescu-Roegen, 1976, pp. 275–279) are nothing other than our group axioms i–iv, plus commutativity and the axiom of Archimedes. As he observes without the aid of group theory, the imposition of an Abelian group structure upon an economic production process is tantamount to positing a world where all transformations consist of the reshuffling of some primal substance; such reshufflings can result in no new emergent properties other than those already inherent in the primal substance (p. 288). In somewhat simpler terms, qualitative novelty is precluded by the symmetry of the Abelian group. This is further corroborated by Georgescu-Roegen's description of what he calls "weak cardinality" (pp. 281–282), which is nothing other than the axioms posited by physicists in order to characterize "gauge symmetry" (C. L. Smith in Mulvey, 1981; and t'Hooft, 1980).

Why has abstract algebra been neglected in economics? Again we must return to the influence of the development of physical science upon conceptions of mathematical formalism in economic theory.

§19. Relatively recently, developments in particle physics have prompted some physicists to reconceptualize the progressive thrust in the history of their discipline as the unfolding of manifestations of symmetries in nature (Galison, 1983, p. 49; Elliott and Dawber, 1979). This revised standard chronicle begins with the recasting of the laws of motion in terms of energetic considerations—precisely those touched upon above in section §6. The goal of a unified theory of nature was given further impetus in the early twentieth century by the development of a theorem by Emmy Noether, which included an early application of the theory of continuous groups (Brewer and Smith, 1981, pp. 16 et seq.). Noether's theorem demonstrates that corresponding to every invariance or symmetry property of a variational theory there exists a conservation law. For example, the statement that the results of most physical experiments do not depend upon their orientation (i.e., the direction in space in which they are pointed) is more formally expressed as the axiom of rotational invariance; and this, in turn, is equivalent to the law of the conservation of angular momentum. Likewise, statements about the invariance of a phenomenon with respect to its temporal location are equivalent to the postulation of the law of the conservation of energy, as well as to the axiom in much of physics that laws of motion are symmetric with respect to the time axis. In this manner, many seemingly separate hypotheses concerning physical phenomena were subsumed under one general pattern.

The power of this approach only became apparent in the twentieth century, after the twin revolutions of relativity theory and quantum mechanics, only to become paramount upon the rise to dominance of subatomic physics (Rosen, 1983). The theory of relativity grew out of an imposed symmetry to the effect that the known laws of motion should be symmetric and invariant relative to any moving observer; and this deceptively simple condition provoked a profound revision in the very algebra of space and time, from the Galilean group to the Lorentz group. Quantum mechanics escalated the dependence of physics upon symmetry principles to a greater degree: "The quantum numbers tell us what kind of symmetries we mean.... Thus, when we come to the smallest objects in the world, we characterize them in quantum mechanics just by their symmetry, or as a representation of symmetries, and not by specifying properties such as shape or size" (Heisenberg in Buckley and Peat, 1979, p. 14). The implementation of this precept is evident in the quark model, where it serves to impose some structure upon a confusing proliferation of types of subatomic particles (Elliott and Dawber, 1979). Group theory was there applied to reduce all known particles (and a few yet to be discovered) to combinations of a small number of abstract qualities. Even more recently, theories of gauge symmetry are the main contenders in the quest to provide a grand unified theory of the four fundamental forces of nature (t'Hooft, 1980).

The lesson of interest for economists resides not in the mere fact that group theory has progressively become more and more indispensable in physics, but rather in the novel attitudes toward mathematical formalism which it has engendered. As physicists have become increasingly resigned to the role of the observer as an inextricable facet of any physical phenomenon, they also have become less sanguine about the existence of any independent preordained natural metric. In their practice, the specification of a metric has come to be seen as the generalization of an equivalence relation, which imposes a symmetry group upon a given state space (Rosen, 1983, p. 142). Hence modern mathematical formalism in physics tends to consist of the postulation of judiciously chosen symmetries with an eye toward the self-conscious construction of the meaning of natural order. Systems with very few salient features are asserted to possess powerful symmetries. For example, in mechanics the absence of all forces is defined as spatial symmetry. In any case where things persist in shooting off to the right, this is interpreted as evidence that we have discovered some external force or influence. The moral of this tale would seem to be that when faced with the phenomenological confusion besetting an empirical question, the first step is to ask: what symmetries am I willing to suggest characterize this situation? The next step is to define order as regular alterations of that symmetry. "Order is broken symmetry" (Salam, in Mulvey, 1981, p. 111) is the slogan of late-twentieth-century physics.

We have already had occasion to observe in section §10 that the track record of economics in justifying its favored conceptions of order has left something to be desired. Instead of stressing the importance of research into the meaning and implications of successful coordination of economic activity, economists attempted to create the impression of natural order by appropriation of a physics metaphor, and then found the critical notions of competition, equilibrium and so forth dictated to them by their newly adopted mathematical procedures.

Although perhaps the most legitimate research program in economics should generate its own mathematical tools simultaneously with its development of the economic theory, the present author is not at all sanguine about the likelihood of that prospect. The history of the economists' envy of the physicists is a heavy burden, not easily or lightly discarded. The interaction of physical and social metaphor pervades our thought in more ways than we might at first imagine. Moreover, mathematical expertise has itself become so separated from practical application in the modern disciplinary boundaries of the university, that sociological forces also militate against that scenario (Kline, 1980). A more realistic and modest proposal would be that, if we are to get our mathematical metaphors from physics, let us at least do it self-consciously, and with greater discrimination and subtlety than did our neoclassical forebears. Instead of arbitrarily appropriating this or that particular physical model as a metaphor, perhaps it would be more useful to contemplate the larger pattern of mathematical theory in the physics of the twentieth century. In this respect, the deployment of symmetry concepts and abstract algebra provides a framework for the conceptualization of order which is not tethered to any particular physical model. In the older, pre-Kuhnian sense, it can serve as a paradigm of explanation.

And so we arrive at the kernel of truth within Defense$_1$: the question of the appropriateness of mathematical techniques in economics cannot be separated from the conception of order in economic theory. Such an awareness must foster a skepticism toward prepackaged mathematical techniques taken from the physical sciences. The trepidation with which some would regard such a research program might derive from an impression that it would involve repudiation of three centuries of economic thought, leaving us to start, as it were, with a blank slate.

Luckily, the situation is not so drastic as all that.

§20. When and if we revise our understanding of what it means to conduct a self-conscious mathematical economics, we shall also revise our roster of whom we believe to have been legitimately creative mathematical economists. Contrary to the claim of Schumpeter quoted above in section §13, we should like to seriously entertain the idea that Marx was a seminal mathematical economist. By this statement we do not intend to refer to the schemes of expanded reproduction, or the algebra of the transformation problem found in volume III of *Capital*. Neither do we desire to praise the labour theory of value as an insightful manipulation of quantitative concepts.[12] Instead, the specifically mathematical contribution of Marx to economic theory is to be found in the first six chapters of volume I of *Capital*, in the discussion of the problems surrounding the conceptualization of a commodity. These chapters display the beginnings of a self-conscious examination of the problems of symmetry and order described above in section §19, and as such might serve as a point of departure for a reconstruction of mathematical economics.

It is very easy for the modern reader to discount the early parts of *Capital*, where Marx searches for the "common element" that permits the comparison of different commodities, as a regrettable metaphysical residuum of his Hegelian training. A different perspective will reveal this to be an intemperate attitude. The first consideration that should help us read these passages in a new light is the realization that much of the history of economic thought has been absorbed with a question that remains unresolved to this very day: Are "normal" trades the exchange of equivalents, or not? What is the meaning and significance of equivalence of value? The rise of neoclassical theory acted to banish this problem from overt discussion, but did not resolve it. One might initially think that neoclassicism settled the issue by placing itself squarely in the camp of those who maintained trade was of nonequivalents, in the sense that the total utilities to each transactor of any given commodity are divergent; but in practice, the situation is not so clearly defined. First, problems of the trade of equivalents have been recast so as to be subsumed under controversies over the cardinality of utility and/or various inconsistent claims with respect to the interpersonal comparison of utility. Second, the issue was avoided, in part, through the imposition of the law of one price as a condition of equilibrium (Bausor, this vol., chap. 4). Third, the presumption of the trade of equivalents has surreptitiously reentered neoclassical theory through such expedients as the discounting of future utility in order to consititute a present price, and the definition, popular in financial theory, of an efficient market as one which arbitrages away all divergent valuations.

Marx deserves attention because he correctly identifies the question of the trade of equivalents as the necessary point of departure for a mathematical economics; it is the other side of the coin of a theory of economic order. Equivalence in trade provides the benchmark and the definition of the putative voluntary character of trade, as was argued by many before Marx (cf. Mirowski, chap. 5, forthcoming). More importantly for our purposes, in the most elementary sense, there can be no equilibrium of nonequivalents in the absence of a prior specification of an equivalence relation. The absence of all forces for change are conceptualized as the equivalence of some critical index. But then, once an equivalence relation is posited for trade, then the stability of nonequivalent "equilibria" becomes adventitious and problematic. This is one way to understand the vagaries of the history of game theory (see this vol., chap. 7), as well as the history of neoclassicism: the law of one price, in conjunction with the imposition of an "auctioneer" or trade coordinator whose job it is to enforce it, are required in order to impose a single metric upon an otherwise chaotic agglomeration of preferences.

This insight can be rephrased in terms of Georgescu-Roegen's work quoted above in section §16. Laws generally take the form of simple linear relations because two or more cardinal variables have an immediate connection: there is no qualitative residual which remains uncaptured in the statement of the law. To insist that "normal" trades are exchanges of nonequivalents is to condemn economic theory to the partial and flawed quantification of economic relations, and thus to relinquish all hope of finding economic laws. To posit the equilibrium trade of nonequivalents is to assert that a set of fundamental quantitative considerations directly govern trade, and yet are beyond the ken of mathematical expression. To state this in terms of the physics metaphor: since there exists no symmetric ground-state which is characteristic of the absence of all forces, there are no guidelines as to how one should conceptualize the manifestation of forces outside of the ground-state (Weyl, 1952, p. 25).

The trade of equivalents is not an empirical issue. For Marx, it was a prior condition for the quantitative comprehension of a capitalist economy. If one accepts this viewpoint, then most of the Marxian prose about the search for an illusive common element shared by all commodities can be reinterpreted in more modern terms as a search for the appropriate abstract algebra to provide the structure requisite for capitalist exchange, and which would serve as the vehicle for the equivalence relation. In this reading, the first six chapters of *Capital* are divided up into preliminary remarks on the conditions any such algebra must meet, then a sequence of successive abstractions or approximations to the algebra from pure barter to a fully monetized economy, and finally to the invocation of symmetry conditions isomorphic to the equivalence relation for the purpose of isolating broken symmetries. Notably, these discussions of the algebraic characteristics of trade take place entirely prior to any specification of the mechanisms of price setting.

Accepting the trade of equivalents as a theoretical imperative, Marx asks what format the abstract algebra should assume. He then proceeds to assert a thesis, broached above in section §16, that economic quantities are not isomorphic to the algebras which characterize their physical constituents: "This common element cannot be a geometrical, physical, chemical or other natural property of commodities. Such properties come into consideration only to the extent that they make the commodities useful" (Marx, 1977, p. 127). Thus Lancaster's insight that the metric of use is not the metric of exchange was broached over one hundred years ago. Next, as a corollary to this first thesis, he insists that a physical commodity cannot be used to measure itself in exchange (Marx, 1977, p. 140). Translating this into more modern concerns, *contra* Clower, commodities do not virtually trade for themselves. Although it would be excessive to credit Marx with understanding of the formal aspects of this problem, this condition is a necessary prerequisite for the presence of an identity element in group theory. If for every a, the result $a \times a = a$, then there can exist no unique a^{-1}. Moreover, the construction of any equivalence relation must begin with the imposition of the postulate of reflexivity (i.e., $a = a$), a condition virtual self-trade tends to undermine (Rosen, 1983, p. 26). Denial of virtual self-trade analytically posits an algebra of commodity trade separate and distinct from an algebra of physical qualities. Comprehension of this fact prompts doubts about the logic of any economic theory asserting that any commodity is by itself sufficiently capable of serving as "numeraire."

After these preliminary considerations, there follows a section of *Capital* that has baffled many commentators. Here Marx posits a sequence of four "forms of value": the simple relative form, the expanded relative form, the general form, and the money form. This profusion of differing forms of value would surely seem superfluous unless one understood them as successive algebras which potentially might characterize exchange. In order to justify this interpretation, let us recast them in terms of modern algebra.

A *simple relative* algebra would correspond to our elaboration of Clower's simple barter economy. Within this format, for every bundle of commodity a traded for a bundle of commodity b, $a \textcircled{T} b = b$. Marx here insists that this is an incomplete and degenerate conception of value: "The expression of the value of the commodity A in terms of any other commodity B merely distinguishes the value of A from its use-value, and therefore merely places A in an exchange relation with any particular single different kind of commodity, instead of representing A's qualitative equality with all other commodities and its quantitative proportionality to them" (Marx, 1977, p. 154). In other words, this conception of the operation of exchange precludes any algebraic group structure.

To illustrate this point, consider the following four-good barter economy, consisting of endowment bundles (a, b, c, d).

Table 6–1:   Marx's Simple Relative Form of Value

$\textcircled{T}$?	a	b	c	d
a	?	b	c	d
b	a	?	c	d
c	a	b	?	d
d	a	b	c	?

Ignoring for the moment the question of what should be entered on the diagonal, we can immediately observe that this particular specification of barter can never be represented by an algebraic group, because a group table can only display a single appearance of any element of the set in any row or columm. Even if we should attempt to impose an external identity element upon this structure by replacing all of the question marks with e, each element would still lack a unique identity. This occurs because $b \textcircled{T} a = c \textcircled{T} a = d \textcircled{T} a = a$, so that appending a further trade for a, we find $b = c = d$. These exchanges fail to display a distinct identity and a distinct inverse, or as Marx puts it, there is no coherent expression of value. Further, this is a closed and finite system, and as such, is incapable of expressing the abstract unity of trade amidst the phenomenal diversity of goods, the quantitative character of value as distinct from the qualitative differentiation of physical manifestation of endowment bundles. Just as in Clower's case, there can be no number in this system. There are no symmetries, so there is no conserved entity. Equivalence is not sufficiently defined.

The movement to an *expanded relative* algebra is due to the recognition that value in exchange cannot arise in an isolated barter situation, but rather must be itself premised upon the supposition of an infinite expansion of commodities, even if this expansion is only virtual.[13] The quantitative conception of value is not contingent upon or limited by the (arbitrary) actual endowments present in the marketplace. In modern terms, the "expanded relative" algebra postulates an operation upon an infinite set. A single particular generic commodity is asserted to conform to the operation of the addition of integers:

Table 6–2:   Marx's Expanded Relative Form of Value

+	0	1	2	3	4	....
1	2	3	4	5	....	
2	3	4	5	6	....	
3	4	5	6	7	....	
4	5	6	7	8	....	
:	:	:	:	:		
:	:	:	:	:		

Initially, this form of value seems to violate Marx's proscription that a commodity cannot trade for itself. A more careful interpretation would suggest that some specific commodity is made subject to the algebra of addition of its own units independent of the operation of trade. Notice that these units are not "natural", but rather externally imposed and enforced, since we have as yet no analytical idea of the reasons why traders may decide to hold this commodity. Superimposed upon the algebra of this particular commodity is the operation of exchange for other endowments, which, as yet, possesses no algebraic structure. If we designate the unit of the chosen algebraic commodity n, then the operation of trade can be represented by a roster of permissible trades:

$$4n \, \textcircled{T} \, a = a; \quad (4n \, \textcircled{T} \, a) + (4n \, \textcircled{T} \, a) = a + a'; \ldots$$
$$12n \, \textcircled{T} \, b = b; \, (12n \, \textcircled{T} \, b) + (12n \, \textcircled{T} \, b) = b + b'; \ldots$$
$$27n \, \textcircled{T} \, c = c; \text{ and so on.}$$

In the expanded relative form, one might jump to the conclusion that by means of the operation of exchange all commodities become subject to the same algebra of addition as the chosen algebraic commodity, but this would be premature. As Marx suggests, "The defects of the expanded relative form are reflected in the corresponding (simple) relative form" (Marx, 1977, p. 156). We can observe that the operation of exchange still cannot constitute a group, because all trades still take the form of $x \, \textcircled{T} \, y = y$. One might object that the existence of the algebraic commodity could be employed to obviate this criticism in the following manner: repeat the trade $4n \, \textcircled{T} \, a = a$ three separate times, and then reverse the operation so that $3a \, \textcircled{T} \, 12n = 12n$, $12n \, \textcircled{T} \, b = b$, and therefore $3a = b$. The flaw in this reasoning is that the algebra of the particular commodity cannot be assumed to apply to other commodities without the imposition of further severe restrictions. In this instance, there is as yet no unique identity element corresponding to the operation of exchange, so there is no reason to believe that the repetition of any given trade will produce the identical result. (That is, we do not have reason to believe that $(4n \, \textcircled{T} \, a)$ followed by $(4n \, \textcircled{T} \, a)$ results in $2a$.) Even more critically, we have no reason to believe that the operation of exchange has an inverse; for example, that $4n \, \textcircled{T} \, a = a$ implies that $a \, \textcircled{T} \, 4n = 4n$. These are not merely technical caveats. Allowing these amendments to the theory of value would presuppose that exchanges have been standardized in such a manner that a sequence of trades over time can be treated as isomorphic to multiple trades at a single point in time and space, although a little introspection should reveal that there is little in our experience that would render this axiom self-evident. Moreover, as we indicated in section §18, neither is it obvious that all trades are commutative. An imposition of commutivity would imply that any trade that is contracted can be undone, that the activity of exchange is reversible, and that some value characteristic of commodities is conserved. Finally, it is not obvious that the order in which trades are consummated has no influence upon the final outcome. In the expanded relative form, the only thing that may legitimately be said to be conserved is the identity of the single algebraic commodity. Therefore, the equality relation defined over the exchange operation remains deficient and degenerate because the terms on both sides of the equation cannot change places across the "equals" sign (Marx, 1977, p. 157). In more technical terms, a semigroup will only possess an equivalence relation if the operation is transitive, reflexive, and symmetric (Ljapin, 1974, p. 36).

The *general form* of value carries the elaboration of symmetries two steps further. First, it posits the requirement that only generic ("freely reproducible") commodities be taken under consideration, and that these commodities be treated symmetrically with the numeraire commodity of the previous "expanded relative" form. Thus each generic commodity, considered in isolation, is required to conform to the infinite algebraic group of addition. Each of these additive groups is symmetric, which implies that the global quantity of the commodity is conserved with respect to the agglomeration of commodities into bundles. Economically, apples can be added to apples; oranges can be added with oranges. The additive group of each of the commodities is isomorphic to that characteristic of the other commodities; indeed, they are identical. They thus all share the same identity element, namely, the zero. In economic terms, we are no longer tethered to a given configuration of endowments in a particular marketplace; instead we now contemplate an infinitely expandable economy.

Only at this stage of value are goods being treated as if there were no qualitative distinctions being made between any finite sequences of their generic units; the traders view them as indifferent manifestations of the same economic object. Thus it is only at the stage of the general form of value that the attributes of the traders themselves and not just the physical attributes of the commodities enter into the proceedings. A prerequisite of a regularized algebra of exchange is the existence of traders socialized to accept and acquiesce in the very existence of generic commodities.

The second aspect of the general form of value is the introduction of the conception of exchange as the composition of mappings of the individual groups associated with each generic commodity. In the example presented in Table 6–3, exchange is portrayed as a mapping of the "units" of commodity A into the "units" of commodity B according to the map α; whereas the reverse exchange is portrayed as a map β from B to A. When presented in this manner, the composition of mappings from one commodity group to another is entirely general, and therefore can express any conceivable configuration of price determination. The imposition of certain restrictions upon the mappings will begin to delimit the forms which prices may assume. For example, if the mappings $\{\alpha, \alpha', \beta, \beta', \gamma, \gamma'\}$ are all "onto," then all quantities of the second commodity are assigned some quantity of the first commodity in exchange. If the composition of these mappings is "one to one," then there is at most one quantity of the second commodity which is assigned to some quantity of the first commodity in exchange. Unless the composition of mappings is not both one to one and onto, trades will not be determinate, at least in the sense of leading to unique outcomes.

Even with these assumptions, this "general form of value" is inadequate to quantify the operation of exchange. One way to see this is to note that, in the general form, prices are not expressed as ratios; rather, they are complicated functions of the quantities of both commodities involved, may not be additive, and may not be the same for different units of the same commodity. Moreover, the operation of exchange is not yet well-defined, because the absence of closure in the second step of Table 6–3 precludes the imposition of the simplest algebraic structure. The heart of the problem is that the mappings have not yet been sufficiently abstracted from the identities of the commodities themselves.

The gist of Marx's general form of value is that the algebraic properties of commodities do not determine the algebraic properties of exchange. Trade itself must also be conceptualized as a group. As (Marx, 1971, p. 143) put it in his critique of Samuel Bailey:

[The object is to explain] ... the proportion in which one thing exchanges for an infinite mass of other things which have nothing in common with it ... for the proportion to be a fixed proportion, all those various heterogeneous things must be considered as proportionate representations of *some common unity*, an element quite different from their natural appearance or existence."

In order to achieve this status, there are further stringent restrictions which must be imposed. First, the mappings of commodities must comprise a closed set. Second, there must be an identity element in this set: some exchange which preserves all the other mappings and endows the operation with quantitative stability. Third, each mapping must have an inverse: an exchange which "undoes" the previous exchange. The appearance of the question marks in Table 6–3 signals the absence of the latter attributes: there is as yet no map which takes a commodity group back into itself, and there is no clear idea of the outcome of the reversal of an exchange, such as the composition of α and β.

Our discussion in section §18 above of the incoherence of virtual self-exchange should make us very wary of the "natural" assumption that the identity element in exchange is provided by the self-identity of the commodity itself. One thing we do not observe in markets is people swapping identical commodities. This means that the commodity groups developed in the expanded relative form of value cannot provide the basis for the group properties of exchange. Instead, what is required is that the very notion of a mapping of a commodity group has to be redefined in terms of a map from the commodity to some index M such that:

$$A \xrightarrow{\alpha} M, M \xrightarrow{\alpha} A; \quad B \xrightarrow{\beta} M', M' \xrightarrow{\beta} B; \quad C \xrightarrow{\gamma} M'', M'' \xrightarrow{\gamma} C.$$

What is this intermediate mapping which will serve to render trades a quantitative phenomenon? The artifact which provides an identity element for the group of exchange (as opposed to the groups of generic commodities) is *money*.

Thus we arrive at Marx's fourth and final form of value, the money form. In every value form prior to the money form, prices were not expressed as numbers because the structure of exchange could not meet the requirements of an equivalence relation. Only by means of the imposition of a group structure which exhibits the same composition of mappings independent of the theory of price will the act of exchange be the exchange of equivalents. Money is the artificially instituted invariant of any price system, the identity map in the group of exchange. Now we can begin to rephrase Clower's insight, and to make it more precise: a monetary system must exhibit certain attributes which cannot be found in an economy constituted solely of arbitrary physical endowments, and one of these attributes must be the existence of a unique money commodity. As (Marx, 1977, p. 190) wrote, "a duplication of the measure of value contradicts the function of that measure." Restating it in the terminology of abstract algebra, a group may only possess one identity element.

Table 6–3: Marx's General Form of Value

First Step: Individual Commodity Groups

commodity A

0	1	2	3	4....
1	2	3	4	5....
2	3	4	5	6....
3	4	5	6	7....
:	:	:	:	:

commodity B

0	1	2	3	4....
1	2	3	4	5....
2	3	4	5	6....
3	4	5	6	7....
:	:	:	:	:

commodity C

0	1	2	3	4....
1	2	3	4	5....
2	3	4	5	6....
3	4	5	6	7....
:	:	:	:	:

Second Step: Trade as a Composition of Commodity Groups

	A	*B*	*C*
A	?	α	α'
B	β	?	β'
C	γ	γ'	?

$$A \xrightarrow{\alpha} B \qquad A \xrightarrow{\alpha'} C \qquad C \xrightarrow{\gamma} A$$
$$B \xrightarrow{\beta} A \qquad B \xrightarrow{\beta'} C \qquad C \xrightarrow{\gamma'} B$$

Table 6–4   Money Form of Value

1	α	β	γ	α/β	α/γ	β/α	γ/α	$\cdots$
α	1	$\dfrac{\beta}{\alpha}$	$\dfrac{\gamma}{\alpha}$	$\dfrac{1}{\beta}$	$\dfrac{1}{\gamma}$	$\dfrac{\beta}{\alpha\,\alpha}$	$\dfrac{\gamma}{\alpha\,\alpha}$	$\cdots$
β	$\dfrac{\alpha}{\beta}$	1	$\dfrac{\gamma}{\beta}$	$\dfrac{\alpha}{\beta\,\beta}$	$\dfrac{\alpha}{\beta\,\gamma}$	$\dfrac{1}{\alpha}$	$\dfrac{\gamma}{\beta\,\gamma}$	
γ	$\dfrac{\alpha}{\gamma}$	$\dfrac{\beta}{\gamma}$	1	$\dfrac{\alpha}{\gamma\,\beta}$	$\dfrac{\alpha}{\gamma\,\gamma}$	$\dfrac{\beta}{\gamma\,\alpha}$	$\dfrac{1}{\alpha}$	
$\dfrac{\alpha}{\beta}$	β	$\dfrac{\beta\,\beta}{\alpha}$	$\dfrac{\beta\,\gamma}{\alpha}$	1	$\dfrac{\beta}{\gamma}$	$\dfrac{\beta\,\beta}{\alpha\,\alpha}$	$\dfrac{\beta\,\gamma}{\alpha\,\alpha}$	
$\dfrac{\alpha}{\gamma}$	γ	$\dfrac{\gamma\,\beta}{\alpha}$	$\dfrac{\gamma\,\gamma}{\alpha}$	$\dfrac{\gamma}{\beta}$	1	$\dfrac{\gamma\,\beta}{\alpha\,\alpha}$	$\dfrac{\gamma\,\gamma}{\alpha\,\alpha}$	
$\vdots$								

Finally, in Table 6–4, we observe actual prices. In this table, there are no longer any physical commodities *per se*. There are only abstract quantities of money which act as the linear mappings from one commodity group to another. The entire table is based upon the principle that one money unit equals $\alpha(A) = \beta(B) = \gamma(C)$. Because the theory of value is analytically prior to any theory of price, there is no explanation of the actual values (α, β, γ); a further theory is required to make them determinate. All the table says is (in the first row) the price of α units of A is one money unit, the price of β units of B in terms of A is β/α, the price of γ units of C in terms of A is γ/α, the price of α/β units of A in terms of money is $1/\beta$, and so on. Although the set of generic commodities generating money prices is only of order three in this example, the resulting group of exchange is of infinite order, but is closed and has unique identity and inverse elements, as can be observed from the structure of Table 6–4. Prices are explicitly rational numbers, and the group is Abelian, as can be observed from the skew-symmetry of the table.

The Abelian character of the money form of value is very critical to the understanding of the way in which a money economy differs from a barter economy. The existence of money creates the transitive structure of exchange. In the example in Table 6–4, one unit of B is traded for β units of money, which can then be traded for α/β units of A. These α/β units of A are then traded for money, which in turn is used to purchase C at the rate of γ/α. The final result of $(\alpha/\beta) \times (\gamma/\alpha) = \gamma/\beta$ is the same ratio which would be found in a more direct exchange of B for money and the result for C. Only in the money form of value is this conception of equivalence in exchange well-defined.

Having persevered through this difficult section, the reader may still be puzzled by the insistence that the operation of exchange conform to a group structure. Have we labored mightily only to demonstrate the obvious, that prices are expressed as rational numbers in a monetary economy? On the contrary: we are now prepared to explicitly define the prerequisites of legitimate quantitative exchange in a monetary economy. They are: (1) The commodity should preserve its identity through the exchange process (Sohn-Rethel, 1978); (2) buying nothing should cost nothing; (3) the order in which the items are presented for purchase should not influence the total amount paid for an aggregate; (4) dividing the aggregate into subsets and paying for each subset separately should not affect the total sum paid for the aggregate; (5) if an item is bought and then returned, the net result should be zero; and (6), everyone should pay the same price for the same item. In other words, we have identified legitimate trades as *symmetric* trades. (Actually, the group matrix is skew-symmetric.) One should not interpret this stricture to mean that all trades conform to these conditions in any and all circumstances; casual empiricism suggests the opposite. One should instead interpret these conditions as the ideal, or the benchmark, of legitimate exchange: these are the ideal conditions which sanction the imposition of rational numbers (in the guise of prices) upon exchanges. Another way of stating this is to say that rational prices require that *value is conserved in exchange*. As long as trades are constrained to be legitimate in this sense, then "value" exists as a phenomenon apart from the physical characteristics of any particular commodity, possessing a stability that is consistent with expression as a rational number. The fact that value as a quantity assumes a separate existence suggested to Marx that value was embodied in the commodity in the form of abstract labor time; but we should observe that the former idea is neither necessary nor sufficient for the latter to be true.[14]

The critical importance of the symmetry conditions and the group structure of exchange for Marx was that it provided a framework within which he could examine what was, in his view, the most vexing and most significant problem in all of political economy: where did the "extra'" or surplus value come from? What are the ultimate wellsprings of economic expansion? Marx saw quite clearly what neoclassicals forget: "With reference to use-value, it can indeed be said that exchange is a transaction by which both sides gain. It is otherwise with exchange value" (Marx, 1977, p. 259). If the rules of legitimate exchange imply that value is conserved in the process of trade, then the process of legitimate trade cannot be the locus of economic growth. "In its pure form, the exchange of commodities is the exchange of equivalents, and this is not a method of increasing value" (Marx, 1977, p. 261). If we were to construct an analogy with twentieth-century physics, we would see the search for the ultimate source(s) of profit and growth as the search for the locus of broken symmetry. This is the logical beginning of a theory of economic order. Since a buyer is also a seller, a producer also a consumer, the explanation of surplus must be located in some subset of the economy where the basic symmetries of legitimate trade are either absent or broken. This structure of explanation must hold whether or not one is a partisan of the labor theory of value. It follows directly from the fact that prices are quantitative.

§21. It is a pity that Marx's work on the formal aspects of value just happened to antedate the formal development of group theory. Later in the century, searching for a developed formalism, economics turned to nineteenth-century physics to provide the paradigm, and as a direct result of that initial choice, economists became advocates of the dogma that exchange was "naturally" quantitative, believing that their discipline was founded on physical algebras provided by nature. As Marx put it with his customary ascerbity, it encouraged "the illusion to arise that all commodities can simultaneously be imprinted with the stamp of direct exchangeability, in the same way it might be imagined that all Catholics can be popes" (Marx, 1977, p. 161).

There is nothing simple about a commodity, and there is nothing natural about the quantitative fact of its exchange. If we might state the major thesis of this paper in a direct and provocative manner: only certain forms of mathematics are appropriate to the discussion of the economic sphere in modern society, and only those forms are isomorphic to the artificially instituted algebra of capitalist exchange. The social construction of the algebra of exchange takes place on two levels: the first, Marx's relative value form, is the construction of the generic commodity, such that there are a class of "identical" objects which can be characterized by a single number; and the second, similar to Marx's general and money forms, is the creation of a value index separate from the commodities themselves, which possesses its own (somewhat different) algebraic character. These stages are simultaneously a framework for economic analysis and a rough description of the actual dynamic of capitalist development. Many historians have noticed the trend toward the standardization of commodities and toward the expendability of any particular human personality in the production process as part and parcel of capitalist economic history, but few have understood it as necessarily constitutive of the creation of an algebra which will structure and govern trade. The development of the institutions of money and accounting have also been claimed to accompany capitalist development, but most (with the exception of Sombart and a few others) have seen them as an insignificant subset of technological innovation, whose only purpose is to grease the wheels of a preexistent trade. These historical phenomena, which neoclassical economics has tended to treat as adventitious or of secondary importance, are precisely the locations of the social construction of the algebra of exchange.

The social construction of an economic metric is inherently an historical and institutional phenomenon. Serious research into the evolution of this process would carry us too far afield from our present concerns. Nonetheless, it is critical for our present argument to insist that the construction of the quantitative incarnation of commodities and prices is never comprehensive nor complete: it is an ongoing affair. Money is such a protean institution that, as soon as a government seems to fix its identity through legal tender legislation and the sanction of legitimate credit institutions, the actors contrive and conspire to make it something else (Kindleberger, 1984). Or, in the same vein, as soon as an industry seems to succeed in standardizing a commodity, technological change and product differentiation undoes the situation. The social construction of value is doomed to the same fate as Sisyphus: no sooner is the illusion of the identity through time fabricated, then the very normal operation of the system serves to undermine it.

The history of Western economic reasoning is the story of a futile search for the natural value unit, be it gold, or abstract labor, or the standard commodity, or generic abstract utility. Once discovered, it is always promised that this holy grail will once and for all put an end to the confusion engendered by social change. This quest is quixotic; yet, also, it has been one of the prime motivations behind the mathematization of the economics discipline to date. Had the neoclassical partisans of the mathematical method paid more attention to the foundations of mathematics, they might have become more sensitive to the futility of their venture. After Gödel, few believe that any formal algebra can be both fully complete and fully consistent. Moreover, the economic actors already behave as if they knew it.

To see the quest for a natural economic metric as futile is not to counsel despair, however. Instead, it envisions that the reconstruction of a mathematical economics will be at least as pragmatic as the economic actors whose aims it seeks to describe. The economic actors do not fully "understand" the system (contrary to the faddish peccadillos of the rational expectations school); but they do have a very real need to make causal claims about their activities in the economic sphere. In order to do so, they impose strong symmetries upon the processes of trade, in the form of the six conditions described above in section §20. The postulation of such symmetries is decisive, because it implies the simultaneous construction of an equivalence principle (Rosen, 1983, p. 108). In this instance, it is interpreted as a mandate that legitimate trades are trades of equivalents. The conjuration of equivalence is necessary for the construction of causal statements, in the sense that equivalent states of a cause then imply equivalent states of an effect. In physics, one links causal states with effect states by imposing the restriction that both sets of states possess the same energy. In economics, one causally links the antecedents with the consequences of an exchange by imposing the restriction that both states possess the same value. For the mathematical economist, this will mean that the group properties of any chosen formalism will be severely restricted.

In the most general of theories, the mathematical economist will employ the organizing principle that the symmetry group of the cause should be a subgroup of the symmetry group of the effect (Rosen, 1983, p. 117). This heuristic principle can help further research in two different ways. The first, which Rosen (1983, p. 119) calls the "minimalistic use," takes a known cause and works out the minimal symmetry of the effect. An example of this research strategy has already been developed in this paper. If exchange conforms to a certain algebraic group, then it is a theorem that there can exist but one unique identity element. This theorem can be translated into the economic sphere by showing that any economic system predicated upon two or more monetary units or commodity standards (such as a bimetallic currency) will evince an unstable measure of value. The second way to use the symmetry principle is what Rosen (1983, p. 136) calls the "maximalistic use." Here one isolates a known effect and attempts to locate an unknown cause. If the symmetry characteristics of the effect are known, then the symmetry principle sets an upper bound on the symmetry characteristics of the cause. Quoting Rosen:

> ... the first step towards a theory is to determine the ideal symmetry that is only approximated by the phenomena.... Then to obtain as symmetric a cause as possible we try to construct a theory such that the cause will have a dominant part ... possessing the ideal symmetry of the effect, and another, symmetry-breaking part, which does not have that symmetry. In the (possibly hypothetical) limit of complete absence of symmetry breaking, the dominant part of the cause produces the ideal symmetry of the phenomena, while the symmetry-breaking part brings about the deviation from the ideal symmetry. (Rosen, 1983, p. 136)

The maximalistic use of the symmetry principle could serve to clear up one of the most convoluted and muddled areas in economic theory: the theory of profit. The effect we wish to explain is the expansion of value in the capitalistic process. This is an asymmetry, a change in the magnitude of value over time. To begin the explanation, we posit the symmetric base line of constant value through time. This is the previously discussed exchange of equivalents. Next, we posit a symmetry-breaking phenomenon which induces the deviation from ideal symmetry. One might accomplish this in the same manner as Marx, insisting that the value of the output of a production process is asymmetric with respect to the value of the wage, because the labor contract does not partake of the character of the exchange of equivalents. Or, as the author himself might suggest, the function of credit is to increase the aggregate magnitude of the value unit apart from the trade of equivalents. In either case, causal explanation then limits the potentials of what can be quantified, what algebras may be employed, what is conceived of as being constant, and so forth.

This would be the beginning of a mathematics grounded in economic theory, rather than vice versa.

Notes

[1] The position that the linguistic isolation of mathematicians is justified is softened considerably in (Koopmans, 1957). Nevertheless, the attitude that the isolation is the reader's, and *not* the writer's problem, can be traced back to the work of Walras (for example, Walras, 1960).

[2] See Kline, 1980, pp. 271–272; Wittgenstein, 1976, 1978; Wright, 1980; Hacking, 1984, pp. 101–111; and Putnam, 1983.

[3] Fisher (1926, pp. 85–86) openly displays this fact in a table which presents the correspondences between the physics and economics labels for variables in the same mathematical model. For a detailed commentary, see Mirowski (forthcoming, ch. 5). Although Fisher and the other neoclassicals did not realize it, one area in which the analogy did not carry over into economics was in the law of the conservation of energy. See Mirowski (1984b; 1984c).

[4] It has already been formally admitted that the axioms of revealed preference are isomorphic to a subset of thermodynamics. See Hurwicz and Richter (1979).

[5] There are many similarities between this analysis and the discussion in Georgescu-Roegen (1971) of "Arithmomorphism." See also the discussion in Katzner's essay in this volume, ch. 5.

[6] Quite obviously there exist neoclassical models which allow for inventory accumulation, inflexible prices, price discrimination, and so forth. What this statement means is that such models, by their very structure, cannot be members of the class of Walrasian or Arrow-Debreu models if they allow the so-called "disequilibrium phenomena" to feed back into the determination of a unique general equilibrium. This was the critical insight of Clower (1965). In actual practice, the models that purport to incorporate these phenomena finesse this problem by inevitably being cast in a Marshallian partial equilibrium framework.

[7] For a further elaboration of these issues, see chapter 4 by Bauser. The "law of one price" is a major component of the definition of equilibrium imported from physics. In brief, it states that all trades of generic units of a commodity will be contracted and realized at a single uniform price. Some further discussion can be found in Mirowski (forthcoming, ch. 5).

[8] If some believer in the inevitable progress of mathematical sophistication really needs a contemporary example, let him consult Georgescu-Roegen (1976, p. 286) for a critique of the errors of Frank Hahn.

[9] Partial exceptions to this sweeping generalization are found in Georgescu-Roegen (1971),

Katzner (1983), and chapter 5 of this volume. The author would like to acknowledge the influence of these seminal works.

[10] The Arrow-Debreu predisposition to characterize a commodity by an exhaustive enumeration of the accompanying state of the world (an apple at 8 P.M. on Tuesday on the Boston Common in the rain after a bout of jogging but before a drink with friends ...) would thus appear to undermine the very algebraic attributes upon which it leans so heavily to provide a metric. If, in essence, every commodity is unique in an economic sense, then there are no grounds for quantitive comparison, no cardinality, and certainly no prices. In respect to this problem, see the discussion of Georgescu-Roegen below.

[11] In recent conversations, Robert Clower has informed me that he produced an as-yet unpublished lengthy manuscript in the late 1960s which explored the implications of group theory for the issues broached in his 1967 article. I have not yet seen this manuscript.

[12] I have argued elsewhere that Marx was the last serious expositor of a labor theory of value precisely because developments in mathematics and physics caused substance theories of value to be superseded in the later nineteenth century. See Mirowski (forthcoming, ch. 4).

[13] This insight can be traced back to Aristotle's *Politics*. Aristotle (1962, pp. 21–29) contrasts the wealth of the household and barter trade, which he considers bounded, with exchange for the sake of acquisition, which is potentially boundless.

[14] Unfortunately, Marx's embodied labor values do not possess the properties necessary to qualify them as cardinal numbers. For elaboration, see Mirowski (forthcoming, ch. 4).

References

Aristotle, 1962. *The Politics*, trans. E. Barker, Oxford: Oxford University Press.

Arrow, Kenneth. 1951. "Mathematical Models in the Social Sciences", in. D. Lerner & H. Lasswell, eds., *The Policy Sciences*. Stanford, Cal.: Stanford Univ. Press.

Arrow, Kenneth, and Hahn, Frank. 1971. *General Competitive Analysis*. San Francisco: Holden-Day.

Barnes, Barry, and Shapin, Steven. 1979. *Natural Order*. Beverley Hills, CA: Sage.

Baumol, William, and Goldfeld, Steven. 1968. *Precursors in Mathematical Economics*. London: LSE Reprints.

Bloor, David. 1973. Wittgenstein and Mannheim on the Sociology of Mathematics. *Studies in the History and Philosophy of Science* 4:173–191.

Bloor, David. 1978. Polyhedra and the Abominations of Leviticus. *British Journal for the History of Science* 11:245–272.

Bloor, David. 1983. Wittgenstein: A Social Theory of Knowledge. New York: Columbia University Press.

Bompaire, François. 1932. L'Économie Mathematique D'Apres Comparée de ses Representations les Plus Typiques. *Revue D'Économie Politique* 46:1321–1346.

Bouvier, Emile. 1901. La Methode Mathématique en Économie Politique. *Revue D'Économie Politique* 15:817–850, 1029–1086.

Brewer, J., and Smith, M. 1981. *Emmy Noether* New York: Marcel Dekker.

Buckley, P., and Peat, F. 1979. *A Question of Physics*. London: Routledge and Kegan Paul.

Campbell, Norman. 1957. *What is Science?* New York: Dover.

Charlesworth, James, ed. 1963. *Mathematics and the Social Sciences*. Philadelphia: American Academy of Political & Social Science.

MATHEMATICAL FORMALISM AND ECONOMIC EXPLANATION 237

Chipman, John, et al. 1971. *Preferences, Utility and Demand*. New York: Harcourt Brace Jovanovich.

Clower, Robert. 1965. The Keynesian Counterrevolution. In F. Hahn and F. Brechling (eds.), *The Theory of Interest Rates*. London: Macmillan.

Clower, Robert. 1967. A Reconsideration of the Microfoundations of Monetary Theory. *Western Economic Journal* 6:1–9.

Colvin, Phyllis. 1977. Ontological and Epistemological Commitments in the Social Sciences. In E. Mendelsohn, P. Weingart, and R. Whitley (eds.), *The Social Production of Scientific Knowledge*. Boston: Reidel.

Cournot, A. 1897. *Researches into the Mathematical Principles of the Theory of Wealth*, Trans. N. Bacon. New York: Macmillan.

Debreu, Gerard. 1959. *The Theory of Value*. New Haven: Yale University Press.

Debreu, Gerard. 1984. Economic Theory in the Mathematical Mode. *American Economic Review* 74:267–278.

Dennis, Ken. 1982. Economic Theory and the Problem of Translation. *Journal of Economic Issues* 16:691–712; 1039–1062.

Douglas, Mary. 1966. *Purity and Danger*. London: Routledge and Kegan Paul.

Douglas, Mary. 1970. *Natural Symbols*. London: Barrie and Jenkins.

Durbin, John. 1985. *Modern Algebra*. 2nd ed. New York: Wiley.

Ellerman, David. 1980. Property Theory and Orthodox Economics. In E. Nell (ed.), *Growth, Property and Profits*. Cambridge: Cambridge University Press.

Ellerman, David. 1984. Arbitrage Theory: A Mathematical Introduction. *SIAM Review* 26:241–261.

Elliott, J., and Dawber, P. 1979. *Symmetries in Physics*. New York: Oxford University Press.

Fisher, Irving. 1926. *Mathematical Investigations in the Theory of Value and Prices*. New Haven, CT: Yale University Press.

Galison, Peter. 1983. Rereading the Past from the End of Physics. In L. Graham, W. Lepenies, and P. Weingart (eds.), *The Function and Uses of Disciplinary Histories*. Boston: Reidel.

Garegnani, Pierangelo. 1983. On a Change in the Notion of Equilibrium in Recent Work on Value and Distribution. In J. Eatwell and M. Milgate (eds.), *Keynes' Economics and the Theory of Value*. Oxford: Oxford University Press.

Georgescu-Roegen, Nicholas. 1971. *The Entropy Law and the Economic Process*. Cambridge: Harvard University Press.

Georgescu-Roegen, Nicholas. 1976. *Energy and Economic Myths*. Elmsford, NY: Pergamon Press.

Giedymin, Jerzy. 1982. *Science and Convention*. Elmsford, NY.: Pergamon Press.

Gorenstein, Daniel.1985. "The Enormous Theorem", *Scientific American* 253:104–115.

Grattan-Guiness, Ivor. 1980. *From the Calculus to Set Theory 1630–1910*. London: Duckworth.

Green, H. A. J. 1971. *Consumer Theory*. Baltimore: Penguin.

Hacking, Ian. 1984. *Representing and Intervening*. Cambridge: Cambridge University Press.

Hamermesh, Morton. 1962. *Group Theory*. Reading: Addison-Wesley.

Harcourt, Geoffrey. 1984. Reflections on the Development of Economics as a

Discipline. *History of Political Economy* 16:489–517.

Harman, P. M. 1982. *Metaphysics and Natural Philosophy*. Sussex: Harvester.

Herstein, I. 1964. *Topics in Algebra*. New York: Blaisdell.

Hicks, J. R. 1979. *Causality in Economics*. New York: Basic Books.

Hofstadter, Douglas. 1979. *Gödel, Escher, Bach*. New York: Basic Books.

Hurwicz, Leonid, and Richter, Marcel. 1979. An Integrability Condition with Applications to Utility Theory and Thermodynamics. *Journal of Mathematical Economics* 6:7–14.

Ipsen, D. 1960. *Units, Dimensions and Dimensionless Numbers*. New York: McGraw Hill.

Jevons, W. S. 1970. *The Theory of Political Economy*. Baltimore: Penguin.

Katzner, Donald. 1983. *Analysis Without Measurement*. New York: Cambridge University Press.

Kindleberger, Charles. 1984. *A History of Finance in Western Europe*. Boston: Allen and Unwin.

Kitcher, Philip. 1983. *The Nature of Mathematical Knowledge*. New York: Oxford University Press.

Kline, Morris. 1972. Mathematical Thought from Ancient to Modern Times. New York: Oxford University Press.

Kline, Morris. 1980. *Mathematics: The Loss of Certainty*. New York: Oxford University Press.

Koopmans, Tjalling. 1954. On the Use of Mathematics in Economics. *Review of Economics and Statistics* 36:377–379.

Koopmans, Tjalling. 1957. *Three Essays on the State of Economic Science*. New York: McGraw Hill.

Kornai, J. 1971. *Anti-Equilibrium*. Amsterdam: North Holland.

Krantz, David, et al. 1971. *Foundations of Measurement, vol. I*. New York: Academic Press.

Kyburg, Henry. 1984. *Theory and Measurement*. New York: Cambridge University Press.

Ladrière, Jean. 1972. L'Applicabilité des Mathématiques aux sciences sociales. *Économies et Sociétes* 6:1511–1548.

Lakatos, Imre. 1976. *Proofs and Refutations*. Cambridge: Cambridge University Press.

Lancaster, Kelvin. 1966. A New Approach to Consumer Theory. *Journal of Political Economy* 74:132–157.

Leontief, W. 1982. Letter: Academic Economics. *Science* 217:104–107.

Levine, David. 1980. On the Classical Theory of Markets. *Australian Economic Papers* 19:1–15.

Levinson, Arnold. 1978. Wittgenstein and Logical Laws. In K. T. Fann (ed.), *Ludwig Wittgenstein: The Man and His Philosophy*. New York: Humanities.

Lichnerowicz, André. 1972. Mathématique et Transdisciplinarité. *Économie et Société* 6:1497–1509.

Ljapin, E. 1974. *Semigroups*. 3rd edition. Providence: American Mathematical Society.

Magill, M. J. P. 1970. *On a General Economic Theory of Motion.* New York: Springer Verlag.

Marshall, Alfred. 1920. *Principles of Economics.* 8th ed. London: Macmillan.

Marshall, Alfred. 1971. *The Early Economic Writings.* New York: Free Press.

Marx, Karl. 1971. *Theories of Surplus Value,* Part III, Moscow: Progress Pub.

Marx, Karl. 1977. *Capital, vol. I.* B. Fowkes, trans. New York: Vintage.

McCloskey, Donald. 1986. *The Rhetoric of Economics.* Madison: Univ. of Wisconsin Press.

Meyerson, Émile. 1962. *Identity and Reality.* New York: Dover.

Mirowski, Philip. 1984a. Macroeconomic Instability and Natural Fluctuations. *Journal of Economic History* 44:345–354.

Mirowski, Philip. 1984b. Physics and the Marginalist Revolution. *Cambridge Journal of Economics.* 8:361–379.

Mirowski, Philip. 1984c. The Role of Conservation Principles in 20th Century Economic Theory. *Philosophy of the Social Sciences,* 14:461–473.

Mirowski, Philip. Forthcoming. *More Heat Than Light.*

Moret, Jacques. 1915. *L'Emploi des Mathématiques en Économie Politique.* Paris: Giard & Brière.

Morgenstern, Oskar. 1963a. *On the Accuracy of Economic Observations.* 2nd edition. Princeton, NJ: Princeton University Press.

Morgenstern, Oskar. 1963b. Limits to the Use of Mathematics in Economics. In Charlesworth (1963).

Morishima, Michio. 1984. The Good and Bad Uses of Mathematics. In P. Wiles and G. Routh (eds.), *Economics in Disarray.* Oxford: Basil Blackwell.

Mulvey, J., ed. 1981. *The Nature of Matter.* Oxford: Oxford University Press.

Nagel, E., and Newman, J. 1958. *Gödel's Proof.* New York: New York University Press.

Olson, Harry. 1958. *Dynamical Analogies.* Princeton, NJ: Van Nostrand.

O'Malley, Mary. 1971. *The Emergence of the Concept of an Abstract Group,* unpub. Ph.D. thesis, Columbia University.

Palomba, Giuseppe. 1976. Les Héretiques dans l'Économie Mathématique. *Économie Appliquée* 29:353–407.

Penrose, Roger. 1982. Playing with Numbers. *Times Literary Supplement* May 14:523–524.

Petley, B. W. 1985. *The Fundamental Physical Constants and the Frontiers of Measurement.* Boston: Adam Hilger.

Prigogine, Ilya. 1980. *From Being to Becoming.* San Francisco: Freeman.

Putnam, Hilary. 1983. Models and Reality. In *Realism and Reason.* Cambridge: Cambridge University Press.

Restivo, Sal. 1983. *The Social Relations of Physics, Mysticism and Mathematics.* Boston: Reidel.

Robertson, Ross. 1949. Mathematical Economics Before Cournot. *Journal of Political Economy* 57:524–527.

Rosen, Joe. 1983. *A Symmetry Primer for Scientists.* New York: Wiley.

Samuelson, Paul. 1952. Economic Theory and Mathematics—An Appraisal.

American Economic Review 42:56–69.

Samuelson, Paul. 1972. *Collected Scientific Papers*. Cambridge: MIT Press.

Samuelson, Paul. 1983. The 1983 Nobel Prize in Economics. *Science* 222:987–989.

Sato, Ryuzo. 1981. *Theory of Technical Change and Economic Invariance*. New York: Academic Press.

Schumpeter, Joseph. 1954. *A History of Economic Analysis*. New York: Oxford University Press.

Shackle, G. L. S. 1967. *Time in Economics*. Amsterdam: North Holland.

Sharma, C. S. 1982. The Role of Mathematics in Physics. *British Journal for the Philosophy of Science* 33:275–286.

Shea, William, ed. 1983. *Nature Mathematized*. Boston: Reidel.

Skolem, T. 1970. *Selected Works in Logic*. Oslo: Universitets–Forlaget.

Sohn-Rethel, Alfred. 1978. *Intellectual and Manual Labour*. London: Macmillan.

Takayama, Akira. 1974. *Mathematical Economics*. Hinsdale, IL: Dryden.

Theobald, D. W. 1966. *The Concept of Energy*. London: Spon.

Theocharis, Reghnos. 1961. *Early Developments in Mathematical Economics*. London: Macmillan.

t'Hooft, Gerard. 1980. Gauge Theories of the Forces Between Elementary Particles. *Scientific American* 243:104–138.

Vind, Karl. 1977. Equilibrium with Respect to a Single Market. In G. Schwödiauer (ed.), *Equilibrium and Disequilibrium in Economic Theory*. Boston: Reidel.

Waismann, Friedrich. 1982. *Lectures on the Philosophy of Mathematics*. W. Grassl, ed. Amsterdam: Rodopi.

Walras, Leon. 1960. Économique et Mécanique. *Metroeconomica* 22:1–6.

Walras, Leon. 1965. *Correspondence and Related Papers*. W. Jaffee, ed. Amsterdam: North Holland.

Weintraub, E. R. 1983. The Existence of Competitive Equilibrium. *Journal of Economic Literature* 21:1–39.

Westfall, R. S. 1980. *Never at Rest: A Biography of Issac Newton*. Cambridge: Cambridge University Press.

Weyl, Hermann. 1952. *Symmetry*. Princeton, NJ: Princeton University Press.

Wicksell, Knut. 1958. *Selected Papers on Economic Theory*. Cambridge: Harvard University Press.

Wigner, Eugene. 1967. *Symmetries and Reflections*. Bloomington: Indiana University Press.

Wilder, Raymond. 1965. *Introduction to the Foundations of Mathematics*. 2nd. edition. New York: Wiley.

Wittgenstein, Ludwig. 1976. *Wittgenstein's Lectures on the Foundations of Mathematics*. Cora Diamond, ed. Ithaca: Cornell University Press.

Wittgenstein, Ludwig. 1978. *Remarks on the Foundations of Mathematics*. Rev. ed. Cambridge, MA: MIT Press.

Wong, Stanley. 1978. *The Foundations of Samuelson's Revealed Preference Theory*. Boston: Routledge Kegan Paul.

Wright, Crispin. 1980. *Wittgenstein on the Foundations of Mathematics*. London: Duckworth.

Wussing, Hans. 1984. *The Genesis of the Abstract Group Concept*. Cambridge: MIT Press.

7 INSTITUTIONS AS A SOLUTION CONCEPT IN A GAME THEORY CONTEXT

Philip Mirowski

... he believed that human beings, when it had been clearly explained to them what were their vital needs and necessities, would not only altruistically but selfishly become honest and reasonable: they would sacrifice what might be short term advantages for long term ends. What he never saw was that in politics as in other forms of human activity, human beings are for the most part interested in struggle, in manoeuvrings for power, in risks and even unpleasantnesses; and that these are often in direct opposition to what might reasonably be seen as their long term ends....

This was one reason why he could so often make rings around his opponents by reasoning: he believed in it; while they, although they said they did, ultimately did not. Yet what they felt instinctively, and might have answered [him] by, was traditionally unspoken. They could not say to him in effect—Look, in your reasoning you leave out of account something about human nature: you leave out the fact that human beings with part of them-selves like turmoil and something to grumble at and perhaps even failure to feel comfortable in: your economic perfect blueprint will not work simply because people will not want it to.

Mosley, 1983, pp. 68–69

241

Confounding the Critics

In the history of neoclassical economic theory, there have been two major categories of rejoinders to critics of the theory: one, that the critics did not adequately understand the structure of the theory, and thus mistook for essential what was merely convenient; or two, that the criticism was old hat, and had been rendered harmless by recent (and technically abstruse) innovations with which the critic was unacquainted.[1] The freedom of passage between these defenses has proven to be the bane of not only those opposed to neoclassicism, but also of those who have felt the need for reform and reformulation of economic theory from within. It has fostered the impression that, with enough ingenuity, any arbitrary phenomenon can be incorporated within the ambit of conventional neoclassical theory, therefore rendering any particular change in "assumptions" as innocuous as any other, and thus rendering them all equally arbitrary.

Nowhere has this impasse been more evident than in the confrontations between the various partisans of an "institutional" economics and the adherents of neoclassical economic theory. The early institutionalists, such as Thorstein Veblen, John R. Commons, and Wesley Clair Mitchell, mounted a scathing attack on neoclassical value theory in the first three decades of the century, ridiculing the "hedonistic conception of man [as] that of a lightening calculator of pleasures and pains, who oscillates like a homogeneous globule of desire of happiness under the impulse of stimuli that shift him about the area but leave him intact."[2] The unifying principles of this movement were: (a) an assertion that neoclassical economists were the advocates of a spurious scientism which insisted upon imitating physics without understanding the implications of such mimesis; (b) an expression of an alternative to the above conception of society based upon a study of the working rules that structured collective action and going concerns, such as the corporation, the trade union, the bank and the state; (c) in conjunction with the construction of theories that took as their province the explanation of the evaluation of the working rules and then attendant institutions. The institutionalists' writings on the vagaries of behavior, such as Veblen's book on "conspicious consumption", were intended to show that theories based on individual psychologies were built upon shifting sands; and that, as Commons wrote, "cooperation does not arise from a presupposed harmony of interests, as the older economists believed. It arises from the necessity of creating a new harmony of interests" (Commons, 1934, p. 6).

The initial rebuttal to the institutionalists adopted the first tactic. To cite just one prominent example, Paul Samuelson insisted that nothing substantial would be lost if economists relinquished utility (Wong, 1978), and that institutions were effectively included in the assumptions of neoclassical economic theory (Samuelson, 1965, p. 8). When fully interpreted, this assertion meant that the study of institutions was *separable* from neoclassical economic theory, to the point of being independent of any particular institutional framework (Mirowski, 1981). Economics could cut itself free of the inessential institutional considerations, and preserve its core as the study of rational allocation of scarce means in a thoroughly abstract frame. Veblen and Commons were drummed out of the economists' camp, and exiled to the provinces of Sociology or Anthropology.

With the passage of time, this first rebuttal has fallen into disuse, and the second option has gained favor. Among a certain subset of theorists, it has become acceptable to admit that conventional neoclassical theory is "mechanistic", in the sense that it slavishly imitates certain theoretical structures and procedures in physics, and that this might be undesirable in certain respects. In most cases, this admission is accompanied by an assertion that this flaw has been remedied by the development of new techniques in the theory of games, to such an extent that there is a "new mathematical institutional economics" which has incorporated the concerns of the earlier critics (Johansen, 1983; Schotter, 1981, 1983; Schotter and Schwödiauer, 1980; Shubik, 1975, 1976).

It is a curious fact that the language of the critique of neoclassical theory of the game theorists is so close to that of the earlier institutionalists as to be almost indistinguishable. For example: "The neoclassical agents are bores who merely calculate optimal activities at fixed parametric prices.... No syndicates or coalitions are formed, no cheating or lying is done, no threats are made.... The economy has no money, no government, no legal system, no property rights, no banks ..." (Schotter, 1981, p. 150). "The general equilibrium model is: (1) basically noninstitutional. (2) It makes use of few differentiated actors. (3) It is essentially static. No explanation of price formation is given. (4) There is no essential role for money. (5) It is nonstrategic" (Shubik, 1976, p. 323). However, similarities in languages can be misleading. How justified is the claim that institutionalist concerns have been absorbed by game theorists?

For the purposes of this paper, we shall choose to avoid discussion of the first variant of the neoclassical defense. We shall simply assume that the central concept of neoclassical economic theory is the application of a physical metaphor to the market.[3] This will allow us to concentrate our attention on the second variant: Are recent game theoretic models different in any substantial way from neoclassical theory? Do game theory models capture the concerns that institutionalists believed were ignored in neo-classical economics? How can one judge the various claims made for the superior efficacy of game theory?

Game Theory and Institutional Analysis: Shubik and Schotter

It is a difficult task to discern the wood from the many trees that have passed through the pulper in the cause of game theory. Game theory burst upon the scene in 1944 with von Neumann and Morgenstern's book. The solutions of games were claimed to be isomorphic to "orders of society," "standards of behavior," "economic organizations"; and yet these models also claimed to be following "the best examples of theoretical physics" (von Neumann and Morgenstern, 1964, pp. 43, ix). Forty years of development have revealed that game theory is not the philosopher's stone its progenitors had claimed: more than half of any competent textbook in game theory is occupied with developing taxonomies of the numerous variants of games—cooperative and noncooperative; constant- or nonconstant-sum; static or sequential; extensive, strategic or characteristic forms; cardinal or noncardinal payoffs; various permutations of information sets and sequences of moves; small and large numbers of players; different conceptions of uncertainty; stationary versus nonstationary payoffs and/or strategies—so that the permutations and their attendant solution concepts have far outstripped any claims for generality or unity.

Doubts about the efficacy of game theory have begun to surface—sometimes during inauspicious occasions, such as Nobel Prize lectures (see, e.g., Simon, 1982, pp. 486–487). In this context, it is noteworthy that its most vocal defenders have chosen to reemphasize the potential of game theory to encompass institutional considerations. We shall therefore concentrate our initial attention on the work of the two most prolific prosely-tizers for a "new institutional economics": Martin Shubik and Andrew Schotter.

Shubik has built an illustrious career upon the development of game theory in economics, providing many of the basic theorems and results in that literature, as well as writing the best introductory textbook (Shubik, 1982). In this respect, he is particularly well qualified to judge which areas of game theory should be credited with having made substantial contributions and novel innovations, as well as revealing the motivations behind the prosecution of game theoretic research. In a series of journal articles, Shubik has been persistently critical of Walrasian general equilibrium because it does not explain price formation; it merely *assumes* it. The actors in a Walrasian world have no freedom to make errors or even choices about process, he says; and in this, he sounds very similar to Veblen. More unexpectedly, he is also critical of cooperative game theory: "As an early proponent of the core and of the replication process for studying mass economic behavior, I am completely willing to admit that to a great extent the results on the core have helped to direct attention away from the understanding of the competitive process ..." (Shubik, 1975a, p. 560; see also Shubik, 1982, p. 286). He believes that whole other classes of games tend to be mere repetitions of pregame-theoretic models and add little insight to the corpus; for example, constant-sum games impose conservation rules which hinder the adequate description of process (Shubik, 1975a, p. 557; Shubik, 1972; Mirowski, 1984a).

Where, then, does the advantage of game theoretic techniques lie? Shubik claims that the future belongs to noncooperative nonconstant-sum games. "Noncooperative game theory appears to be particularly useful for the study of mass phenomena in which the communication between individuals must be relatively low and individuals interact with a more or less faceless and anonymous economy, polity or society" (Shubik, 1982, p. 300). Since strategic considerations are linked to a perception of society as consisting of impersonal social forces, and this conception informs Shubik's notion of "institutions", he therefore proselytizes for the appearance of a "new mathematical institutional economics": "... my basic approach to economics is through the construction of mathematical models in which the "rules of the game" derive not only from the economics and technology of the situation, but from the sociological, political and legal structure as well" (Shubik, 1982, p. 10).

Shubik's research programme is not so very different from the seventeenth-century dream of Hobbes, that "in the same way as man, the author of geometrical definitions can, by starting from those arbitrary definitions, construct the whole of geometry, so also, as the author of the laws which rule his city, he can synthetically construct the whole social order in the manner of the geometers" (Halévy, 1972, p. 494). Just as with Hobbes, there is some equivocation in deciding what is *necessary* and what is *adventitious*; we are referring in this case to the notion of social structures "external" to what is identified as the "economy". Shubik has, in places, suggested that institutions are merely ad hoc rules (Shubik, 1975a, p. 558), of which he is providing mathematical descriptions. In other places, he suggests he is actively constructing optimal rules with regard to various problems, such as the treatment of bankruptcy (Shubik, 1975b, p. 526; Dubey and Shubik, 1979). In either event, Shubik's claim to be including "sociological, political and legal structures" is in practice, reduced to the mathematical specification of rules which impinge upon the operation of a market whose basic constituents—tastes, technologies, and endowments—are essentially the same as in the conventional Walrasian models. These rules have a different analytical status than the tastes, technologies, and so forth, because they are not treated as "natural" or fundamental givens, but rather as arbitrary intrusions from outside the sphere of the economy.

The arbitrary character of the rules is only confronted once, to my knowledge, in the Shubik corpus. In (Shubik, 1974, p. 383) he asks the two revealing questions: "Should we assume that the laws and customs are to be modelled as rules of the game which are given and never broken? . . . Why should individuals accept fiat money or the laws and customs of trade in the first place?" Both questions are not answered: they are instead relegated to be outside the competence of the mathematical institutional economist, and by implication, outside of the sphere of the "economic".

It is possible to attempt a summary of Shubik's cannonical institutional model. He distinguishes between "market games", which can be represented by a characteristic function, because the payoff of any subset of players is independent of the activities of the complement (i.e., all other traders); and a "strategic market game", in which the activities of all traders are linked by an explicit price formation mechanism and a distinct monetary system. One valuable insight of Shubik's work has been to show how the neoclassical economists' notion of "externalities" pervades the entire price system through a demonstration that realistic descriptions of the trading process preclude the possibility of treating traders' options and objectives as independent of one another. Nonetheless, he retains the neoclassical predisposition to see prices mainly as the means of conveyance of information. He writes:

> The key aspect of many economic activities that differentiates them from the viewpoint of information processing and coding from say political or societal activities or from abstract games is that a natural metric exists on many of the strategies. In mass markets, for example, for wheat, the information that two million tons were produced last season is probably more useful to most buyers and sellers than is a detailed list of the quantities produced by each individual farmer. (Shubik, 1975a, p. 560)

A strategic market game is modelled as a noncooperative nonconstant sum game. It consists of a list of traders[4] and their endowments, the postulation of a market structure as a set of rules governing the process by which traders may convey information about bids and offers, as well as rules for the clearing of markets, and the utility functions of and strategies available to each player. The specification of market structure may become quite complicated, including the role of a bank, the rules for bankruptcy, and so on (Shubik and Wilson, 1977). Another further assertion of Shubik is that the specification of the generic types of strategies pursued by the traders captures the presence or absence of "trust" in the market. The predominance of historical strategies—i.e., where a player's move is conditional upon the past moves of a set of players—is said to represent a situation of low trust. On the other hand, the acceptance of state strategies, where a player's move depends solely upon the present state of the game, is said to represent a situation of widespread trust. There is a hint, but no more, of an evolutionary argument embedded in this distinction: as markets become more anonymous and threats, by their very nature, become less specific, state strategies slowly displace historical strategies. Shubik explicitly links this development to the spread of the use of money, which he calls "the symbol of trust" (Shubik, 1974, p. 379).

Perhaps the most striking characteristic of Shubik's published work is the relative unpretentiousness of the claims made for its efficacy. He admits that game theory enforces a symmetry upon the personalities of the players which belies any serious intrusion of personal detail, while also abstracting away from social conditioning and role playing; he also admits that game theory requires a fixed and well-defined structure of payoffs. Even more significantly, he explains that "there is as yet no satisfactory blending of game theory with learning theory" (Shubik, 1982, p. 358). The impression conveyed is that game theory is one of many techniques of social analysis, with its own strengths and weaknesses; the matter of choice of analytical technique is left to the individual reader without any explicit discussion. This attitude is encouraged by statements that one should choose the solution concept to fit the preconceived objective: "The [Walrasian] price system may be regarded as stressing decentralization (with efficiency); the core shows the force of countervailing power; the value offers a "fairness" criterion; the bargaining set and kernel suggest how the solution might be delineated by bargaining conditions ..." (Shubik, 1982, p. 382). One cannot help, however, but receive a different impression from the collected body of his writings. There intermittent claims are made that game theoretic models are necessary prerequisites for the integration of macroeconomic and Walrasian microeconomic theory, and ironically, that Nash equilibrium points of strategic market games frequently include the conventional Walrasian general equilibrium (Dubey and Shubik, 1979, p. 120). It would appear that all the different solution concepts really are subordinate to the one "real" solution, the Walrasian general equilibrium.

Shubik's circumspection contrasts sharply with the claims made by the other prominent mathematical institutional economist, Andrew Schotter. Schotter (1983, p. 692) writes, "game theory is the only tool available today that holds out hope for creating an institutionally realistic and flexible economic theory." Schotter reveals that he is aware that other economists, such as John R. Commons, also have tackled these issues, but feels that such research can be written off as ineffectual without any extended critical discussion, simply because it is not phrased in game theoretic terms.

In certain respects Schotter resembles Shubik: Schotter, also, disparages Walrasian theory for leaning on the *deus ex machina* of the auctioneer rather than directly confronting process (Schotter, 1983, p. 674); and, as well, repudiates cooperative game theory and the solution concept of the core, because after limit theorems that showed the core converged to the Walrasian general equilibrium (Debreu and Scarf, 1963; Aumann, 1964) "what we have left is an economy that is not any richer institutionally than the neoclassical analysis, which merely assumed that this degenerate set of market institutions existed at the outset" (Schotter, 1983, p. 682). Schotter gives voice to what many have said privately: these results stole the thunder from game theory by demonstrating that it added little or nothing to the analytical content of Walrasian general equilibrium (Schotter, 1981, p. 152).

It is here that Schotter begins to diverge from Shubik. Whereas the latter seems to pursue a live-and-let-live policy in the house of neoclassicism, the former is critical of the modern general equilibrium trick of handling time, uncertainty, externalities, and a host of other complications by redefinition and expansion of the commodity space. (A Hershey bar at 6 P.M. on Tuesday on the Boston Common in the rain is different from a Hershey bar at 7 P. M. etc., etc.; and presumably is traded in a separate "market". See chapter 6 in this volume.) "When market institutions fail, as in the case of economies with uncertainty and externalities, the neoclassical economist does not, as he should, try to explain what alternative sets of institutions would be created to take their place" (Schotter, 1981, p. 151). It is the stress on the creation of institutions that Schotter believes sets him apart from Shubik and others. Shubik, as we have observed, has a tendency to define institutions as ad hoc rules which act to constrain or restrict the operation of the market; Schotter, on the other hand, insists that institutions are *solutions* to games (Schotter, 1981, p. 155; Schotter, 1983, p. 689). Initially, the distinction might seem to be excessively subtle: although Shubik will not commit himself on where his "rules" come from, he is not hesitant to suggest bankruptcy rules are a reaction to a perceived market failure, and then examine the spectrum of possible rules to discover which are "optimal." But Schotter insists this conception is wrong because he does not believe institutions are consciously constructed; instead, behavioral regularities "emerge endogenously" or "organically." In his book, he makes a preliminary attempt at developing a taxonomy of different kinds of institutions (Schotter, 1981,

p. 22), but quickly abandons all but one category as not being sufficiently "organic." His rationale is worth quoting in its entirety:

> If the social institutions we are investigating are created by a social planner, their design can be explained by maximizing the value of some objective function existing in the planners mind. . . . On the other hand, if the form of social organization created is the outcome of a multilateral bargaining process, a bargaining theory would be required. (Schotter, 1981, p. 28)

A number of references to the Australian school, and particularly Hayek, are provided in support of this conception of an institution.

Again, appearances suggest an affinity with the earlier institutionalists' stress on the unintended consequences of both conscious choices and evolutionary drift. For this reason, it is all the more important to be clear and precise about how Schotter conceptualizes an institution. In his scenario, institutions do not lead a separate or semiautonomous existence: "Social and economic institutions are informational devices that supplement the informational content of economic systems when competitive prices do not carry sufficient information to totally decentralize and coordinate economic activities" (Schotter, 1981, p. 109). Institutions are stopgaps or *pis aller* which evolve naturally whenever a market is not capable of producing a Pareto optimal outcome. The failure of the market to produce these outcomes is not explored in depth, nor are there any suggestions of the ubiquity or the determinants of the presence or absence of failure; and in this it stands in stark contrast to the work of Shubik. Without any motivation, all market failures are attributed to the existence of prisoner's-dilemma structures, given presumably by "states of nature". The overall picture is of a market that organically heals itself, with health defined as the conventional Walrasian general equilibrium.

Schotter has provided us with a canonical model which can be easily summarized. His model starts by *assuming* "that the only institution existing is the auctioneer-led market institution, whose origin is left unexplained by the model" (Schotter, 1981, p. 120). Schotter's "market" is not Shubik's "market": for all practical purposes it is not strategic; its only glitch is that it does not clear in any short sequence of "gropings" for the correct vector of Pareto-optimal prices, due to the fact that preferences are not strictly convex (Schotter, 1981, p. 124). Traders cannot communicate directly with each other, but must communicate through the "price system" by making *quantity* offers to the auctioneer. It is asserted (Schotter, 1981, p. 125) that this is isomorphic to a supergame played over individual component games which are both stationary and of the form of the prisoner's dilemma. The purported reason the payoff is of prisoner's-dilemma form is that it is assumed that if all parties cannot arrive at agreement upon the same aggregate quantity of the commodity both bid upon and offered, *no trades are executed*.

Before we summarize the technical details of the supergame, it will be instructive to examine the structure of one of these component "moves" or subgames. Table 7–1 is a presentation of the situation presented graphically in Schotter (1981, p. 125). Let us restrict our attention to two traders each with endowments of a single commodity. Because utility is not strictly convex, auctioneer-provided equilibrium prices are tangent to utility functions at more than one point: here, for simplicity's sake, let us assume there are only two possible trading points: A, where trader 1 (seller of commodity X) ends up with less of his endowment, and B, where he ends up with more. Because utility is "flat" in this region, both traders end up with the same level of utility whichever quantity is traded at the fixed price. However, if no trade is executed (because the traders could not agree upon relative quantities), they would be stuck with their initial endowments, and their concomitant lower utility levels. It is a curiosity of Schotter's graph that he neglects to discuss the presence or absence of symmetry in the level of utility of the two traders, because as one can readily observe, this game is not of the prisoner's-dilemma format. The problem here is not that the equilibrium point is suboptimal: it is only that there are a *multiplicity of equally desirable equilibria* and that the game does not allow any external coordination to agree upon which of these indifferently acceptable equilibria will be settled upon. If utilities are not comparable and side payments are not allowed, there are only two possibilities as one adds more traders to the market: (1) everyone is psychologically identical up to a scalar multiple, and the number of multiple equivalent equilibria proliferate; or (2) people have different utility functions, and as the number of traders increases, the solution shrinks to a single Walrasian general equilibrium, which the auctioneer effectuates. Schotter seems not to have noticed that this is not an intrinsically noncooperative game, and that only in the most idiosyncratic of special cases of utility functions is there any problem of coordination.

Far from being a niggling criticism, this observation reveals that contrary to his statement in section 4.2 (Schotter, 1981), the "market model" is not isomorphic to the supergame model in chapter 3 (Schotter, 1981), because the latter model is predicated on the Nash equilibrium point solution concept applied to a sequence of generic prisoner's-dilemma games, which the former clearly is not.

Let us assume that Schotter has found a way of recasting his model of the market process so that it is in the form of a prisoner's dilemma. From whence come his claims of "evolution" and "organic developments"? First he must postulate a fixed prisoner's-dilemma situation that is repeatedly played over and over again by an identical set of players. Players are assumed to "learn" from past plays of the game, but this learning is constrained to a very small subset of experience: they are allowed neither threat strategies nor to be different from other players, and cannot "remember" past the last immediate play of the game. Technically, allowable strategies are restricted to a mixed strategy over best responses in which the probabilities attached to each response are updated with a mechanical Bayesian procedure (Schotter, 1981, p. 72). The rule is so constructed that it will eventually converge to a pure-strategy Nash equilibrium point if that strategy is played at some juncture in the game. For Schotter, an institution is any one such Nash equilibrium of a fixed game converged upon after repeated play. He does not claim to have identified the single unique institutional outcome of the situation: there are in general multiple Nash equilibria; all he can guarantee is that the Markov chain of mixed strategies will eventually converge upon one of the equilibrium points, which is an absorbing state.

Table 7–1:   A Trading Subgame

		Trader 2	
		A	B
Trader 1	A	10, 20	3, 6
	B	3, 6	10, 20

One point needs elucidation not received in Schotter's book. The necessity for the single component subgame to be of the form of a prisoner's dilemma derives from the narrow conception of learning implied in the mechanical Bayesian updating rule. The question arises, as it does in all Austrian theory, how the institutional regularity is to be "policed" if it is, in fact, "organic" or "evolutionary". If the game is not of the prisoner's-dilemma form, there is no longer any unique way for a player to "punish" the others for behavior undesirable from his point of view (Schotter, 1981, p. 83). This can be easily observed by again looking at table 7–1. Suppose trader 1 in the last around of play has chosen A while trader 2 has chosen B. Clearly both of their situations could be improved, but how can trader 1 teach this to trader 2? No message can be sent that would not involve the recall of the pattern of all plays previous to the last, and that is prevented by the Bayesian updating rule, due to the fact that mixed strategies are allowed. In other words, no strategy is explicitly identified as punishment by the structure of the game.

Schotter, like many other latter-day Austrians, shies away from explicitly discussing *learning*, as opposed to the transmission of a discrete and seemingly prepackaged commodity called *knowledge*, because the former suggests a social process, whereas the latter conjures up the grocer's dairy case (Field, 1984). This is done largely by mathematical sleight-of-hand: assuming that everyone's psychology is identical (Schotter, 1981, p. 88), and ruling out what Schotter calls "disguised equilibria," that is, situations where the opponent's choice of strategy cannot be divined from the actual outcome or payoff. In effect, he defines the "problem" to be so straightforward and unambiguous that only one choice can be made: it is not so much learning as it is mechanism. Any discussion of the influence of history is rendered pointless, since only state strategies (in Shubik's terms) are allowed, or indeed, make any sense, given that the situation is so well defined. It should not surprise us, then, that at the end of the narrow corridor through which we are allowed to pass, we arrive at—voilà—a Walrasian general equilibrium (Schotter, 1983, p. 185–186). It is difficult to maintain that this model transcends the passive cooperation of the zombies found in conventional neoclassical general equilibrium. The question posed at the beginning of this section remains: where has game theory gotten us?

The Rules of the Game: Game Theory and Neoclassical Economics

What is a game? It is, as quite correctly perceived by von Neumann, a set of rules, a set of objectives or payoffs, and a ranking of those objectives by the set of players. If all of these sets are *discrete* and well defined, they may be expressed in the format of mathematical formalism; and then further manipulation of the symbols can serve to suggest potential outcomes. However, it is also true, as Wittgenstein wrote in his *Remarks on the Foundations of Mathematics*, "A game, a language, a rule is an institution" (Wittgenstein, 1978, VI 32). The copula "is" in this quote should not be confused with an equals sign, for the relationship is neither commutative nor symmetrical. To say that a game is an institution is not necessarily to say that an institution is a game.

Game theory and neoclassical market theory start from an identical premise: market trades are not adventitious, but possess a regularity and stability which permits them to be causally explained. So what is the constancy postulated by game theory? The first, and least discussed postulate,[5] is the persistence and constancy of the players (Heims, 1980, p. 307). Within a static one-shot game the persistence of the players' identities may be ignored; but with any repetition or learning this condition becomes critical.

The constancy of humans, and therefore the putative constancy of human nature is the key to the translation of any game into mathematical formalism. If humans are not to be treated with all their individual quirks and idiosyncracies (that is, are to be the subject of generalization), then their communication and behavior must be treated symmetrically. If one merely assumes that language is always adequately shared, that the content of a transmitted message is identical to the content received, and that interpretation is not problematic, then the people who are the subject of the analysis must be substantially "the same", no matter what happens.

The second postulate of game theory is the assumed constancy of the rules. As we have observed, this appeared to be the bone of contention between Shubik and Schotter. Shubik seemed content to accept the rules as arbitrarily fixed; Schotter claimed that the rules were solutions to super-games. Examination of Schotter's model revealed that the rules were no more flexible than in Shubik's models; if anything, Schotter mistakes arbitrary psychological rigidities for rule structure. As with the previous postulate, this problem is not apparent in one-shot games, but only attains importance upon repetition. The rules are what exist to be learned by the players, although this is often obscured by mathematically posting the game in strategic form.[6] We shall return to this issue shortly.

The third postulate of game theory is the relative stability of the objectives and the environment. Interestingly enough, this is not an endogenous outcome in game theory, but must be given a priori as part of the mathematical formalism. Many pages have been written about the necessity of expendability of cardinally measurable payoffs, and especially the requirement of cardinal utility, but few have realized that this is merely the tip of the iceberg. A game must have a single-valued objective function which somehow summarizes the jumbled, confused, and sometimes unconsciously contradictory desires and drives of human beings. Further, this index must generally conform to the axiom of Archimedes (Krantz et al., 1971, pp. 25–26), which translates into the requirement that all potential outcomes be comparable before the fact; or more prosaically, every man must have his price. It is of paramount importance that these rankings be stable,[7] for without them, there is no sense in which a game can be "solved".

Now, the most important aspect of these postulates is not their tenuous connection to "reality" (game theorists have been historically thick skinned when it comes to empirical disconfirmation of solutions and/or assumptions), but rather what passes for analysis and explanation. Given the fixed actors with their fixed objectives and the fixed rules, the analyst (and *not the actors*) prereconciles the various sets, insists the prereconciled outcome is the one that will actually obtain, and calls this a "solution". The critical role of the three postulates of constancy becomes evident: without them, there is no preordained reconciliation to be discovered. The process in which the actors take part is irrelevant, because the deck has been stacked in a teleological manner. Insofar as the three postulates are "naturally" given, equilibrium is identified with harmony and natural order, while conflict and disharmony can only be expressed as disequilibrium.

This caricature is crudely drawn, and the game theorists would surely complain (at least there, if not in their published work) that the world is not that simple. I should think they would aver that the distinction between cooperative and noncooperative games was invented precisely to conjure up a more subtle and penetrating analysis of harmony and conflict. I would like to suggest that the promise of game theory to encompass conflict and strategy in a rigorous manner is more than a little illusory, and is rooted in a confusion over the role of the analyst in the solution of games.

The clearest definition of a cooperative game has been provided by Shubik (1981, p. 165): Pareto optimality is taken as an axiom, sidepayments of utility or other payoff unit are permitted outside of the actual structure of the game, and communications and bargaining of an unspecified nature are permitted and presumed to take place (at least virtually, in that the value of each potential coalition must be well defined). Cooperation is not modelled; it is subsumed in the various payoffs to coalitions. In the presence of the three postulates, the players know what the analyst knows, and both the players and the analyst "agree" upon the feasible and desirable outcomes. It is no surprise that early partisans of cooperative games have lately been repudiating their premature enthusiasm: in this scenario, "natural order" is imposed by the analyst.

The distinctive characteristic of noncooperative games is that the players and the analyst no longer "think" the same things: in essence, the analyst would like to impose a solution that the players would not choose as a result of obeying the rules. The conflict is not located among the players as much as it resides in the tension between the rule-governed situation and the Pareto optimum. The analyst, obeying his own self-denying ordinance, resists simply imposing the naturally given optimum (or optima), and then is challenged by the need to provide a description of simple rule-governed stability in the presence of infinite degrees of freedom. The analyst is faced with the prospect of constructing some definition of the rationality that is not transparently a reflection of the natural givens.

This impasse has surfaced whenever someone tries to explain what a Nash equilibrium point means or signifies (Johansen, 1982; Harsanyi, 1982; Shubik, 1981; Friedman, 1977). Mathematically, the Nash EP is the maximum point or points on a compact convex set of the "best replies" of each player's strategy set. The Nash EP is often motivated by appealing to some lack of knowledge or ability to compare goals among players, but this is not strictly true. Each player knows all the relevant information about the other players, and has the ability to prereconcile the entire process in his own head. The only difference from a cooperative game is that the rules create the potentiality that rationality is indeterminate, in that the interpretation of strategy sets becomes an issue.

It is well known that every finite N-person game has at least one Nash EP if mixed strategies are allowed. This mathematical existence proof does us a disservice, however, once we realize that mixed strategies are only rational if deployed outside of a one-shot static game (Shubik, 1981, p. 155). Therefore, a noncooperative game can in most cases only be seriously discussed if it is repeated; more generally, after Wittgenstein, we can say that no one is capable of following a rule only once. Games, if they are to describe behavior rather than a set of prearranged natural conditions, must be repeated. But it is precisely in repetition that the notion of a fixed strategy set slowly unravels: more and more ad hoc assumptions must be made about how each player interprets the sequences of the other players' moves over time. In general, the solutions to a sequence of noncooperative games will not be the sequence of individual solutions to each of the component games (van Damme, 1981; Friedman, 1977, p. 199). It is in this sense that rationality, as conceived in game theory, is indeterminate.

At this juncture we once again return to the postulates of constancy. Shubik is right to point out that it is a misnomer to call the Nash solution concept "rational expectations", because there is no guarantee that the outcome will meet the *analysts'* criteria of rationality (i.e., Pareto optionality) (Shubik, 1981, p. 153). He suggests it is more appropriate to think of a Nash EP as displaying "consistent expectations," in that conjectures about players' behavior match ex post outcomes. However, the definition of consistency is a function of the time frame over which the Nash equilibrium is defined; once that is realized, it follows directly that all Nash EP require our three postulates of constancy. How else could we possibly "construct" consistency solely from the payoffs of the game, unless the players, the rules, and the objectives where identical through time?

Contrary to the claims often made in the literature on supergames, those models cannot encompass historical change. Works that claim to include change of players over time—(Schotter 1981, pp. 127–139) for example—in fact specify the sequential agent characteristics so that they are functionally identical. In contrast, works, such as that of Friedman (1977), which vary the payoffs over time, do so in such a way that the change can be specified independent of history (i.e., are stationary). If changes in strategy sets are allowed, they are restricted to stationary Bayesian revisions, by their very structure myopic and ahistorical. There is no published work that attempts to change all three postulates simultaneously. This poor showing cannot be excused as a temporary situation contingent upon further mathematical effort and virtuosity. It is a corollary of the neoclassical notion of rationality, which can only augment the psychological abilities of *homo rationalis* in order that all interactions must be virtually prereconciled in their heads, whether or not they actually occur. This conception, of course, is exactly what caused the older institutionalist school to renounce neoclassical economics.

It is easy to be lulled by all the language of "conflict", "retaliation", and "enforcement" into believing that the solvable supergames portray processes. Harsanyi (1982) and Aumann (1981) both define the Nash EP as a self-enforcing equilibrium, but we should now understand this to mean that the solution would persist if the postulates of constancy held and if the analyst imposes an arbitrary set of rules governing how players interpret each other's moves. These requirements wreak havoc with any commonsense notion of this enforcement of rules. Neoclassical economists want to portray a world where there is no active coercion, because rationality polices itself. What causes this goal to elude their grasp is that there is no such thing as a self-justifying rule (Levison, 1978). Quoting Wittgenstein: "However many rules you give me—I give a rule which justifies *my* employment of your rules" (Wittgenstein, 1978, I 113). "The employment of the word 'rule' is interwoven with the employment of the word 'same'" (Wittgenstein, 1978, VII 59). The exercise of rationality, as opposed to the twitches of a zombie or a machine, depends upon active interpretation of whether the rule applies in the particular instance, and on whether to regard anomalies as exceptions or failures to abide by the rule. Rationality is the deployment of judgment as a process, which cannot itself be justified by a rule at the risk of falling into an infinite regress (Field, 1979).[8]

This is nowhere better illustrated than in the proliferation of solution concepts and individual solutions in game theory. As soon as someone proposes a "rational" solution to a particular game someone else generates a counterexample that questions its rationality. For example, Morgenstern and Schwödiauer (1976) criticize the core as being dominated by other imputations if the players are aware of the theory of the core. Or, Johansen (1982, p. 430) points out that if player X knew player Y was experimenting with his options, and had any basis for guessing the pattern of player Y's experiments, then player X would in general choose strategies outside of the Nash equilibrium. van Damme (1981, p. 37) shows that in certain game structures, "a player can punish the other as badly as he wishes and therefore each player can force the other player to steer the system to any state he wishes. So all kinds of behavior (even rather foolish) can appear when one plays according to a history dependent EP." Aumann (1981) reports that the solution points of supergame depend critically upon the discount rate used to calculate the present value of future payoffs; I believe no one has yet indicated how vulnerable these results are to the paradoxes arising out of the Cambridge capital controversy (Harcourt, 1982, pt. V). We have already noted that the Nash EP for a one shot noncooperative game is not identical to a Nash EP for the same game repeated over and over again.

Game theorists have opened the Pandora's Box marked "rationality," and do not know how to close it again. Walrasian general equilibrium was based upon a direct appropriation of a metaphor from physics, and this meant that the natural givens of the analysis would directly determine the optimal outcome (Mirowski, 1984b). Planets in motion are passive and do not talk back, and neither did the passive Walrasian trader. The natural world is stable and unchanging,[9] which allowed postulations of laws that were independent of their spatial or temporal location. The Walrasian laws were also stationary and static. Then game theorists proposed to discuss bargaining, which led to cooperative games, which begat noncooperative games, which begat discussions of process, which allowed the transactors the freedom to differ in their interpretations of the roles of others and the constancy of the world, all of which is now undermining the older construct of mechanistic rationality. This is not happening because game theorists have willed it so—in fact, much effort is spent demonstrating that special sorts of solutions to special sorts of games converge to Walrasian equilibria. It is happening because game theory exposes the weaknesses of the physical metaphor that all the excessive mathematical formalism served to obscure. Game theory does not, however, suggest what to put in its place. It cannot conceptualize the reduction of a language or of an institution to a game.

Rules are not Homogeneous

The word "institution" has been so far used loosely; the time has arrived to suggest a more precise definition. In view of the criticisms voiced in the previous sections of this paper, it may prove illuminating to conceptualize institutions as consisting of three tiers of rules. In the first tier are the rules most familiar to game theorists: these are rules grounded in stable, persistent, and independent givens of the analysis. These rules are in some sense "policed" by the stability of the environment. A good example of this type of situation is provided by prisoner's-dilemma games describing the overgrazing of a commons or the depletion of a fish species. Insofar as the "payoff" is well defined and not socially defined (i.e., fish caught or animal fed), and the players are fairly homogeneous, Nash equilibria can explain certain regularities in behavior. We could refer to these situations as "natural" rules.

The rules in the second tier are based upon the recognition that human rationality cannot be an algorithm, but must constantly be flexible and prepared for change. These rules are social, consciously constructed, and consciously policed. Into this category would fall property rights, money, religion, the family, and much else that comprises social order. The rules of this class cannot be explained as the outcome of underlying natural forces, because their enforcement mechanisms are not "natural": they possess neither persistence nor independence from the phenomena. We could refer to those situations as *bootstrap* rules.

The third tier of rules derives from the recognition that the first two classes of rules must interact over time. For example, the overgrazing game will be influenced by the institution of money, and any natural regularity of behavior may be destabilized or redefined by the penetration of market relationships: here, the "payoff" itself becomes partly socially defined. The exercise of human rationality itself transforms the environment. The recognition that there may be temporal regularities to the relative dominance or importance of natural rules versus bootstrap rules leads to the metarationality of evolutionary regularities. Unlike the first two classes of rules, evolutionary regularities by their nature cannot be teleological: they reflect interactions of natural rules and bootstrap rules beyond the imagination of any player.

It should be clear from previous comments that most neoclassical economists would insist that a scientific economics would only recognize explanations that linked any given social phenomenon to its natural rules (Mirowski, 1981). Explanation in this framework is satisfied to take as given tastes, technologies, and endowments, and to identify equilibrium with the extremum of some objective function. Why can't all social processes be reduced to their natural rules? To reiterate, this program leads to a logical contradiction. All natural rules must be subject to human interpretation. Natural constraints do not inexorably compel us to do anything, because human reason intervenes. This freedom is what provides us with all the multiform variation that comprises the history of the human race. To put it in Wittgensteinian terms: A rule does not certify its own correct application. To pretend that it does so is to appeal to other rules, and can only lead in a circle. Whether a reason or an activity conforms to a rule in a particular case is a problem in reasoning and interpretation, having to do with judgments about when situations are "the same". We may feel compelled to follow a rule, but the rule itself cannot compel us.

There are also those who believe that the world is only comprised of bootstrap rules. Let us call this opinion *conventionalism*. Why cannot all social phenomena be reduced to bootstrap rules? This position also meets an insuperable logical difficulty: knowledge of this theory of social phenomena tends to undermine its efficacy. To argue that all social regularities are consciously instituted is to argue that the only prerequisite for change is will; a society based upon this premise cannot ultimately enforce or maintain the stability required to define rules. In other words, just as the natural world is intrinsically incapable of defining the totality of social life, so too is the belief that might makes right. Even if the world of language, markets, and culture were ultimately organized by bootstrap rules, these rules would themselves be asserted by some actors to be grounded in natural rules, in order to provide stability and diffuse responsibility.

What then, is the function of the evolutionary regularities? These must be present because bootstrap rules influence natural rules, and vice versa. They are the locus of the understanding of change. The determination that a natural situation is producing regularities in behavior is itself a function of society's conception of science; and, as twentieth-century philosophers of science have come to argue, science consists largely of bootstrap rules. As our understanding of what is natural evolves, it cannot help but change the formal relations of bootstrap rules to natural rules in social life. These changes are not purely erratic: a good example of this is provided by Wesley Clair Mitchell in his "Role of Money in Economic History." He argues that money cannot be cogently explained by the prosaic notion that it made life naturally easier for traders. "When money is introduced into the dealing of men, it enhances their freedom. For example, personal service is commuted into money payment.... Adam Smith's obvious and simple system of natural liberty seems obvious and natural only to the denizens of a money economy" (Mitchell, 1953, p. 200). More significantly, Mitchell proposes that the penetration of the money economy into social life altered the very configurations of rationality, to the extent of encouraging particular conceptions of abstraction, quantification, and thus ultimately, the ontology of modern Western science. Here we have socially constructed rules, slowly transforming the understanding of natural constraints through the rational interpretative structure, finally changing the natural rules themselves.

What has all this to do with game theory and economic theory? It clearly and concisely provides a framework within which to evaluate the claims that there is a new mathematical institutional economics in the offing. Neoclassical economists will only sanction explanation in terms of natural rules. This is a reflection of their perennial search for a natural order, an invisible hand, and so forth. Since bootstrap rules and evolutionary regularities cannot be reduced to natural rules, their project is doomed to failure. One need only compare Schotter's "explanation" of the rise of money as a game theoretic solution to a naturally given problem of transactions costs to Mitchell's broad interpretation of the influence of money on economic life to see this failure.

There are other economists who believe that conscious and deliberate planning will solve all economic ills; they are partisans of the view that the world is nothing but a collection of bootstrap rules. Since neither natural rules nor evolutionary regularities can be reduced to bootstrap rules, this research project is also doomed to undermine itself.

Game theoretic explanations of human institutions fall into one of these two categories. Contrary to Schotter, all phenomenal rules cannot be reduced to their underlying natural rules. Contrary to Shubik, the postulation of rules as boostrap or ad hoc leaves explanations without any firm foundations. A theory of institutions must operate simultaneously on all three levels. The mathematical formalism of game theory is best suited for the discussion of natural rules. It can be used to *describe* bootstrap rules. But it also reveals that notions of rationality and equilibrium are distorted beyond recognition in those models, to the point that neither the existence nor efficacy of those rules can be said to be illuminated by the analysis. Since evolutionary rules are not teleological, they are not suited to game theoretic structures.

In conclusion, game theory is not a substitute for a theory of institutions. It can only be one component of such a theory, a theory committed to the explanation of change as well as of complacency.

Notes

[1] This history of the critique of the concept of the maximization provides a clear example of the peripatetic migration between one defense and the other. For recent examples of the former, the 'straw man' defense, see Boland (1981); for the latter, the insinuation of sour grapes, see Wong (1978).

[2] The quote is from Veblen's "Why is Economics Not an Evolutionary Science?" reprinted in Veblen (1919). The best introduction and summary of the thought of the institutionalists is still chapters 14 and 15 of Mitchell (1950).

[3] Evidence for this statement is provided in Mirowski (1984b), and in chapter 6 of this volume.

[4] Sometimes there is postulated a continuum of traders, i.e., a nonatomic agglomeration, who therefore cannot be subject to a discrete list. This assumption is often used to "prove" that Nash equilibria converge to Walrasian competitive equilibria.

[5] This absence of discussion may provide a counterexample to the common opinion that mathematical models, by their very nature, make assumptions more clear and transparent than common speech. As such it illustrates a thesis developed in this volume, chapter six.

[6] "There is a not completely innocent modelling assumption that any finite game in extensive form can be reduced to a game in strategic form, which is equivalent to the original description of the game from the viewpoint of the application of solution theory" (Shubik, 1981, p. 157).

[7] We say "stable" and not "constant," because of the tradition of probabilistic concepts of utility dating back to the original work of von Neumann & Morgenstern (1964).

[8] Perhaps this explains Schotter's final chapter (1981) with its discussion of sociobiology. One way to short-circuit the infinite regress is to locate "fundamental" rules in our genes.

[9] At least until the twentieth century, when physics left the economists behind.

References

Aumann, R. 1964. Markets With a Continuum of Traders. *Econometrica* 32:39–50.

Aumann, R. 1981. Survey of Repeated Games. In *Essays in Game Theory and Mathematical Economics in Honor of Oskar Morgenstern*. Mannheim: B.I.

Boland, Lawrence. 1981. On the Futility of Criticizing the Neoclassical Maximizing Hypothesis. *American Economic Review* 71:1031–1036.

Commons, John R. 1934. *Institutional Economics*. New York: MacMillan.

van Damme, E. E. 1981. History-Dependent Equilibrium Points in Dynamic Games. In O. Moeschlin and D. Pallaschke (eds.), *Game Theory & Mathematical Economics*. Amsterdam: North Holland.

Debreu, G., and Scarf, H. 1963. A Limit Theorem of the Core of the Economy. *International Economic Review* 4:234–246.

Dubey, Pradeep, and Shubik, Martin. 1979. Bankruptcy and Optimality in a Closed Trading Mass Economy Modelled as a Noncooperative Game. *Journal of Mathematical Economics* 6:115–134.

Dubey, Pradeep, and Shubik, Martin. 1980. A Strategic Market Game with Price and Quantity Strategies. *Zeitschrift Für Nationalökonomie* 40:25–34.

Field, Alex. 1979. On the Explanation of Rules Using Rational Choice Models. *Journal of Economic Issues* 13:49–72.

Field, Alexander. 1984. Microeconomics, Norms and Rationality. *Economic Development and Cultural Change* 32:683–711.

Friedman, James. 1977. *Oligopoly and the Theory of Games*. New York: Elsevier-North Holland.

Halevy, Elie. 1972. *The Growth of Philosophical Radicalism*. London: Faber.

Harcourt, Geoffrey. 1982. *The Social Science Imperialists*. Boston: Routledge Kegan Paul.

Harsanyi, John. 1982. Noncooperative Bargaining Models. In M. Deistler, E. Furst, and G. Schwödiauer (eds.), *Games, Economic Dynamics and Time Series Analysis*. Wein: Physica-Verlag.

Heims, Steve. 1980. *John von Neumann and Norbert Wiener*. Cambridge, MIT Press.

262   THE RECONSTRUCTION OF ECONOMIC THEORY

Johansen, Leif. 1982. On the Status of the Nash Type of Noncooperative Equilibrium in Economic Theory. *Scandinavian Journal of Economics* 34:421–441.
Johansen, Leif. 1983. Mechanistic and Organistic analogies in Economics: The Place of Game Theory. *Kyklos* 36:304–307.
Krantz, D., Luce, R., Suppes, P., and Tversky, A. 1971. *Foundations of Measurement.* New York: Academic Press.
Levinson, Arnold. 1978. Wittgenstein and Logical Laws. In K. T. Fann, ed. *Ludwig Wittgenstein: The Man and His Philosophy.* New York: Humanities.
Mirowski, Philip. 1981. Is There a Mathematical Neoinstitutional Economics? *Journal of Economic Issues* 15:593–613.
Mirowski, Philip. 1984a. The Role of Conservation Principles in 20th Century Economic Theory. *Philosophy of the Social Sciences* 14:461–473.
Mirowski, Philip. 1984b. Physics and the Marginalist Revolution. *Cambridge Journal of Economics* 8:361–379.
Mitchell, Wesley Clair. 1950. *The Backward Art of Spending Money.* New York: Kelley.
Mitchell, Wesley Clair. 1953. The Role of Money in Economic History. In F. Lane and J. Riemersma (eds), *Enterprise and Secular Change.* Homewood, IL.: Irwin.
Morgenstern, O., and Schwödiauer, G. 1976. Competition and Collusion in Bilateral Markets. *Zeitschrift Für Nationalökonomie* 36:217–245.
Mosley, Nicholas. 1983. *The Rules of the Game.* London: Fontana.
von Neumann, J., and Morgenstern, O. 1964. *The Theory of Games and Economic Behavior.* 3rd edition. New York: Wiley.
Rosenberg, Alexander. 1979. Can Economic Theory Explain Everything? *Philosophy of the Social Sciences* 9:509–529.
Samuelson, Paul. 1965. *Foundations of Economic Analysis.* New York: Atheneum
Schotter, Andrew. 1981. *The Economic Theory of Social Institutions.* Cambridge: Cambridge University Press.
Schotter, Andrew. 1983. Why Take a Game Theoretical Approach to Economics? *Economie Appliquée* 36:673–695.
Schotter, A., and Schwödiauer, G. 1980. Economics and the Theory of Games: a Survey. *Journal of Economic Literature* 18:479–527.
Shubik, Martin. 1972. Commodity Money, Oligopoly, Credit and Bankruptcy in a General Equilibrium Model. *Western Economic Journal* 11:24–38.
Shubik, Martin. 1974. Money, Trust and Equilibrium Points in Games in Extensive Forms. *Zeitscrift Für Nationalökonomie* 34:365–385.
Shubik, Martin. 1975a. The General Equilibrium Model is Incomplete and Not Adequate for the Reconciliation of Macro and Micro Theory. *Kyklos* 28:545–573.
Shubik, Martin. 1975b. Mathematical Models for a Theory of Money and Financial Institutions. In R. Day and T. Groves (eds.), *Adaptive Economic Models.* New York: Academic Press.
Shubik, Martin. 1976. A General Theory of Money and Financial Institutions. *Economie Appliquée* 29:319.
Shubik, Martin. 1981. Perfect or Robust Noncooperative Equilibrium: A Search for

the Philosopher's Stone? In *Essays in Game Theory and Economics in Honor of Oskar Morgenstern*. Mannheim: B.I.
Shubik, Martin. 1982. *Game Theory in the Social Sciences*. Cambridge: MIT Press.
Shubik, Martin, and Wilson, Charles. 1977. Optimal Bankruptcy Rule in a Trading Economy Using First Money. *Zeitscrift Für Nationalökonomie* 37:337–354.
Simon H. 1982. *Models of Bounded Rationality*. Cambridge: MIT Press.
Veblen, Thorstein. 1919. *The Place of Science in Modern Civilization*. New York: Huebsch.
Wittgenstein, Ludwig. 1978. *Remarks on the Foundatlons of Mathematics*, rev. ed. Cambridge: MIT Press.
Wong, Stanley. 1978. *The Foundations of Paul Samuelson's Preference Theory*. Boston: Routledge Kegan Paul.
Wright, Crispin. 1980. *Wittgenstein on the Foundations of Mathematics*. London: Duckworth.

Index